Case Studies on Information Technology in Higher Education: Implications for Policy and Practice

Lisa Ann Petrides
Teachers College, Columbia University, USA

IDEA GROUP PUBLISHING
Hershey USA • London UK

Acquisition Editor: Mehdi Khosrowpour
Managing Editor: Jan Travers
Development Editor: Michele Rossi
Copyeditor: Maria Boyer
Typesetter: Tamara Gillis
Cover Design: Connie Peltz
Printed at: Sheridan Books

Published in the United States of America by
        Idea Group Publishing
        1331 E. Chocolate Avenue
        Hershey PA 17033-1117
        Tel: 717-533-8845
        Fax: 717-533-8661
        E-mail: cust@idea-group.com
        http://www.idea-group.com

and in the United Kingdom by
        Idea Group Publishing
        3 Henrietta Street
        Covent Garden
        London WC2E 8LU
        Tel: 171-240 0856
        Fax: 171-379 0609
        http://www.eurospan.co.uk

Library of Congress Cataloging-in-Publication Data

Case studies on information technology in higher education : implications for policy
and practice / [edited by] Lisa Ann Petrides.
        p. cm.
    ISBN 1-878289-74-8
        1. Education, Higher-- Data processing--Case studies. 2. Educational technology--
Case studies. 3. Information technology--Case studies. I. Petrides, Lisa Ann, 1961-

LB2395.7 .C39 2000
378'.00285--dc21   00-031925

British Cataloguing in Publication Data
A Cataloguing in Publication record for this book is available from the British Library.

NEW from Idea Group Publishing

Case Studies on Information Technology in Higher Education: Implications for Policy and Practice

Table of Contents

Section IV: REFLECTIONS ON A CHANGING ENVIRONMENT

Preface

The forces of transformation in higher education are all around us. Privatization, globalization, and lifelong learning are just a few of the drivers in this competitive and continually changing environment. While it is often argued that many of the pressing problems of higher education can be ameliorated by technology, this book focuses on both the successes and failures associated with integrating information technology in colleges and universities. As higher education strives to maintain goals of quality, efficiency, and effectiveness, information technology is now playing—and will continue to play—a critical role in this process. However, the significance of that role is what appears to be in question. These factors contribute to the need to examine issues, trends, controversies, challenges, and opportunities facing higher education leaders and administrators as they begin to assess the value of information technology in their own institutions.

With the advent of easier-to-use and more cost-effective technology solutions, there is no longer the need to go through complex systems, intermediaries, and analysts. For the first time, education leaders and administrators have direct access to the information processes and systems that they require. Additionally, the ubiquitous presence called the Internet has ushered in a new era. Not only has information technology itself changed, but so too has the relationship between the public and private sectors, challenging long-held beliefs about the role of universities and traditional education structures. Additionally, higher education has come to rely on industry to find conceptual tools and technologies that it can apply, even though higher education is distinct in many ways from industry (e.g., organizational structure, governance, culture). There are scores of good books available on information technology in industry; however, most have little or nothing to do with its applications in higher education. Perhaps what is most exciting about this field today is that the time is ripe for higher education to frame an internal dialogue about these issues.

The void that this book fills is threefold. First, educational leaders and practitioners need to enter the conversation based on the voice of their own experiences, as there has been very little written specifically about information technology in higher education. Secondly, the field of higher education has been very resistant to change in thinking about information systems and organizational transformation, and therefore this book brings together the perspective of a broad-based coalition of educators and practitioners from across the academy in order to explore these issues. Lastly, as higher education is at a crossroads in terms of the way the business of education is conducted, not only in terms of restructuring processes but also in terms of the core mission of higher education, this book brings the most important issues back to the center – teaching and learning.

This book demonstrates examples of the integration of information technology in higher education and explores the ways in which the application of information technology in higher education is both similar to and different from industry. This set of case studies attempts to bridge the gap between the application of information technology in industry and its application in higher education, as well as to assist students, practitioners, and researchers of higher education in their understanding and application of information technology.

The scope of the book covers a wide range of fields including communications, computer science, education, health sciences, management systems, and physiology. It encompasses a variety of topics such as strategic planning, management, knowledge production, distance learning, early technology adopters, course management, access, cultural change, and collaboration. There are also a range of institution types profiled, from community colleges to research universities, including public and private universities. The purpose of the case studies is to address and analyze issues that are common to higher education institutions as a way to highlight pressing problems and offer effective solutions.

How To Use This Book

This book was designed to be used by administrators, teachers, students, information technology practitioners, policy-makers, and knowledge managers. It can be used by administrators to acquire a better sense of the issues they face in integrating information technology in their institutions. Teachers and students in educational administration, management, and information science can enjoy the practical hands-on approach to case study analysis and will be able to apply research and theory to their practical experience. Information technology practitioners can benefit from real-life examples that will help assess the maze of options and challenges facing them on a day-to-day basis. Policy-makers will gain a deeper understanding of the short- and long-term effects of the efforts of others, and in doing so be guided toward better decisions based on the needs and perspectives of various stakeholders. Knowledge managers will see first hand how the information needs of an organization can be translated into knowledge-based systems.

There are several types of cases in this book. The majority of them are case studies written in narrative form that provide the reader with detailed context and analysis about a specific institution's experience with information technology. There are also research-related cases that discuss the findings of an implementation or design of information technology, and there are point-of-view cases that present thought-provoking analysis of the changes and transformations occurring in higher education as they relate to information technology. The chapters are intended to be used as stand-alone cases; however, in their totality, the cases provide an overarching framework for the integration of information technology in higher education.

Each case contains several open-ended questions at the beginning of the chapter. The purpose of the questions is to provide the reader with a guiding backdrop to think about the main issues in the case. There is also a set of discussion questions provided at the end of each case that can be used to generate or lead a discussion after the case has been read.

Acknowledgments

This book of case studies was a collaborative effort among many educators, researchers, and practitioners. The authors represented in this book are among the pioneers, early adopters, and risk-takers in information technology in higher education. And for the tremendous amount of time and effort that it takes to put together a case study, I have tremendous gratitude and appreciation for the authors who have shared their insight and experiences, because they have indeed made this book possible.

This book would also not have been possible without the determined efforts of Sharon Khanuja-Dhall, who from early on helped to create and sustain the vision for this project, along with Pablo Reguerin. Major editorial contributions were made by the following people: Tyler Kendall, Sharon Khanuja-Dhall, Marc Chun, and Victoria Manos. I would like to express my appreciation to the anonymous reviewers for their significant contribution to the quality of this book.

I would like to thank my colleagues at Teachers College, Columbia University, for their support and assistance in helping me to cast a much wider net around my work, that is, to conceptually locate this book in a broader context. Specifically I would like to acknowledge: Linda Powell, Lee Knefelkamp, and Greg Anderson.

I would also like to acknowledge Mehdi Khosrow-Pour at Idea Group Publishing, whose foresight at the book's inception helped turn an idea into reality and for his guidance that helped bring it to completion, and to the rest of the staff at Idea Group Publishing for all of their organizational and editorial efforts.

Lisa A. Petrides
New York City
February 2000

Chapter I

Introduction

This book brings together in one volume a compilation of case studies that provides examples of the integration of information technology in higher education. The book is divided into four thematic sections with each chapter serving as a stand-alone case. When taken together, the cases provide a framework for understanding the conditions necessary for integrating information technology in higher education, and keep teaching and learning in the forefront. The four sections are: Planning and Management Processes, Impact on People and Culture, Teaching and Learning, and Reflections on a Changing Environment. Within each of the four sections, the cases portray particular institutions, entities, or events where the intersection of information technology converges with a process, policy, or practice.

SECTION I: PLANNING AND MANAGEMENT PROCESSES

This section includes six case studies that focus on the planning and design processes in information technology. A critical component of planning and the management of information technology is the development and implementation of these processes, which include issues of strategic planning and policy development. These cases illustrate the importance of building and maintaining the necessary human and technology infrastructure in the planning and management processes.

The first case, **Designing and Implementing a Learning Organization-Oriented Information Technology Planning and Management Process, by Penrod and Harbor**, provides an overview of the processes of implementing a broad-based strategy to address its information technology needs, including the use of strategic planning and the development of an information technology governance structure. Next, **Penn State's World Campus": Mainstreaming a Virtual Campus Initiative, by Ryan and Miller**, illustrates the complexity of planning a technology-based innovation to meet the need for lifelong education in an information society. It discusses the strategies used in the development of a major distance education campus and the lessons learned in the first full year of operation. The third case, **Policy Processes for Technological Change, by Smith, Lewis and Massey**, focuses on the policy processes that are key to managing technological change as higher education administrators maneuver their way through the challenges accompanied by information technology.

The fourth case, **Information Management in Higher Education Administration: A Slow Drive on the Information Superhighway, by Edirisooriya**, explores the ways in which information management in higher education administration is far behind its business sector counterparts. This case illustrates the impact of such practices on its institutions and stakeholders and offers an explanation for the current predicament. The fifth case, **Development of a New University-Wide Course Management System, by Jafari,** examines the importance of developing and implementing course management systems that function as enterprise systems, specifically how they are able to link and interface with database resources and services already in place in the university. The case discusses issues of pedagogy, usability and operational cost benefit. The last case in Section I, **The Selection and Implementation of a Web Course Tool at the University of Texas at Austin, by Decker, Schulman, and Blandy**, offers a centralized approach to Web course development for faculty use. This case illustrates the challenges encountered and the lessons learned in initiating such a plan, given the institutional and personnel constraints of a large, historically decentralized research university.

It is evident from each of these case studies that the planning and implementation of information technology are both challenging and critical to its successful utilization. As the institutional environment shifts with the use of information technology, so too must the planning and management processes.

SECTION II: IMPACT ON PEOPLE AND CULTURE

Planning and management are important to the successful implementation of information technology, but so too are the people and culture of each organization. Section II consists of five case studies that examine the intersection of information technology with people and culture in higher education institutions. These cases demonstrate the spectrum of similarities and differences on the impact of information technology on an institution's people and culture.

The first case, **Access to Internet-Based Instruction for People with Disabilities, by Burgstahler**, discusses the ways in which The Americans with Disabilities Act (ADA) of 1990, which requires that programs and services made available to the public also be made accessible to people with disabilities, should be applied to Internet-based instruction as a way to make learning accessible to all. The case discusses access issues, presents design guidelines, and provides an example of an accessible course. The second case, **Social Impacts of Computer-Mediated Communication on Strategic Change Processes, by Cecez-Kecmanovic and Busuttil**, explores how computer-mediated communication can be used to facilitate strategic decision-making within an organization, with varying and sometimes controversial social impact. The third case, **Implementing Relational Database Systems: Implications for Administrative Cultures and Information Resource Management, by Serban and Malone**, discusses the changes required when computing services and administrative divisions rethink data ownership and utilization. This case also describes the cultural and technological transformations that occurred during the implementation process and their impact on information resource management.

The fourth case, **The Politics of Information Management, by Petrides, Khanuja-Dhall, and Reguerin**, investigates the control and governance of information management and the ownership of student data. It profiles a departmental unit's efforts to conduct decentralized short- and long-term planning in a highly centralized environment. The last case in Section II, **Risks and Rewards: Good Citizenship and Technologically Proficient Faculty, by Sechrist and Finnegan**, looks at two technologically proficient faculty members who exhibit organizational citizenship behaviors in a system where technological expertise is neither recognized nor rewarded in tenure and promotion decisions.

From the ADA to organizational citizenship behavior, each of these case studies illustrates the impact that people and culture have on information planning and implementation. Assessing the people and culture of any higher education institution is a critical element in successfully integrating information technology.

SECTION III: TEACHING AND LEARNING

This section is composed of five cases that bring the focal point of information technology to the core mission of higher education institutions—teaching and learning. These cases examine the ways in which information technology has the potential to transform teaching and learning as information technology becomes tightly integrated into face-to-face and virtual classrooms. The potential collaboration, critical thinking, and content development exemplify how information technology has the ability to transform the teaching and learning process.

The first case, **Higher Education Culture and the Diffusion of Technology in Classroom Instruction, by Smith**, examines the values and beliefs of the academic profession. It looks at how academic culture discourages a pro-innovation social climate and may hinder the diffusion of technological innovation in the classroom. The second case, **The Impact of Information Technology on Roles and Role Processes in Small Groups, by Heckman, et al.**, explores the use of collaborative work in a technology-mediated communication environment. It also discusses the prerequisite conditions necessary for success in technology-mediated learning teams. The third case, **The International Negotiation Modules Project: Using Computer-Assisted Simulation to Enhance Teaching and Learning Strategies in the Community College, by Raby and Kaufman**, illustrates the use of computer-assisted simulation as a tool to enhance teaching and learning strategies in understanding international issues and perspectives. This case demonstrates how information technology in the classroom can be used to improve students' ability to work collaboratively, enhance computer literacy, and improve critical thinking skills.

The fourth case in Section III, **The Harvey Project: Open Course Development and Rich Content, by Stephenson**, describes the creation of an Internet-based collaboration of teachers, researchers, and students who are brought together for the purpose of developing content for the teaching of physiology, which is to be provided free of charge to all academic users. The final case in Section III, **The Role of Computers and Technology in Health Care Education, by Hart**, examines the assumption that the health sciences are automatically propelled to the forefront of information technology use in classrooms, laboratories and clinics just because there is an increasing reliance on computer-based medical systems.

This section underscores the importance of keeping the core mission of higher education at the forefront of information technology. Within this section, the transformative potential of information technology is illustrated by the unique execution and integration of technology, whose purpose is to improve the learning experience.

SECTION IV: REFLECTIONS ON A CHANGING ENVIRONMENT

The common thread throughout this book is the focus on change—from strategic planning to classroom learning. The final section of the book contains four cases that reflect the changing environment of information technology in higher education. Whether it is administration, governance, teaching or learning, this section provides a synthesis of the issues facing institutions of higher educational today.

The first case, **Why Not Reengineer Traditional Higher Education?, by Berge**, poses the question of why educational institutions seem incapable of radical redesign or reinvention. It explores the ways in which information technology can be used to either change the way the business of education takes place, or simply to pave over the same road that it has always taken. The second case, **Forces of Change: The Emergence of a Knowledge Society and New Generations of Learners, by Nasseh**, examines the emergence of two new generations of learners—a widespread return of adult learners and the incoming Internet-generation of students—and the ways in which educational institutions will need to prepare students to work in a knowledge-based society and economy.

The third case, **Adopting Information Technologies for Instructional Environments, by Kumari,** looks at information technologies that have created a turbulent environment for change in higher education and have caused institutions, faculty, and administrators to rethink their role in variations markedly different than from the past. In particular, this case investigates the role of faculty as early adopters of information technology and explores the interplay between particular technologies and teaching practice. The final case in Section IV, **Fostering a Technology Cultural Change: The Changing Paradigms at the University of Minnesota Crookston, by Lim**, describes four paradigm shifts that could be used to help facilitate a long-term cultural change in a higher education institution, and specifically, it develops a model that empowers education to drive technology implementation in higher education.

A Framework for Thinking about Information Technology and Forces of Transformation

The diagram at right suggests a framework for considering the conditions necessary for successful strategies to be designed and implemented when integrating information technology in higher education, and it illustrates the ways in which transformative processes are most likely to occur. The four thematic sections of the book are represented in the diagram. Three of the sections, Planning and Management Processes, Impact on People and Culture, and Teaching and Learning, are represented as cylindrical components in nested layers. At the base of the model are the planning and management processes that must be in place for the system to effectively manage and adapt to the environment. Examples of these processes are found in Section I of this book. These planning and management processes inevitably have an impact on the people and culture within the organization, as is illustrated in Section II. At the top of the nested components is teaching and learning—representing the core mission of higher education. Examples of integrating information technology with teaching and learning are found in Section III.

The gray shaded background in the diagram represents the external environment, which is continually changing. The lightning bolts in the shaded area indicate the external drivers or conditions which serve to influence the system. Environmental factors might include: changing demographics of student population, technological innovations and obsolescence, and competition from commercial education ventures. Chapters that present a more macro perspective of the forces of change in the higher education environment are found in Section IV.

Figure 1: Forces of Transformation

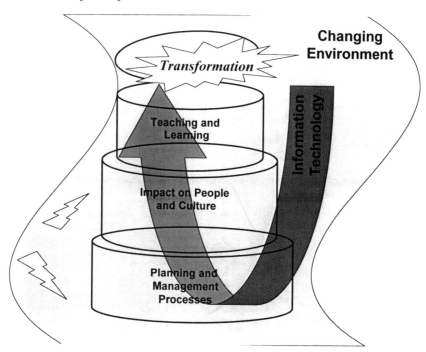

The flow of information technology into the system is depicted by the shaded arrow that circulates from the external environment passing up through planning and management processes, impact on people and culture, and teaching and learning. The curved nature of the arrow illustrates a process of interaction between each of the individual layers, driving towards a transformative interaction across all three, where "true" processes of transformation (or the potential for transformation) occur at the intersection of each of the three layers with information technology. The framework above suggests that the transformation of the education process itself is the result of these interactive forces. Does it work? Does it make sense? How might it apply to your situation?

In conclusion, the cases in this book offer an effective and engaging learning tool for all readers. The case-based approach allows teachers and learners the opportunity to learn from examples across several different disciplines in higher education, to participate in conversations that are practical as well as theoretical, and, perhaps most importantly, to challenge our thinking about information technology in higher education.

Section I

Planning and Management Processes

Chapter II

Designing and Implementing a Learning Organization-Oriented Information Technology Planning and Management Process

James I. Penrod and Ann F. Harbor
University of Memphis

INTRODUCTION

Higher education is changing. Driven by the need to increase productivity, quality, and access while meeting the challenges of competition, universities, especially state-assisted institutions, are seeking ways to do more with less governmental support. Information Technology (IT) is perhaps the enabling tool that will bring transformative change (Oblinger & Rush, 1997). The organizations that have had primary managerial responsibility for IT implementation on many campuses need to change and be restructured if the technology is to live up to its potential.

This case study provides an overview of the process utilized in implementing a broad-based strategy to address the information technology needs of a large public university, the University of Memphis. It deals at length with the planning and creation of an IT governance structure and a strategic planning and management model. In this case, modern theories of organizational change and strategic planning were applied to the creation and improvement of the University's IT structure.

CASE QUESTIONS
- What IT changes are needed to significantly improve a large state-assisted urban campus?
- What organizational structures are necessary to enable meaningful IT decision making?
- What types of "people" changes need to occur and in what time frame?
- What are the major barriers in making planned IT change happen?

CASE NARRATIVE

Background

The University of Memphis (UoM) is the flagship institution of four-year universities within the Tennessee Board of Regents system of higher education. The campus of approximately 20,000 students, with its primary location in the geographic center of the city, is ethnically, socially, and economically diverse. This regional, urban, doctoral granting institution is within a relatively short commute of 1.5 million residents of the mid-South. The institution has two campuses and a growing number of other locations offering courses. It consists of nine schools and colleges and five centers of excellence. The University employs about 2,400 faculty and staff members. An annual state and non-state budget of approximately $220 million meets educational and service needs.

The University of Memphis is a state-assisted institution governed by a state-regulated system office. As an urban university, it strives to provide a stimulating academic environment consisting of innovative undergraduate education and excellence in selected research areas and graduate programs. Exposure to diversity in the composition of the student body, faculty, staff, and administrators enhances educational experiences. The University responds to the challenging responsibility of being located in a culturally diverse region by developing a unique blend of teaching, research, and service that contributes to the general welfare and growth of the region.

Historical Context

Shortly after assuming the leadership of The University of Memphis in 1991, President V. Lane Rawlins recognized that the existing IT unit could not provide the vision and ongoing assistance needed to support the institution as it began a significant change process. Initially, he instituted self-studies and brought in an outside consultant to define the magnitude of needed change. This led to a decision to create a chief information officer (CIO) position and to combine various IT-related units into one.

Thus in the Fall of 1995, the President established a new division of Information Systems (IS) and created the position of Vice President for Information Systems & CIO (VP/CIO). The new unit had responsibility for networking, academic and administrative computing, and telecommunications. As chief information officer, the new Vice President also had responsibility for developing an IT strategic planning process, an associated governance structure, and a much-needed information policy for the institution.

The new IS organization was formed from units that had previously reported to either the Vice President for Business & Finance or the Provost, who each had IT staff with mid-manager or below levels of authority. The need to restructure and redirect the organization was evident. Experienced senior-level administrators were required, and several existing positions within the organization needed to be redefined. The need for different management principles, a renewed service orientation, team-based activities, and a planning focus would lead to a commitment to begin an organizational cultural change toward that of a learning organization.

A learning organization is one that continually expands its capacity to create its future. For such an organization, "adaptive learning" must be joined by "generative learning"— learning that enhances the capacity to create. Characteristics include shared visions, personal mastery, systems thinking, and team learning. Such organizations can also be defined as:

> [...] organizations where people continually expand their capacity to create the results they truly desire, where new and expansive patterns of thinking are nurtured, where collective aspiration is set free, and where people are continually learning how to learn together (Senge, 1990, p. 3).

Shortly after appointment, the new VP/CIO initiated three major multi-year projects relating to information technology. The first involved completion of the basic network infrastructure for the University by connecting all offices and a proportion of classrooms and dormitories to the campus network and selected locations to Internet2. The second project was to develop an integrated, standardized academic system (including support roles) consisting of computing laboratories, classrooms, and faculty offices. The third initiative was to significantly decrease maintenance of the University administrative system by enhancing it with World Wide Web (WWW)-based access and eventually moving to a next-generation administrative system in an object-oriented and relational database environment.

During his tenure, the President appointed several new executive officers and senior administrators to work together with remaining long-term senior administrators and executives in a collegial and collaborative style for the betterment of the organization. The addition of strong executive support and leadership, along with experienced new academic leaders and staff, is allowing needed changes to occur at a more rapid pace than would otherwise be realized (Penrod, 1998).

Restructuring the IT Unit

The requirement to move ahead with significant system upgrades while restructuring the IT unit necessitated an IT strategic planning and management process closely coupled with a well-understood IT decision-making structure. It was equally important to link the IT planning and management model to existing institutional processes such as planning, budgeting, and personnel administration. Additionally, a learning organization component was critical to ensure that adaptive change would occur within the staff.

When the CIO arrived, the institution lagged behind its regional and national peers in IT infrastructure and, consequently, in usage. There was a lack of direct state funding to support institutional IT requirements, in addition to a need for internal restructuring of IT financial support. The first action was the development of both an operational and linked capital budget. Initially, a reserve account and year-end funds addressed major IT-related administrative costs and upgrades. Now the capital budget is directly linked to the operational budget, and meaningful ongoing planning for administrative and infrastructure needs may be conducted.

Students historically paid a very modest technology access fee (TAF) of up to $15 per semester. In the fall of 1997, this fee increased to $50 per semester; then in 1998, it was raised to $100. This enhanced fee provides a steady source of revenue allowing ongoing modernization of academic computing and instructional networking.

The University Strategic Plan called for a concerted effort to enhance the overall image and regional stature of the institution. Because of historical issues—a commuter campus environment and statewide reduction of higher education funding over the last decade—the university often suffered from an image that does not match the quality of existing programs and offerings that are available in certain disciplines. Strategies were devised to address this and to continue to increase overall quality—especially in five designated areas that included information technology, health sciences, international programs, performing arts, and undergraduate academic achievement.

Introducing any significant change in organizational culture is always difficult. An attempt to aggressively move a university forward requires the creation of a plan of action. One of the first exercises in such an endeavor is to define the barriers that exist. Establishing appropriately enhanced ongoing operational and capital budgets in a state university with severe budget constraints is difficult, even when there is presidential support. A major infusion of budget money for academic needs comes from increased fees, and student support was necessary to convince board members of that need.

Money, however, is not the only resource necessary. Initiating a formal IT planning process linked to the institutional planning process was a place to begin. Furthermore, linking IT planning directly to individual behavioral change, management style and practice, and unit and personnel evaluation set the stage for productive use of existing and additional budget allocations. Moving from a traditional data processing-oriented structure to one aimed toward 21st century management processes requires a change in organizational culture. Senge's (1990) learning organization theory provides an appropriate methodology to bring such change. Adaptive change in people requires the individual to determine that he/she wishes to change. If change is truly to occur, it is imperative for organizational changes to be apparent as well. Personal empowerment, professional development opportunities, team-based activities, involvement in decision making, and the linking of personal and organizational values are examples of unit changes that provide a stimulus to motivate individuals.

Against this backdrop, the president authorized creation of the new IS unit and supports its development to help position the University for the future. The need for such action is crucial:

> We are entering a second era of information technology in which the...applications of computers, the nature of technology itself, and the leadership for use of technology are all going through profound change. Organizations that cannot understand the new era and navigate a path through the transition are vulnerable and will be bypassed (Tapscott & Caston, 1993, p. 13).

The initial IS organization consisted of disparate units that had functioned as a divisional group for several months led by an outside consultant. Many had not engaged in any substantial professional development for some time and were not adequately equipped with desktop computing capabilities. Additionally, many individuals were long-term staff members of the university with little or no experience elsewhere. Almost without exception, they did not know what to expect from a new CIO or what the institution expected of them.

The University publication, *The Strategic Plan: Defining Excellence 1995-2000*, called for major IT advancements in both academic and administrative areas. It defined the need for a concerted effort to enhance the overall image and regional stature of the institution. For a variety of reasons, the University's image did not match the quality of programs and offerings that are available in certain disciplines. Responses devised by senior administrators to address this included the advancement of an information strategy. Near-unanimous agreement by senior executives and within the Information Systems Division indicated the need for change that was planned, bold, supported, and nurtured.

The president recognized the need for urgent change in sustaining institutional quality, and the CIO recognized that building a learning organization and implementing a strategic planning and management process were critical components to attaining that shared vision. It was neither necessary nor prudent to spend a lot of time analyzing that situation. Instead, the IT governance structure, enabling quick decision-making, was established within the first three months of the CIO's appointment. The governance process immediately embraced and involved up to 100 key institutional players in a new direction for IT across the University.

The formal structure consists of a senior policy level council (a group with presidential designated decision-making authority) and advisory committees representing academic (primarily faculty), administrative, and student interests. In addition, various role-defined groups also have the opportunity to provide input into decisions that affect them (technical support providers, college-level committees, other administrative groups, etc.). Movement away from a fairly rigid bureaucratic structure within the central IS unit toward a coordinated but distributed organization was called for as rapidly as feasible. Finally, it was essential to define an appropriate role relationship between the central IT organization and other IT units located in academic and administrative departments.

The obvious need for a structural overhaul coupled with an expectation for developing future excellence called for a process of organizational alignment. Alignment takes place when a group of individuals works as one with a deeply shared sense of vision and purpose. Alignment of individuals can be powerful, but it is not enough. The organizational processes, systems, and structures must also be in alignment. When there is reasonable alignment in an organization, learning—individual learning, team learning, and organizational learning—results. It is a powerful energy source (Smith & Yanowitz, 1996). The President and CIO immediately developed, defined, and instituted this IT governance structure with overlapping membership, which began making institutional decisions and defining IT direction. To steer the effort, the president instituted a policy-level body, supported by three advisory committees—academic, administrative and student. The new structure called for the creation of a number of new councils and committees:

Information Technology Policy & Planning Council

This council is entrusted with the primary decision-making authority regarding IT issues. It provides a forum for discussion and approval of all institutional IT policies, IT-related standards, the IT Strategic Plan for the University, and IT issues that require policy-level deliberation. The Council works in conjunction with, and coordinates the activities of, student, academic, and administrative IT advisory committees. This body is also charged with responsibilities to help ensure good cross-functional communication and to ensure that agreed-upon IT plans are carried out. The Council consists of the campus Executive Officers, Deans, the President of the Student Government Association, Faculty and Staff Senate representatives, Internal Auditor, Chairs of Advisory Committees, the University Librarian, and the CIO. The President appoints the chairperson.

Information Technology Academic Advisory Committee

This group advises the CIO on IT matters related to academic issues; provides input to and reviews the academic sections of the *IT Strategic Plan*; establishes priorities of all IT academic projects brought before the committee; participates in the development of IT standards, guidelines, and procedures related to academic information technology; and helps facilitate communication across the campus on all IT-related matters. Membership includes students, representatives of each college, the Library, Research Institutes, the Provost, and the Faculty Senate.

Information Technology Student Advisory Committee

The students advise the CIO on matters related to information technology access for students, matters related to certain academic or administrative issues, and use of student technology fees. The committee helps facilitate communication to student groups across the campus on IT-related matters. Members include student leaders, both graduate and undergraduate.

Information Technology Administrative Advisory Committee

The committee advises the CIO on IT matters related to administrative issues; provides input to and reviews the administrative sections of the *IT Strategic Plan*; establishes priorities of all IT administrative projects brought before the committee; participates in the development of IT standards, guidelines, and procedures related to administrative information technology; and helps facilitate communication across the campus on all IT-related matters. This committee consists of representatives from the Provost's office, each vice presidential unit, the schools and colleges, a representative from the Staff Senate, and representatives from Information Systems.

IT Strategic Planning and Management Model

The IT strategic planning and management model also stressed the necessity of a shared vision for the internal IS staff. From this staff of approximately 100, about 65 percent voluntarily met throughout the fall of 1995 to collectively begin the process of aligning their services and skills with the aggressive initiatives that faced them and to begin building a shared sense of vision, understanding, and buy-in.

The first alignment process was to assess individual core values and then to derive a values statement for the new organization for which there was a consensus commitment. A number of exercises from *The Fifth Discipline Fieldbook* (Senge et al., 1994, pp. 193-234, 297-350), including "Personal Mastery" and "Shared Vision," were used. This resulted in a list of 13 values for the IS organization, which are now posted in each unit office. The fundamental purpose of IS, a broad-based extended mission statement, and a three- to five-year futures scenario were also derived for the new division. The outcome of this initial planning stage was the development of six institutional strategies designed to provide guidelines for moving to the envisioned future. Each of these "pieces" was initially developed by the IS staff in draft form then discussed, modified, and approved by the governance structure. The exercise and rapid defining of institutional strategies, while not without some controversy, serve as the linchpin to future efforts and provide focus to initiatives that have institutional ramifications and require a great degree of collaboration and leadership at all levels.

Planned and bold steps by the institution were required to contend with its peer competitors. Because major shifts in education are being realized by all institutions of learning—older, nontraditional students, virtual classrooms, more learning by discovery, instructors as facilitators of learning, and distributed campuses—it was critical that changes be strategically planned. It was necessary to recognize the relationship between the institution and its IT environment, to make difficult decisions concerning the institution's desired IT future, and to realize the ultimate purpose of IT planning—which is decision making to support the good of the institution (Shirley, 1988).

During the fall of 1995, meetings were held with all college deans and administrative unit heads to understand the current environment and discuss future needs and initiatives. Input was sought during these visits on perceived institutional and IS divisional strengths and weaknesses that influence information technology implementation and support.

Within the IS division, planning centered on making a thorough self-examination and then exhibiting a willingness to make the sometimes difficult decisions to act upon identified changes. Examinations focused upon: how the unit was staffed; how the unit was budgeted and how those resources were utilized; what the physical facilities lacked and how existing facilities could best be utilized; what technologies were in place and what were necessary; what the competencies of the IT staff were and what were the needed competencies; what image was projected to clientele; what was the cultural climate in which the unit operated; and what were the services provided. Strengths and weaknesses in each of these areas and in the internal and external environment in which the unit operated were carefully analyzed.

In examining service offerings, the IS unit first reviewed new service concepts internally, then submitted them for review to the advisory committees, compared recommendations, and came to meaningful agreement. The examination of existing services helped determine which services to eliminate, how the staff felt about those decisions, and how clients felt about the decisions. Some services simply needed modification and some services were unchanged. Having completed that exercise, it was necessary to get the resources properly assigned and aligned to ensure delivery.

An aggressive decision to serve as a beta site for a new administrative systems support platform and outsourcing of University systems development personnel to provide training and leadership occurred during year two of the new administration. Elsewhere within the IS division, alignment of positions and incumbents was taking place. Certain individuals retooled their skills and transitioned successfully, others less so, and a few, not at all—who ended up leaving University employment.

Fiscal Support

External factors required addressing fiscal resource support. The University was suffering severe budgetary constraints, and the forecast for future state assistance continued to be bleak. However, this did not prevent significant IT progress. The University President actively sought funding through traditional avenues but was also very proactive in developing influential constituencies at local and regional levels.

One example of fiscal support and the decision-making process is the campus allocation of student technology access fees (TAFs) that now generate approximately $4 million annually. These fees, closely monitored at the system level, may only be used for purposes that directly benefit the instructional component. Fund usage is endorsed at the IT Policy & Planning Council level, but the real use determinations are made at an operational level. The Associate Vice President for IS, who has budgetary responsibility for TAF, works with IS staff and an infrastructure support group to develop a campus-wide "footprint" for infrastructure and academic computing resources. This proposal is discussed among the deans from not only a campus-wide perspective, but also how it affects individual colleges. Final recommendations are submitted to the IT Policy & Planning Council for endorsement and to the University Budget Committee for approval. This illustrates a process that pushes decision making to the lowest and most practical level, and has allowed significant and meaningful change to occur.

Human Resource Support

Human resource support is also a major concern. Developing and acquiring IT staff to support the new learning organization and the associated planning and management process entails a concerted and coordinated institutional approach. A process of staff self-examination identifies skills necessary for successful IS operation. Once the IT governance structure and the Information Systems staff agree upon desired outcomes and services, designated training and professional development exercises became points of focus. Units that have project responsibility define needs and identify individual training and development plans. The VP/CIO office carves out a significant allocation of the existing budget to support the retraining efforts. Distributed IT support at the college and administrative unit levels is also critical. The Policy & Planning Council collectively identified an institutional strategy that redefined more than 50 existing positions for localized IT support. These Local Support Providers (LSPs) are an important ad hoc working group that meet on a regular basis to discuss tactical roll-out issues such as scheduling, interdepartmental coordination, training, public relations (which must be coordinated), as well as common support concerns.

IS personnel are trained by the VP/CIO Office and professional consultants in what it means to be a learning organization and how that alters the way they work and make decisions—both individually and collectively. This requires them to work in different ways with clientele and builds levels of trust and confidence that had not existed before. This strengthens the IT planning process between constituencies by supporting a shared vision and common goals (DiBella & Nevis, 1998).

The idea of individual adaptive change, previously mentioned, pertains to both management and staff, and encompasses every IS employee. Managers must move from the stance of traditional bureaucrats and technical managers to that of managerial mentors and facilitators (with staff) and relationship managers (across the university). This means that individuals need to commit themselves to an unending path of learning. It also means that individuals must grow accustomed to rapid and ongoing personal change. Neither is easy to do for people who have worked many years in a bureaucratic environment. A change in organizational culture does not come quickly; full realization of a learning organization environment takes a minimum of five years and perhaps much longer (Schein, 1997). Perceptible changes in many individuals, however, are visible three years into the process.

Process Support

Process support is crucial to any change effort. A learning organization model can be successfully implemented only if processes are in place to support it. This can often prove to be one of the more challenging components to meaningful change. It may very well threaten existing internal structures, power, and influence. The IS staff is encouraged to think independently, let common sense be their guide, "communicate-communicate-communicate," "focus-focus-focus," and "just do it" when it makes sense. Query is fundamental and, in a culture where that had not been encouraged to any great degree, change comes slowly (Watkins & Marsick, 1993). Nevertheless, illogical bureaucratic chains-of-command are beginning to dissolve when confronted. Rules, regulations, and perceived constraints are continually analyzed within the decision-making context to make new and better corporate decisions (Mankin, Cohen & Bikson, 1996). Time does not allow consensus on some issues, so when a critical mass of support is secured, action is taken.

Recognition is an invaluable process support mechanism. Lead by a grassroots volunteer committee, the IS staff designed a rewards program that incorporated both contemporary and traditional methods of recognition. It allows recognition to occur at the time it is earned, encourages team values, supports innovation and risk-taking, and respects diversity. This highly successful program (which has very few "rules" associated with it and virtually eliminates collegial competition for competition's sake) helps bring together a staff that celebrates one another's successes (Hesselbein & Cohen, 1999). Another form of recognition is deriving more competitive compensation levels for IT staff through a rigorous exercise of benchmarking and using industry standards to define job roles and responsibilities. The IS organization works closely with Human Resources (HR) to assure equity and parity, and gives exhaustive attention to recruitment and retention mechanisms that work. All IT positions across the institution are linked to the area market.

Few processes can be as supportive as leadership-by-example. There can be little discontinuity between corporate lip service and daily practices, leaders must "walk the talk." Leaders cannot ignore the need for the skills required for managing change, and they can encourage creativity while they take the sting out of failure (Bennis & Beiderman, 1997). To help develop such abilities, the IS unit again works with the HR training department to provide professional development especially in "soft skill" areas. Areas such as conflict resolution, project, time, and stress management require continuous support.

Ongoing attention and focus create nurtured perceptions. "The primary function of culture management during a process of change is to implement and sustain changes" (Galpin, 1996, p. 54). The infusion of new planning and management practices and the associated behaviors expected of the IS staff are carefully and continuously supported from their introduction, thus allowing them to begin the embedding process into the organizational culture. Achieving and sustaining organizational change mandates that the culture of the organization be affected. Changes in organizational culture are supported by tangible reinforcements such as pay-for-performance in selected cases, reassignment of work to better align skill sets with tasks at hand, providing people with meaningful work, and continually communicating the big picture (Floyd & Wooldridge, 1996).

The old performance evaluation process within the Information Systems division has been significantly revised. Evaluations now include self-appraisals, supervisory reviews by line staff, and peer reviews at the management team level (Reddy, 1994). These reflective exercises promote meaningful dialogue between raters and individual staff on issues such as training and development. This allows a planning focus as well as an evaluative process to take place. Merit salary adjustments, when available, directly correlate to staff appraisal scores, and the organization takes great care to ensure equity across the division.

An ombudsperson program exists to provide an avenue for problem resolution when regular organizational channels do not meet an individual's needs or are not appropriate. After nomination by their peers, two individuals appointed by the CIO serve on a rotational two-year term as IS ombudspersons. Internal staff as well as clients are encouraged to utilize the services of the ombudspersons, and the program is publicized in each edition of the campus technology newsletter and on the IS Web site.

Every level within the organization needs leadership. The behaviors of those leaders (whether at the executive, management, or supervisory level) prove to have a tremendous impact on the success of managing change to support the IT strategic planning and management model (Hesselbein, Goldsmith & Beckhard, 1997).

ANALYSIS

Outcomes

The IT strategic planning and management model has met with early success. The fifth IT strategic plan is now in effect, and critical masses of decision makers across the institution have bought into the process. Meetings conducted twice annually with each major academic and administrative unit to determine IT need and solicit feedback work well. The academic deans meet regularly with the associate vice president for IS to specify academic IT needs and to make recommendations to the IT Policy and Planning Council for prioritization. The IS staff is also comfortable with the process and has met stated goals for completing objectives in each of the four prior plans (completing in excess of 90 percent of the initially stated objectives each year). Metrics for ongoing assessments of what constitutes satisfactory service are established and published on the Web monthly and discussed with client groups periodically. The overall IS productivity, as measured by the size of the IT infrastructure in relation to the number of full-time equivalent staff positions, has increased by a factor of five, and there is demonstrable progress on all three of the major IT initiatives that were initially set forth in 1995.

The initiative to move toward a learning organization culture is slow, as expected, but exhibits steady progress. A number of meaningful organizational adjustments are now in place including: providing at least three professional development opportunities for each staff member annually; establishing two ombudsperson roles; initiating ongoing focus groups; selecting, training, and implementing work teams; and creating a process to recognize and celebrate individual and team-based achievement. Regular ongoing workshops on learning organization principles and skills exist for staff members, and a mentoring process for managers is being introduced during this fiscal year. Both formal and informal assessment indicates that the staff is gaining skills and using them in providing service to the client community.

The governance process has been modified somewhat and defined in greater detail over the years (see below) and is functioning effectively and efficiently. The IT Policy and Planning Council meets approximately every six weeks during the regular academic year where it approves IT-related decisions of consequence to the entire University and establishes IT policy. The advisory committees meet monthly, review progress toward objectives, and make recommendations on selected issues. As previously noted, a year ago the institution was selected to participate in the "Institution-Wide Information Strategies" project sponsored by the Coalition for Networked Information.

The Budget Committee for the campus has steadily increased the proportion of institutional budget (augmented by the TAF) allocated for IT-related expenditures. Over a four-year period, that ratio has increased from approximately 3.5 percent to about 6 percent, enabling the University to be fully competitive with its designated peers. The University has moved from near the bottom of its 10 designated peers to near the top in this ratio and other benchmark ratings.

The IT organization is judged to be considerably stronger from both the addition of well-qualified professionals and by the elimination of some who were not performing up to their potential. A number of existing positions were upgraded and/or redefined to better fit the current needs of the institution. Of particular note in this regard is the shift of some half-dozen positions from primarily administrative functions to primarily academic support positions. A strategy for the IS unit to provide the main support for the IT infrastructure and for distributed IT positions to be the primary routine desktop support was approved by the IT Policy and Planning Council in 1997. Since then, approximately 55 LSP positions have been created across the campus. This has enabled reasonably clear roles to be established for IS personnel and for the LSPs, which together provide an improved service level to the campus community.

Successes/Failures and Adjustments

In addition to the major successes noted above, one other should be stressed—support from the executive officers of the university. Without their broad-based level of support, the necessary involvement of faculty and staff would not have been so forthcoming. The failures have come from decisions related to implementation procedures rather than from the more global strategies. It was determined that participating as a beta test site would provide a way to move aggressively to a new administrative system. Once that decision was made, it became obvious that the existing staff needed to be upgraded and augmented to accomplish the goal. It was thought that outsourcing a portion of the staff to the vendor with whom the beta test was to be done would best accomplish this. Due to time constraints and certain legal reasons, the outsourcing decision could not be discussed with the staff until it was to be implemented. This proved to have been an unfortunate circumstance. As one might expect, the staff was initially shocked, then disturbed by the move. After several months, it became evident that the product scheduled for installation would not be the "next generation" system that was desired, and the beta involvement was ended. Shortly after that, by mutual agreement, the outsourced staff returned to the employment of the university. A great deal of time and energy has been exerted to repair the damage, and progress has been considerable, but lingering feelings are still evident at times. Fortunately, a new beta test is underway with a true next generation system, and staff training in new technologies is underway. This staff was also part of the first work teams formed.

Although the governance structure has become a major success, it got off to a rocky start. Appropriate care was not taken to define in enough detail the role of Policy and Planning Council members. It soon became obvious that some members were not carrying out their duties as expected and some were unhappy because they were not as involved in operational decisions as they had anticipated. This occurred simultaneously with the increased TAF, and some deans asked that the increased funds be directly allocated to academic units according to a formula. First, the Policy and Planning Council held a retreat with a facilitator to get all of the concerns from all parties out in the open for discussion. Secondly, the Provost and the CIO came to an agreement to set up a process that would involve all of the deans in helping to put forth recommendations for TAF usage, with the stipulation that it would focus on overall university priorities. Finally, based on the retreat results, the CIO drafted and the President approved a more detailed role definition for the Policy and Planning Council; at the same time, they reconstituted the Council membership to include all of the deans and vice presidents. This created a group that makes IT decisions—one that has the charge and the authority to see that decisions are carried out.

CONCLUSION

Several factors contributed to the renewal of the IS unit and the success of institutional IT strategies. Consistent support and the articulation of that support by the executive officers were essential. Implementing a flexible IT strategic planning and management model purposefully linked to previously existing institutional processes set the stage for initial change and continues to define ongoing, progressive change. Another key component is the definition and evolution of an IT governance structure empowered to make decisions and charged to implement them. The reallocation of existing resources and the development of new funds to support IT initiatives is crucial to current and future success. The adaptation of learning organization principles to routine organizational operation and the infusion of them into the planning and management model seem to have begun a progression toward a new culture. Finally, the involvement of a broad array of people across the institution in governance, decision making, and team-based activities is leading to the "buy-in" so essential to long-term success.

After approximately four years, the IS Division is more than halfway through the timeframe required to acquire the characteristics of a learning organization. If the rate of progress to date can be sustained, the unit should be prepared to provide the quality of service needed by the university to meet goals of the early 21st century.

DISCUSSION QUESTIONS
1. What types of organizational changes have been brought about by information technology in your organization?
2. What are some of the barriers that make it difficult to effect information technology change? How is this different for administration, faculty, students, and support staff?
3. How important is governance structure in information technology strategic planning?

REFERENCES
Bennis, W., & Biederman, P. W. (1997). *Organizing Genius: The Secrets of Creative Collaboration*. Reading, MA: Addison-Wesley.

DiBella, A. J., & Nevis, E. C. (1998). *How Organizations Learn*. San Francisco: Jossey-Bass.

Floyd, S. W., & Wooldridge, B. (1996). *The Strategic Middle Manager*. San Francisco: Jossey-Bass.

Galpin, T. (1996). *The Human Side of Change*. San Francisco: Jossey-Bass.

Hesselbein, F., & Cohen, P. M. (1999). *Leader to Leader*. San Francisco: Jossey-Bass.

Hesselbein, F., Goldsmith, M., & Beckhard, R. (Eds.) (1997). *The Organization of the Future*. San Francisco: Jossey-Bass.

Mankin, D., Cohen, S. G., & Bikson, T. K. (1996). *Teams and Technology: Fulfilling the Promise of the New Organization*. Boston: Harvard Business School Press.

Oblinger, D.G., & Rush, S.C. (1997). *The Learning Revolution: The Challenge of Information Technology in the Academy*. Bolton, MA: Anker Publishing Company.

Penrod, J. I. (1998). Information technology governance and strategic planning. *CNI-Institution-Wide Information Strategies*. Retrieved April 24, 1998, from the World Wide Web: http://www.cni.org/project/iwis97rep/iwis97.html.

Reddy, W. B. (1994). *Intervention skills: Process Consultation for Small Groups and Teams*. San Diego: Pfeiffer & Company.

Schein, E. H. (1997). *Organizational Culture and Leadership*. San Francisco: Jossey-Bass.

Senge, P. M. (1990). *The Fifth Discipline*. New York: Doubleday.

Senge, P. M., Kleiner, A., Roberts, C., Ross, R., Roth, G., & Smith, B. (1999). *The Dance of Change*. New York: Doubleday.

Shirley, R. C. (1988). Strategic planning: An overview. In Kramer, M. (Series Ed.) and Steeples, D. W. (Vol. Ed.), *New Directions for Higher Education: Vol. 64. Successful Strategic Planning: Case Studies* (pp. 5-15). San Francisco: Jossey-Bass.

Smith, B., & Yanowitz, J. (1996, Third Quarter). The role of leadership in a learning organization. *Prism: Leadership and the Accelerating Organization*, 58-59.

Tapscott, D., & Caston, A. (1993). *Paradigm Shift: The New Promise of Information Technology*. New York: McGraw-Hill.

Watkins, K. E., & Marsick, V. J. (1993). *Sculpting the Learning Organization: Lessons in the Art and Science of Systemic Change*. San Francisco: Jossey-Bass.

Chapter III

Penn State's World Campus©: Mainstreaming a Virtual Campus Initiative

James H. Ryan and Gary E. Miller
Pennsylvania State University

INTRODUCTION

Pennsylvania State University's World Campus© enrolled its first students in January 1998. The World Campus is one of several "virtual campus" initiatives within higher education in the United States and abroad. Penn State built the World Campus as its 25th campus, fully integrating it into the mainstream of the University's academic life as part of an institution-wide web of innovation. It completed its first full year of operation in June 1999, initially offering courses in 10 credit and noncredit certificate and degree programs in some of Penn State's most highly regarded disciplines. At that time, the World Campus had admitted 861 students and generated 896 individual course enrollments. It had also attracted national attention as a "bellwether institution" in the emerging online learning field.

The idea of a "virtual university" has moved distance education into the mainstream of higher education. The creation of the World Campus illustrates the complexity of planning a significant technology-based innovation directed at positioning a major comprehensive university to meet the need for lifelong education in an information society. This case study provides a detailed examination of the strategies used in the development of a distance education campus and the lessons learned in the first year of World Campus operation.

CASE QUESTIONS

- How does a major, comprehensive university create a community of interest to launch and sustain a large-scale innovation in online learning?
- How can the business practices and academic policies of the institution be adapted to facilitate the full integration of technology-based distance education?
- How can use of technology to serve off-campus students be developed in a way that stimulates use of technology throughout the academic program?

CASE NARRATIVE

Background

The Pennsylvania State University has been a pioneer in distance education since 1892 when it was one of three American universities that initiated collegiate-level correspondence study in response to the development of Rural Free Delivery. In the century that followed, Penn State experimented with many new technologies. The basic correspondence study model evolved into a multiple-media system with the addition of audio and video cassettes, CD-ROM, computer software as new media for delivering course content, and the use of broadcast and cable television to reach new audiences at home. The fax and email, which now complement "snail mail" in the delivery of lessons and assignments, greatly improve the speed and effectiveness of instructional feedback. At the same time, the University has been a pioneer in other kinds of telecommunications-based distance education. As early as the 1960s, the University used an internal television cable system to deliver accounting and engineering classes to multiple classrooms. In the 1980s, it joined the Appalachian Educational Satellite Program and was a founding member of the National University Teleconferencing Network which experimented with the use of satellite and, later, telephone-based interactive video in order to reach students at distant locations and to distribute courses to multiple campuses.

By the 1990s, there were two distinctly different approaches to distance education. Correspondence study offered students significant flexibility and control over the time, place, and pace of instruction. At the same time, it did not allow students to interact with each other. The "distributed classroom," which used satellite and other technologies to extend the classroom to distant sites, gave students the ability to interact spontaneously with their instructor and other students, but it limited their control over the time, place, and pace of study. Correspondence study had become an accepted means for universities to extend undergraduate courses; on the other hand, the distributed classroom was generally used for professional graduate study, especially in engineering. These appeared to be diverging methods. The development of the World Wide Web was to change the direction of distance education. The Web promised not only to give the student the flexibility associated with correspondence study but also, at the same time, access to a highly interactive learning community.

In 1992, a University-wide task force reviewed the status of Penn State's distance education programs and recommended that the distance education function be moved into the mainstream of the University's academic life. Citing changes in society's need for education as a result of the impact of technology on the workplace, William Kelly, associate professor of theater and integrative arts and chair of the task force, noted:

> It was astounding how clearly the task force believed that distance education must become one of the central strategies in the University's future plan, if the University is to seriously hold on to its national and international preeminence in teaching, research, and service.

The task force recommended six actions that would permit Penn State to:

> [...] advance and support the use of distance education across the full range of academic pursuits and endeavors and move rapidly and aggressively to develop programs of the highest academic quality within each of its constituent units.

As a result of the task force report, the existing distance education program was organized into a larger Department of Distance Education under the Vice President for Outreach and Cooperative Extension. A University-wide Distance Education Advisory

Committee was established to guide the movement of distance education into the mainstream. Grants from the AT&T Foundation funded an initiative, Innovations in Distance Education, which was designed to introduce more faculty to distance education, create faculty-based principles for teaching at a distance, and sponsor a series of invitational policy symposia that explored administrative and academic policy needs. Innovations in Distance Education involved senior faculty from every college of the University and helped to create a broader awareness of distance education throughout the University.

By 1996, the Distance Education Advisory Committee had made recommendations on several major policy issues. One important achievement was a Graduate Council review of the residency requirement for professional master's degrees. The Graduate Council approved new standards that made it possible to offer professional master's degrees at a distance. The Advisory Committee also produced a "Programmatic Vision for Distance Education" that positioned distance education as a point of innovation for teaching. It noted:

> [...] distance education ...creates a highly interactive, learner-centered environment that is marked by increased access to faculty expertise and increased access to information resources.

The report set the stage for discussion of a virtual campus for Penn State.

While these changes in distance education were underway, the University itself was beginning a major transformative process. The goal of the process was to position Penn State as a leader in the integration of teaching, research, and service in order to engage better the needs of society in the 21st century. Among the new initiatives were several designed to enhance the use of technology in the curriculum: Project Vision, which promoted the use of laptops in general education courses at several of the University's regional campuses; the Schreyer Institute, an internal think-tank for curricular reform; the Leonhard Center, which focused on pedagogic innovation in the engineering curriculum; and a University-wide revision of general education designed to promote active and collaborative learning.

Several significant organizational changes were also underway, including the transformation of 17 two-year campuses into a collection of regional colleges, each able to offer baccalaureate degrees that met local needs, and a merger with Dickinson School of Law. Another major organizational change was the creation of the Office of the Vice President for Outreach and Cooperative Extension. This new unit brought together the University's primary outreach organizations – Cooperative Extension, Continuing Education, Public Broadcasting, and Distance Education – into a single, coordinated administrative unit.

It was in this environment of innovation that President Spanier announced plans to study the feasibility of a World Campus in September 1996. As a first step, he appointed a study group, chaired by the Vice President for Outreach and Cooperative Education, and consisting of a number of key academic and administrative leaders. The World Campus Study Group included a representative of the Council of Academic Deans, the Acting Dean of the University Libraries, the Budget Officer, the Vice Provost for Enrollment Management, the Vice Provost for Undergraduate Education, the Vice President for Research and Dean of the Graduate School, the Executive Director of Computer and Information Systems, a regional college dean, the Associate Vice President for Distance Education, several faculty experienced in distance education, and an academic department head. The group met one evening each week from November through March. Their report recommended that the University proceed with the development of the World Campus and laid out the basic organizational, financial, and programmatic principles that have since guided its development.

As the work of the Study Group progressed, discussions were held with each academic dean to identify possible programs for development through the World Campus. A list of 90 ideas was generated and tested against program criteria: academic reputation, readiness, appropriateness for technology, market interest, and sustainability. Twenty-five programs were subjected to market research, and from this was developed a final list of 10 programs with strong likelihood for success.

Discussions were begun with the Alfred P. Sloan Foundation, which resulted in a formal proposal for start-up funding submitted in May 1997. It was approved in June, and the World Campus was officially underway.

In September 1996, Penn State, building on its experience in both correspondence study and distributed classroom distance education, embarked on a major new direction in its use of technology in distance education. It announced its intention to create a new distance education campus that would use asynchronous learning technologies and pedagogies made possible by the World Wide Web to establish new "virtual" learning communities among motivated adult learners nationally and internationally. Penn State's World Campus would become the University's 25th campus, providing access to undergraduate and graduate degree programs, certificate programs, and just-in-time professional development programs. The University would enhance its highly regarded Distance Education student services capabilities—developed through a century of support for correspondence study students—to support learner needs in this new online, asynchronous learning environment.

The goal of the World Campus was simple: to use information technology to aggregate sustainable populations of new students nationally and internationally in signature programs that represented Penn State's greatest academic strengths, and to do so in a way that would not only be self-supporting but that would generate a new source of income for participating academic units.

Organization and Structure

The World Campus is organized within the Department of Distance Education, one of four delivery units administered by the Vice President for Outreach and Cooperative Extension. It is led by the Associate Vice President for Distance Education and Executive Director of the World Campus. Just as the University itself is a matrix organization, with academic units and administrative units representing the two axes of the matrix, the World Campus operates as a networked, virtual organization within this larger matrix, bringing together staff from several organizational units that house the core competencies needed to launch and sustain the venture.

The core organizational unit is the Department of Distance Education, which includes the administrative and program development leadership, an existing and well-developed Student Services unit, an Instructional Design and Development unit, a distance education book store, and a Business Office. Existing Distance Education processes and practices, most of which are geared toward the correspondence study model of distance education, were enhanced to meet the needs of the World Campus.

Other core services are provided by the centralized resources of Outreach and Cooperative Extension. The Outreach Office of Program Development Services (PDS) provides market research, client development, and advertising and promotion support. The Director of Program Development Services joined the Distance Education Management

Team as a permanent member; a dedicated Marketing Manager coordinates activities across all World Campus programs; and several new PDS staff were hired to accommodate the increased workload. The Office of the Vice President provides leadership and staff support for internal and external public relations, fundraising, financial planning, and policy development.

The World Campus virtual organization extends beyond Outreach and Cooperative Extension to include other units throughout the University whose participation is essential to the long-term integration of the World Campus into the University mainstream.

The most obvious and important partnership is with the academic units. The World Campus functions as a delivery unit of the University. All World Campus programs extend the programs and faculty of the University's 17 academic schools and colleges. This partnership between academic and delivery functions is an important feature of the World Campus.

Faculty who teach in the World Campus are the same faculty members who teach resident students. The long-term vision was that the World Campus would have an impact on the use of technology in both environments. To facilitate this, the World Campus created a partnership with the University's Center for Academic Computing to ensure an integrated instructional design and development support service. The Center has had a long-standing commitment to encouraging and facilitating the development of instructional computing by faculty. The World Campus funded several instructional design positions within the Center, complementing existing staff in the Distance Education Instructional Design and Development unit. The purpose was to ensure consistency and synergy between World Campus initiatives and similar efforts directed to resident students. This has also ensured that decisions about technology and software platforms took into account both distance education and resident needs. Therefore the technical platform for the World Campus was fully integrated into the University's overall technology platform and support.

Other partnerships have also emerged. For instance, the University Libraries has appointed a Librarian to support World Campus programs; World Campus administrators have been invited to serve on the Administrative Council for Undergraduate Education and the Graduate Council; and the Distance Education Student Services functions—including registration, records maintenance, advising, and transcript validation—are in the process of being fully integrated into the University's general student data system.

The World Campus has created several teams to ensure coordination and communication in this networked, matrix environment.

- Each World Campus program is built around a Program Team, which includes the senior faculty coordinator from the sponsoring academic unit, a World Campus program manager, an instructional designer, a marketing manager, and a student services representative. Each member of this team represents a functional team that supports the World Campus generally.
- Directors of the various functional teams, along with core World Campus leadership, meet weekly as the Distance Education Management Team, chaired by the Associate Vice President for Distance Education and Executive Director of the World Campus. This group is expanded twice a month to include the directors of the marketing units and key individuals from instructional design and development.
- A World Campus Strategic Management Group (SMG), chaired by the Vice President for Outreach and Cooperative Extension, focuses on resource management issues,

organizational development, and strategic planning. It includes the Outreach leadership most responsible for supporting the World Campus.

- A World Campus Steering Committee ensures leadership and coordination throughout the University. This group represents the highest-level leadership of University-wide support units. Members include the Vice Provost for Undergraduate Education, University Budget Officer, Vice Provost for Computer and Information Systems, Vice Provost for Enrollment Management, the Dean of the Libraries, a Dean of regional campus colleges, and appointed representatives of the Council of Academic Deans, the Graduate Council, and the Faculty Senate. It was charged by the University Provost to facilitate the full integration of the World Campus into the organizational fabric of the University.

- An External Advisory Board meets twice annually to advise World Campus leadership on trends in technology and distance education and on how to improve business processes. The Advisory Board includes senior-level representatives from AT&T, CSC Corporation, IBM, International Thompson, Lucent Technologies, *Newsweek*, and other corporations, as well as leaders of nonprofit organizations such as A*DEC, the Alfred P. Sloan Foundation, and the Corporation for Public Broadcasting.

This organizational structure ensures inter-unit coordination on the operational and strategic level, university-wide coordination at the policy level, and communication with external organizations for benchmarking best practices.

The World Campus was established as a cost center within the University. This responded to two concerns: (1) that the investment in this new initiative not draw down resources already committed to campus-based instruction, and (2) to establish new sources of income for academic units that were tied directly to reaching new students. The financial objective of the World Campus was to recover full cost and, over time, to produce net revenue for participating academic units.

Over the past few years, some universities have created for-profit subsidiaries to capitalize their online learning initiatives. This was considered early in the development of the World Campus. However, the administration quickly decided that this would set the World Campus apart from the mainstream of the University and work against the goal of full integration of the World Campus into the academic community.

A business plan for the World Campus was developed that used a mix of internal reallocation of resources, external gifts and contracts, and tuition income for start-up funding, with the goal that the World Campus would achieve sustainability through tuition, contracts, and grants by the end of its fifth year of operation. A gift of $1.3 million from the Alfred P. Sloan Foundation was supported by an equal investment through reallocation of existing staff resources in Outreach and Cooperative Extension and one-time University support of $600,000 per year for two years. This funded the development of 10 new programs during the first two years of operation. Additional corporate grants provided partial support for other programs. A second Sloan grant of $1 million in July 1999 is supporting development of several additional programs.

A revenue-sharing policy was developed to stimulate the development of new income streams for participating academic units. Under this plan, the initial development costs were set aside, to be recovered through net income. A set of rate cards was developed to allow program teams to define their real costs. As programs are offered, the first goal is to recover the annual operating cost. After that, net income is distributed as follows: 50 percent returns to the sponsoring academic unit, 30 percent is used to recover initial investment, and 20 percent stays with the World Campus to cover risk costs. When the initial investment is fully recovered, the sponsoring academic unit's share of net income increases to 80 percent. The recovered initial investment is set aside in a "reinvestment fund," which will be used to seed new programs in future years.

As the World Campus developed, students at other campuses became interested in taking World Campus courses, and therefore financial processes to support this intercampus use of these courses are under development.

World Campus Programs and Policies

Development of certificate and degree programs for the World Campus is a clear partnership activity. Academic authority for World Campus programs resides in Penn State's 17 colleges and schools. Each program must be approved by the academic department, the college, or school, and, for degree programs, by the appropriate University-level authority (Vice Provost for Undergraduate Education or Graduate Council). In addition, programs must meet criteria set by the World Campus Study Group Report:

- The program must have a strong academic reputation.
- Faculty must be available and interested in proceeding.
- The program must be appropriate for delivery by the available technology.
- There must be a strong, identifiable market.
- Students must be willing to pay for the program, and the tuition level must be determined based on cost and market factors.
- The program must be scalable to reach the number of enrollments needed to sustain it over time.

Each program is subjected to market research as part of the approval process and, later, to help define marketing and pricing plans.

Sponsoring academic units have full academic responsibility for the program, including curriculum authority, academic quality, assessment, and credentialing. They are responsible for assigning a senior faculty coordinator and individual teaching faculty to the program. The World Campus provides funding support for these faculty when time is purchased on a course-by-course basis. Integration of World Campus assignments into a faculty member's ongoing workload is an important strategic goal of the World Campus.

While most World Campus programs are multi-course certificate and degree programs, provision has also been made to develop individual courses in areas where there is strong student interest. One example is "Commentary on Art," a lower-division Art course that is offered entirely online. In order to serve the critical mass for online courses, the University has set aside funds over the next four years to support the development of individual courses that meet both World Campus and residential campus needs. This fund has brought course and program planning for the World Campus into closer contact with academic planning at other campuses of the University. As a result, the World Campus increasingly works in coordination with the Academic Council on Undergraduate Education and with the academic deans at the University's regional colleges. In addition, the World Campus has become more closely linked to other online learning initiatives of the

University, including the Campus Course Exchange, a policy vehicle through which academic units can share technology-based courses.

The success of an online educational program depends to a great extent on the ability of the University to provide the kind of learner support that students get on campus. Students must be able to be admitted and register for courses, pay their tuition and fees, receive their course materials, obtain academic advising, gain access to course audits and transcripts, and get help for technical and administrative problems, all at a distance from campus.

The World Campus builds on a strong student services function that has been developed over time to support other forms of Distance Education at Penn State, especially the Independent Learning program—the successor to Penn State's pioneering work in correspondence study. This program generates more than 19,000 course registrations each year. The staff of registration assistants and academic advisors provides a base on which to build the learner support function for the World Campus.

Still, many changes are needed. Most Independent Learning courses are "rolling enrollment" courses; students can enroll at any time and study at their own pace. The student services computer system is defined by this requirement. On the other hand, most World Campus courses are cohort-based. In addition, they require that students have a University account to give them access to online services. These two factors require significant adaptation of existing processes.

Several online innovations were also developed. The World Campus represented the first time that students could seek admission, register for courses, and pay their tuition and fees entirely online. An online catalog was also created and included samples of course materials with each course listing. An online technical support site was created, along with "World Campus 101," an orientation Web site that helped prospective students learn more about the World Campus learning environment so that they knew what to expect when they registered for a course.

These were pioneering student services activities for Penn State. However, they also built on innovations designed originally for on-campus students. One example is CAAIS, the Computer Assisted Academic Information System, a Web-based intelligence system designed to improve the delivery of policy information to students. Plans are now underway to fully integrate the Distance Education/World Campus registration and records system into the University's primary student database. This will greatly simplify the work of entering World Campus students into the system and, at the same time, facilitate the process of tracking how other Penn State campuses use World Campus courses.

Marketing

Marketing is one of several functions that involved a cultural change within the University. Most traditional academic units are not directly involved in marketing their campus-based programs. The World Campus, however, exists in a very competitive market environment. Each program must be marketed directly to target audiences, nationally and internationally. Typically, the academic unit is closely involved in defining and helping to reach the market. Marketing efforts for the World Campus fall into three basic categories: partnership development, targeted promotion, and institutional awareness.

Partnership Development

In keeping with the "signature program," niche-market approach to World Campus programming, initial World Campus marketing and recruiting activities have been very focused on specific target audiences. A marketing representative serves on each program team and works with the faculty to identify potential target audiences. To date, every World Campus program has a relationship of some sort with a national or international professional association or industry that helps create an awareness of the program with the primary target audience. In some cases, professional associations have certified a World Campus program so that it can be used for continuing professional education credit within the association. Other associations have endorsed programs and provided access to their members for promotion or provided space at conferences to help members become aware of programs. One association has provided direct financial underwriting support for a program in architectural engineering.

Companies have also provided start-up funding as part of a partnership. The AT&T Learning Network, for instance, provided funds to stimulate the development of a certificate program in educational technology for teachers and then helped to promote the program nationally. Similarly, the Alliance for Employee Development (a management/labor partnership in the communications industry) helped to fund development of a certificate program in Customer Relations Management to enhance career opportunities for its union members.

Targeted Promotion

Initial World Campus programs have been centered on a particular profession or industry. Most promotion has been focused on reaching these prospective students directly through mail, telephone, and advertising in professional publications. As the World Campus has matured and more programs have become available, cross promotion of programs has been added to the marketing mix. Beginning in summer 1999, World Campus program information was combined with the diverse array of Independent Learning courses in a single Distance Education view book and catalog that will be mailed to as many as 10,000 addresses per month, putting the targeted promotion into a broader context.

Institutional Awareness

Institutional awareness for the World Campus involves two components. First, there is a need to create and sustain awareness of the World Campus within the institution. Second, in addition to program promotion, there is a need to position the World Campus for "top of mind" awareness with external constituencies.

The World Campus represents a major new institutional initiative for Penn State. It has been essential that its mission and goals be widely communicated throughout the University and that the academic community be aware of its status, growth, and benefits. This operates at several levels. At the leadership level, the University President has included updates on the World Campus in his annual State of the University Address. World Campus leadership has also provided annual updates to the University's Board of Trustees. The initiative is discussed regularly with the President's Council and the Council of Academic Deans. World Campus administrators and staff have been appointed to represent it on key University committees, including the Graduate Council, the Faculty Senate, and the Administrative Council on Undergraduate Education. Periodic presentations about the World Campus have been made to academic department heads and faculty groups within key colleges. Reports on major achievements are also published in *Intercom*, the University-wide newsletter, and the *Outreach Magazine*, reaching 11,000 members of Penn State's academic community.

With the rapid growth of online courses and "virtual" campuses, distance education has become a very competitive element of higher education. It was important to position the World Campus as a leader within this competitive environment. This has involved presentations by administrators and faculty at major higher education and industry conferences. As a result, the World Campus has been featured in articles about distance education in various national newspapers, and in the higher education press.

Long-Term Commitment

Penn State has made a long-term commitment to the full institutionalization of the World Campus. This commitment is illustrated by changes in University policy following the announcement of plans for the World Campus:

- The Graduate Council has reexamined its residency requirement for professional master's degrees in order to establish standards for achieving the goals of residency in a distance education environment.
- The Administrative Council for Undergraduate Education has adopted new program approval policies that identify distance education and the World Campus as a "location" for the purposes of program approval.
- A revenue-sharing plan for World Campus programs has been developed and approved as part of an overall costing and revenue-sharing policy for Outreach and Cooperative Extension.

Two other changes mentioned earlier illustrate the degree to which the World Campus's approach to online learning is being accepted by the University community. First, the University has set aside $250,000 per year over four years to fund the development of courses that meet the needs of the World Campus but that also address needs of resident students at the 24 traditional Penn State campuses. At the same time, the World Campus is being integrated into plans for a Campus Course Exchange that will facilitate the sharing of online courses among campuses.

Challenges for the Future

The organizational structure within which the World Campus operates reflects a vision of the World Campus as the single delivery unit for distance education initiatives within the larger university. The challenge of integrating a new and quite different organization effectively into the broader University planning and coordination community is an ongoing and very important challenge. Full institutionalization of an asynchronous learning network requires a team approach at all levels, from academic program design to marketing to registration and student support. Many World Campus functions and programs require new working relationships within the institution. Working with academic units to define and develop program ideas is a complex, multistage process. The challenge is to build this new delivery system into the strategic plans of all academic colleges, the operational support plans of administrative units, and into the business practices of the university, generally.

Technology integration is a specific strategic challenge. Integrating World Campus programs with university-wide technology systems and university-wide technical and pedagogic standards for online teaching and learning is a critical issue. The commitment to technology integration not only increases the ability of the World Campus to respond to faculty innovations, but it also serves as a catalyst for change and development within the larger University.

Integration of online teaching into the regular teaching expectations of faculty is another important challenge. Initial feedback from faculty revealed a concern that the level of interaction characteristic of early World Campus courses is well beyond that required by resident instruction and would be unsustainable over the long term. As a result, the instructional design team is developing guidelines for faculty participation in online courses to maximize the effectiveness of interaction within an acceptable faculty workload.

The convergence of the residential, intercampus, and outreach teaching/learning environments—a growing phenomenon in higher education today—will necessitate policies that cut across delivery units. Many organizations throughout Penn State will be or are being affected by these changes. The World Campus Steering Committee, whose members link to all major areas of the University, will continue to play an important integrating role in this process of policy integration and institutional transformation.

Ongoing evaluation has identified other areas that need to be addressed in strengthening World Campus processes and services. For example, students' focus on technology difficulties indicates a need to improve technology platforms as well as to better orient students toward effective problem solving for those difficulties that do not originate in the World Campus. Additionally, the 71 percent satisfaction rate compared to expectations indicates a need to manage student expectations better through promotion/marketing efforts and a need to meet appropriate expectations at a higher level.

The World Campus needs to refine its evaluation process continually to ensure that the right questions are being asked and that actionable information is being gathered. Although the relatively high levels of student satisfaction reported here are gratifying, data related to specific targets for improvement are needed. For this reason the evaluation instruments must more closely examine the extent to which the design, delivery, and instructional approaches used are supporting or enabling activities that allow stakeholders—particularly students and faculty members—to reach their objectives. To this end, a new approach to evaluation was piloted beginning in Fall 1999.

ANALYSIS

Penn State's World Campus was created in order to allow Penn State to meet the changing need for education in an information society. Its goal, as stated by President Spanier, is to "respond to the needs of adult learners in the information age through the creative use of educational technology which will extend signature Penn State undergraduate and graduate programs to them, nationally and internationally." At the same time, the World Campus was envisioned as part of an institution-wide change process. As the World Campus Study Team noted in its report, the World Campus "will be at the center of a fully institutionalized web of education and learner support innovations that will serve students better and foster change across an entire academic environment."

While the World Campus takes Penn State in a major new direction in the use of information technology to provide access to students worldwide, several lessons have been learned in the early development process about how the introduction of online learning subtly shifts the balance in the traditional academic equation to shared authority.

For example, distance education programs require substantial initial investment and development and only reach financial viability after creating common course templates and attaining significant student enrollments. As a result, distance education programs must be market based in order to ensure that they can attract and sustain enrollments that will recover the initial cost of development over several years. This marketing orientation can be an initial source of stress with academic units, which rarely have had to deal so directly with the financial aspects of curriculum development.

Partly due to the need to aggregate markets, external partnerships are important for program development, funding, marketing, and special support services. Whether the partnerships are with professional associations, employers, or more traditional founda-tions, partnerships also put stress on the academic units because they unbalance the traditional academic decision-making process. However, many faculty also see these partnerships as opportunities for professional networking that can enhance campus-based programs (through enhanced student internships, for example) and stimulate new funded research or consulting.

Individual faculty find that they require special support in order to develop effective online courses. They also discover that teaching online is simultaneously invigorating, demanding, and satisfying. Nevertheless, learning to work in a team environment can be a significant cultural change for otherwise independent faculty.

Online distance education also changes the complex relationships between the students and the University, the students and the faculty, and the students and their peers. Clearly, distance education increases access to education on the part of students who might otherwise not be able to continue their education. However, it does so in a market environment where the subtle distinctions between "customer" and "student" tend to disappear. Students participate in distance education because of program reputation, opportunity for career advancement, costs, and convenience. The challenge of bringing these "customers" to see themselves as fully empowered members of an academic learning community is fundamental to the design of online learning. This challenge comes into sharper focus when faculty begin to mingle older, working, distant students with more traditional students on their campuses into a single online community.

That said, most online students are very positive about their experiences. They report that strong learner support services (advising, career development, and technical trouble-shooting, etc.) are essential. They also report that they are attracted not by the technology, but by the need for the educational program itself. Technology is an enabler, not an end in itself.

As a University-wide initiative in online distance education, Penn State's World Campus does not exist in isolation. On the traditional campus, most faculty and students use email regularly to interact outside the classroom. Many faculty are experimenting with instructional Web sites and online methodologies. Several special faculty support units have evolved within individual colleges. Perhaps most important, the institution has made a commitment to pedagogical approaches (active and collaborative learning, for instance) for which technology-based learning is especially well suited. The diversity of initiatives creates a sense of competition but also makes it difficult for some to see the true breadth of institutional change that is underway. As a result, strong internal partnerships are critical to success. Institutional acceptance of distance education—and of the online teaching/learning environment, generally—must be nurtured, and incentives for participation must be developed. From policies to platforms, distance education must be mainstreamed and fully integrated within the institution along with other related innovations.

An ongoing environment of assessment for all elements of the program—students, faculty, technology, services, and competitors—and a commitment to communicate the results with key stakeholders are essential for growth.

During academic year 1998-99, Dr. Evelynn Ellis, an administrative fellow in the Office of the Vice President for Outreach and Cooperative Extension, conducted a series of interviews with faculty, department heads, and deans. The interviews focused on issues of faculty satisfaction and institutionalization. She learned that the primary concerns within the academic community for this new initiative relate to the ability of faculty to integrate World Campus participation into the workload and reward structure of the University and incentives for faculty to participate, given the competing priorities of on-campus teaching and research. Intellectual property issues have also emerged as concerns. These issues are being addressed by the Academic Senate and other University committees.

The goal is to develop evaluation instruments that then become embedded in ongoing World Campus processes. The World Campus contracted with the Center for the Study of Higher Education at Penn State to conduct a formal evaluation of some set criteria. Other data are being gathered through the market research process and through collection of data on student response to instructional design, student services, etc. During its formative stages, the World Campus is being evaluated on six criteria:

1. Does it provide access to Penn State academic programs to new students?
2. Is student learning effective?
3. Do students like the experience of learning through the World Campus and will they recommend it to others?
4. Is the World Campus an effective teaching environment for faculty?
5. Do faculty like the experience of teaching through the World Campus and will they recommend it to others?
6. Can the World Campus build a financially sustainable operating base?

CONCLUSIONS

President Graham Spanier noted in introducing the World Campus concept, "I believe the World Campus will change the shape of the land grant university in the 21st century." The World Campus is, in itself, a significant innovation at a major university. However, it developed within an environment of innovation at two levels. At one level, it is a product of the revitalization of Penn State's century of commitment to distance education. At a broader level, it is one of many ways that Penn State is using its historic strengths in outreach and technology to create a new kind of engagement between the university and society that integrates the traditional roles of teaching, research, and service. This institution-wide web of innovation is essential to understanding the implications of the World Campus for the University.

The World Campus is a highly visible initiative operating on a national and international scale. While only a small percentage of Penn State's 5,000 faculty are directly affected by it at this time, that number will grow as the number of World Campus courses increases and begins to have an impact on resident instruction and as interest grows among the University's external constituencies—especially the key industries that recruit Penn State graduates, support internships and cooperative programs, and fund faculty consultation and research. The long-term implications of the World Campus on Penn State—and on the role of the land grant university—are yet to be felt.

The World Campus is one of several "virtual campus" initiatives within higher education in the United States and abroad. It is being developed at a time when commercial enterprises are using distance education technology to compete directly with nonprofit public and private universities. Not surprisingly, some universities have decided to copy their commercial competitors by creating for-profit subsidiaries both to capitalize on their virtual campuses and to allow them the freedom from institutional and governmental policies that otherwise would limit the institution's ability to respond to rapidly changing market needs and interests.

Penn State has chosen to build the World Campus as the 25th campus within the university's core infrastructure which has had significant implications for funding, organizational development, and policy development. As former Provost John Brighton noted during a discussion with the Council of Academic Deans, "When we made the decision to mainstream the World Campus, we made the commitment to work through the issues and problems that accompanied that decision."

Regardless of how it is funded and organized, creation of a new distance education initiative of this scale represents a major long-term commitment by a university. It is not simply a financial commitment, but a commitment of human resources and of institutional energy to create the policy environment and organizational culture needed to realize the vision over the long term.

DISCUSSION QUESTIONS

1. How can distance education be mainstreamed within a University?
2. What are the benefits of mainstreaming distance education within a traditional University?
3. What are the lessons learned from this distance education initiative that can be applied to other universities?
4. Is the market focus for distance education programs the same or different than for residential programs? What are the similarities and differences?
5. What are the ways in which interactivity, faculty expertise, and learner support are necessary for successful distance education initiatives?

ADDITIONAL RESOURCES

- Several key Penn State planning documents are available on the World Wide Web. These include the 1992 report of the Task Force on Distance Education and the 1996 Programmatic Vision for Distance Education. These can be found at: http://www.outreach.psu.edu/de/de Reports.html.
- The results of the three-year Innovations in Distance Education (IDE) initiative include faculty projects, the Guiding Principles and Practices for the Design and Development of Distance Education, and reports from three invitational policy symposia. These can be found on the World Wide Web at: http://www.outreach.psu.edu/DE/IDE.
- The World Campus may be visited at: http://www.worldcampus.psu.edu.

Chapter IV

Policy Processes for Technological Change

Richard Smith, Brian Lewis and Christine Massey
Simon Fraser University

INTRODUCTION

Universities, among the oldest social institutions, are facing enormous pressures to change. There have always been debates about the university, its purpose, its pedagogical program, and its relationship to other social and political structures. Today, these debates have been given renewed vigor and urgency by the availability of advanced information and communication technologies for teaching and learning. These include computers and computer networks, along with the software and telecommunications networks that link them together. When these technologies are used to connect learners at a distance, they are called "telelearning technologies." When referring to their use more generally, to include local as well as remote teaching innovations, they are sometimes called "technology mediated learning" (TML).

Despite much media attention and recent academic criticism, pressures on universities are facilitated, but not caused, by telelearning technologies. Change in universities is not simply a result of forces acting upon universities, but is the result of a complex interaction of internal and external drivers. The use of telelearning technologies intersects with a host of social, political, and economic factors currently influencing university reform. Technology, in this context, has become the catalyst for change, reacting with other elements in a system to spark a reaction and a change in form and structure.

This chapter examines policy processes for the introduction of technology-mediated learning at universities and colleges. It is based on the results of a two-year research project to investigate policy issues that arise with the implementation of telelearning technology in universities and colleges. The focus was on Canadian institutions of higher learning, but the issues raised are common to higher educational institutions in other countries. The study scanned a large number of institutions, reviewed documents, and interviewed key actors including government and institutional administrators, faculty, and students, to discover the range of issues raised by the implementation of telelearning technologies. This chapter discusses these issues and findings.

CASE QUESTIONS
- What policies or processes are in place to guide change in colleges and universities? Who knows about these policies and participates in them?

- What are the forces behind technological change in higher education organizations? Are they external or internal?
- Can technology be used as a tool for achieving meaningful and positive change or is it an end to itself?
- In what ways can technology be used to increase access to education?

DOING THE RIGHT THING AND DOING THINGS RIGHT

Organizations implementing telelearning technologies often find themselves facing a variety of new issues not encountered when delivering courses in traditional formats. For example, telelearning technologies can provide access to courses for a broad range of new users. What kind of new or different support services will these new students require? On the flip side of the access issue, students are often concerned about who will have access to files that have stored their electronic discussions, how their identities are safeguarded, and how long these files will be stored. These concerns regarding the implementation of telelearning technologies can be broadly classified as concerns on how to implement these technologies, or "doing things right."

These micro issues of implementation, however, quickly raise questions about "doing the right things," the larger, often politically charged questions that form the policy environment for telelearning technologies. These issues are about why telelearning technologies are used and often evoke preconceived notions of economy, society, and education. These issues are concerned with power relations and the very nature of educational institutions. Examples of these issues would be the purpose of education, the role of professors/trainers, and the goals of business-education partnerships — not only "how" a subject is taught, but what, when, why, by whom, and for what purpose. These broad policy debates, while easily becoming polarized, can help to define an institution's goals so that choices about implementing telelearning technologies become clearer.

Clearly, the two aspects of telelearning policy, "doing things right" and "doing the right things," are linked and both must be dealt with in organizational policies and practices. The importance of sound policy processes that can deal effectively with both aspects cannot be overstated.

One could argue that universities already have well-established mechanisms in place to make these kinds of decisions. After all, universities have long traditions of collegial decision-making. But it is a peculiar feature of decisions about technology that these well-worn processes are seldom respected, as the wisdom of how and why to use technology is expected to be apparent to all.

The issues raised by telelearning technologies suggest a need for a systematic approach that honors collegiality while ensuring that the difficult questions can be dealt with in ways that do not overwhelm the process but serve to facilitate choices about implementation. One danger is that policy processes focus solely on "doing things right," trying to avoid controversy with broader political questions. The decisions that result from such processes risk being dismissed by those affected as ill considered and will not be supported. Another danger is that "doing the right thing" questions can overwhelm all discussion, with no progress made on making any decisions for the institution. In the end, decisions are often made anyway, but without consultation, behind the scenes, and as surreptitiously as possible, to avoid getting caught up in an endless and unproductive process.

POLICY PROCESSES
Drivers for Policy Processes

Telelearning technologies serve to amplify a variety of pressures acting on universities and colleges today. For example, the post-secondary sector is experiencing greater competitive pressures than ever before. Institutions can no longer count on their geographical "turf" as being safe from poaching by other institutions. New public and private institutions are emerging to offer popular programs. Telelearning technologies serve to magnify these competitive pressures as online courses attract students from all over the world and as entirely "virtual" institutions are created with no campus infrastructure and no tenure.

At the same time, the demand for post-secondary education is increasing. This demand is coming increasingly from adult workers who are returning to school to upgrade their skills and seek higher professional degrees. These students are seeking more flexible schedules, up-to-date curriculum, and high levels of support services. The more traditional student cohort is seeking similar flexibility as more of these students have part-time jobs and are taking longer to complete their degrees. In this case, telelearning can be an opportunity for universities and colleges to expand their student base and to create new revenue streams through the remote delivery of courses.

The temptation for university administrators in the face of these threats and opportunities is to try to respond quickly, that is, without consultation with their existing constituencies in faculty and students. Consultation, as seen later in the chapter, takes many forms but it is first and foremost an attempt toward inclusiveness in the decision-making process. It is more important than ever that universities establish policy processes that can help them establish priorities and directions to guide planning and to enable rapid responses to threats and opportunities.

Strategic Planning

Strategic planning is a business concept that has migrated recently to universities and colleges as they seek processes to direct their future development. The process can be initiated for a number of reasons. Many institutions feel the need to identify a "niche" for themselves in an expanding marketplace by identifying specific areas where the institution will focus its efforts. In other cases, a strategic plan is useful for convincing others — the Senate, faculty members, and students — that change is necessary (Tamburri, 1999, p. 10).

But the translation of strategic planning from business practice to one appropriate to post-secondary institutions is not automatic. Strategic planning cannot be applied in universities and colleges in the same way in which it is applied in the private sector. Organizational goals in higher education are often vague and, even when well defined, contested. The division of responsibility for priority setting between disciplinary units and the organization as a whole is unclear. But vagueness can be a virtue within post-secondary institutions. Individual units are continually scanning their own discipline's environment and are making informed judgements about their specialized unit. These judgements may conflict with judgements made for the organization as a whole. In the end, contradicting strategies may coexist in the university at the organizational level and at the level of the individual unit (Norris & Poulton, 1991).

Cynthia Hardy argues that many university strategic plans display a fatal lack of emphasis on implementation. She shows how an "executive management" model of strategic planning cannot be imported into universities since it assumes a unitary organization with a common goal. In fact, universities are pluralist organizations where different groups often have competing visions. This means that difficult decisions, such as the reallocation of funds or the elimination of programs, never occur or are made in ways that treat everyone equally since the plan avoids conflict by ignoring how power is distributed and how decisions are really made within the institution (Hardy, 1992).

In light of these concerns, Olcott (1996) suggests a variation on strategic planning specifically designed for aligning institutional academic policy with distance education practice. The need for alignment will become more important as distance education continues to move progressively from the periphery to the core of institutional functions. Olcott argues for a reciprocal adaptation of both distance education units and institutional policy and practice; distance education systems must adapt to create an environment that values mainstream academic norms, and institutional practices must recognize the advantages of the distance education approach. This rapprochement can be achieved by avoiding traditional areas of discontent and agreeing on a commitment to educational values such as quality, access, and responsiveness. He suggests a range of areas where policies can be reformed: recognition of distance education teaching for tenure and promotion purposes, academic residency requirements, and intellectual property.

Strategic Planning for Technology

While strategic planning has begun to play an important role in university and college planning processes, what is different today is the addition of a new function for information technology—teaching and learning.

> All too often, computing plans are focused on technology itself, rather than on how technology enables faculty and students to achieve some of the key instructional or research goals of the institution (Hawkins 1989, cited in Nedwek, 1999).

Still, while many universities may be aware of the need for planning, fewer have successfully extended this process to information technology. The 1998 Campus Computing Project report is instructive. Just under half of U.S. colleges reported having a strategic plan for information technology:

> [Fully] 60 percent do not have a financial plan for information technology and less than a third have a plan for using the Internet in their distance learning initiatives (Green, 1998).

While information technology planning for educational technology is still not widely observed, there are some lessons that we can draw from information technology planning generally. A study of 150 technology officers in universities in the U.S. found that approximately 10 percent of respondents participated in no technology planning at all, saying that it was a frustrating, time-consuming endeavor that distracts instead of contributes to their day-to-day tasks. Nonetheless, this study found that a majority of technology officers devoted a considerable amount of time to strategic planning. The successful processes were able to distinguish between the two functions of technology planning: socioeconomic goals and strategic goals (Ringle & Updegrove, 1998). Socioeconomic goals for technology planning were issues concerned with process. In this case, the goals for a planning exercise were to:

1. Align technology with other institutional priorities
2. Disseminate knowledge about technology needs and constraints
3. Build alliances with key decision-makers
4. Lobby for and obtain financial and other resources
5. Address existing technology needs
6. Keep an eye on the leading edge

These process goals were the most important function of technology planning for these technology officers. The second function of technology planning—the strategic—is concerned with technical issues. Given the speed at which the technology is changing, few technology officers were confident in being able to predict their institution's needs two or three years down the road. For this reason, technology planning needed to focus primarily on the process issues and not get bogged down in technical details (Ringle & Updegrove, 1998).

Ringle and Updegrove's (1998) findings correspond to this chapter's findings about the important role of policy processes for institutional telelearning policy. Technology needs will change quickly and unpredictably. It is crucial, however, that a forum exists for addressing the role and function of technology in the institution. This same study found that the least successful technology plans were those that were marginalized and set apart from overall institutional strategic planning (Ringle & Updegrove, 1998).

John Daniel addresses the development of technology strategies for teaching and learning extensively in his book, *MegaUniversities and Knowledge Media: Technology Strategies for Higher Education.* He makes the point that change works best if it is supported by peer groups and training and if research results are used to demonstrate the reasons for change. It is unrealistic to expect single technology decisions for entire universities. However, the organization as a whole can support technology in strategic ways while allowing units to determine the best way in which to carry out this priority for their students and discipline (Daniel, 1996).

Alberta's Learning Enhancement Envelope program, which provides funding to that province's post-secondary institutions for technology-enhanced learning, makes an institutional technology plan a requirement of funding. As a result, institutions in this province are developing a body of knowledge about technology planning for teaching and learning.

In Canada, the Standing Committee on Educational Technology of BC has developed a guide to educational technology planning. Their plan describes an inclusive process with advisory and communication processes to assist in getting "buy-in" from different internal groups. They avoid the common pitfalls of strategic planning by focusing on implementation. A regular process of revision ensures that any plan is not set in stone for a period of longer than two years, allowing for negotiation and adaptation to new circumstances. The plan is meant to be flexible and adaptable to the specific cultural and institutional circumstances of different colleges and universities (Bruce et al., 1999).

Fair Process
Another danger of strategic planning within universities is that they fall prey to internal lobbying and opposition. As a result, controversial proposals are eliminated before they

reach fruition (Tamburri, 1999, p. 11). This is not to say that it is necessary to create division in order to create change. Kim and Mauborgne (1997) note that it is more important that decision-making processes be fairly carried out than that they accommodate everyone's interests. Fair process was the key factor in the cases they studied on the diffusion of new ideas and change in organizations. Kim and Mauborgne identify three key elements to fair process: first, it engages people's input in decisions that directly affect them; second, it explains why decisions are made the way they are; and third, it makes clear what will be expected of organizational members after the changes are made (1997).

Clearly, fair process can only do so much. Policy processes must negotiate between a set of prior normative issues and a set of practical issues associated with achieving a particular outcome or decision. A successful policy process for change achieves a balance between these two elements, satisfying employee needs for procedural justice with the organization's need to reach decisions and to move forward.

Organizational Change

Much of the discussion so far has concerned organizational change in our universities and colleges. According to Hanna, for change to occur in established organizations, three conditions must be met: (1) enormous external pressures; (2) people within the organization who are strongly dissatisfied with the status quo; and (3) a coherent alternative embodied in a plan, a model, or a vision (Hanna, 1998, p. 66).

It is this third condition that presents perhaps the greatest challenge to higher education institutions as they chart their course in this emerging environment. Sound policy processes are a crucial part of the development of this alternative plan since "the collegial tradition of academic governance makes it unlikely that a technology strategy developed without extensive faculty input would have any impact" (Daniel, 1996, p. 137).

It has been suggested that the challenge to using educational technology effectively in universities and colleges is threefold (Morrison, 1999):

1. Technical: adequate support and training
2. Pedagogical: helping faculty reorient their teaching to best exploit the technology
3. Institutional: reorienting the institution to the effective deployment of educational technology

The first two issues can be addressed with changes in policy and funding. The final step, however, requires something more difficult—leadership and vision.

Organizational change in universities and colleges, therefore, requires a delicate balance of collegial and collaborative policy processes that are championed by a leader with a vision for the institution. Such grandiose organizational change projects are clearly not suited to all institutions — most would surely fail. All, however, are capable of beginning to address the place of educational technology in their teaching and learning.

Part of the process is simply to allow innovation to make its way through the institution more effectively. Universities and colleges have been described as organized along a "loose-tight" principle. That is, as long as an organizational member's behavior is generally aligned with organizational values, individual creativity and innovation are supported. If the individual's behavior moves outside the realm of these core values, the organization "tightens" as a response to guide behavior back to the core values (Olcott, 1996).

Part of the challenge for post-secondary institutions in finding their way with telelearning is to create an environment in which it is not only safe to experiment on the periphery, but also where it is safe to fail in the center; where it is "safe to take the risks needed to improve learning and teaching in times of constant, accelerating change" (Gilbert, 1998). The alternative is to have innovation continually at the margins without ever affecting the core. Kay McClenney observed this trend about innovation in U.S. colleges. She notes that despite mounting pressures for change, most innovative practices are kept at the margins of institutions, thus relieving pressure on the college to truly transform the institution (Gianini, 1998).

PUTTING IT ALL TOGETHER: TEACHING AND LEARNING ROUNDTABLES

One of the most useful models for introducing pedagogical and technological change is the Teaching, Learning and Technology Roundtable (TLTR) program coordinated by the Teaching, Learning and Technology Group (TLT Group), an affiliate of the American Association for Higher Education (http://www.tltgroup.org). The TLTR program provides a set of tools for institutions to help shape goals, facilitate discussion, and organize the implementation of strategies, outside of the bureaucratic structure. A set of structured activities helps evaluate institutional values and pedagogical principles over the use of technology. For example, participants are asked what it is they most value about their institution and would hate most to lose. Only then is technology examined to see how it might support stated values and principles.

A TLTR-style committee should approach its membership strategically. In general, it should be broadly representative of key units in the institution. It is important to have the support of senior-ranking individuals, but they need not be members. The most useful members will be at the operational levels — those who either work with technology or would be expected to.

One of the strengths of the TLTR model is that it places telelearning issues firmly within the context of "doing the right thing" questions. Many technology-planning exercises have failed because they were marginalized from broader questions of institutional mission and purpose. A TLTR group ensures that there is a forum within the institution for those with concerns about the use of technology to have their issues dealt with.

Another strength of the TLTR model is that it is a broad set of organizing and operating principles that can be adapted to local circumstances. Steven Gilbert suggests that TLTR groups not assume a formal policy function in their institution. Some TLTR groups, however, have found that over time, their credibility within the institution is such that they are asked to take on a policy role. Each group will establish itself differently. The TLT Group sponsors national events to help local TLTRs get started and to allow established Roundtables to share experiences and strategies. In this way, local strengths are supplemented by a national network of support.

Finally, the greatest contribution that TLTRs seem to make to institutional telelearning policy is in their communication function. Staff and faculty from dispersed units in the institution discover shared experiences and learn about useful innovations. Support units discover ways in which they can more effectively support telelearning activities. For decentralized institutions, like many universities and colleges, this is an important achievement.

The University of Ottawa and Carleton University jointly sponsored a TLTR workshop in 1998 to begin these processes at their institutions. They have developed an excellent resource on TLTR at (http://www.edteched.uottawa.ca/ottacarl/TLTR/). Although it is still early in the process, several other Canadian institutions have expressed interest in the model and are considering adopting it or trying parts of it in their own sites.

CONCLUSIONS

This chapter has shown that policy processes are critical to the development of sound policies and strategies for telelearning technologies. Based on this research, the following institutional policy processes should be considered:

1. Use a transparent process of deliberation and implementation.
2. Make decisions based on research. Since academic culture values research, the basis for technology decisions needs to be clearly communicated and documented.
3. Enable faculty to feel in control of the technologies and that they fulfill an academic purpose.

The issues associated with online learning are quickly and easily polarized, linked as they are to fundamental ideas about the purpose of education, the role of professors, and the sharing or wielding of power.

Based on this research on policy processes, there are two key areas that need further study. First, there is a need for more research on the impact of policy processes. In the area of telelearning technology, studies are being done to evaluate the technology in terms of cost-benefit, learning outcomes, and pedagogical approaches. More research is also needed on the most effective way to enable universities and colleges to make decisions in this area.

Second, on a broader scale, there is a need for research on the management of change in universities that recognizes and works to uphold those values that make universities unique public institutions — including an unfamiliarity with and even an abhorrence of "management" itself. It is also important that whatever guidelines are developed, these must be sensitive to the variations and differences between universities.

As higher education administrators, teachers, and students seek to maneuver their way through the challenges ahead, they will need to find ways to negotiate change, identify priorities, and find solutions that work. In this context, policy processes become critical. This study has shown that the selection and application of appropriate policy processes for the introduction, application, and use of technology-mediated learning plays a key role in managing technological change in an institution.

DISCUSSION QUESTIONS

1. Which of the policy processes discussed here seem to fit with your organization? What steps would you take to see these processes put in place?
2. Who is involved in the technology planning process in your organization? Could more people be involved in the process?
3. Is the process of technology planning regarded as legitimate by the members of your organization? What role do students play? What about teachers? Others?
4. What are the drivers of change in your organization?

5. Should organizational change be included as part of an information technology strategic plan?

REFERENCES

Bruce, R., Bizzocchi, J., Kershaw, A., Macauley, A., and Schneider, H. (1999, May). Educational technology planning: A framework. Victoria, British Columbia: Centre for Curriculum, Transfer and Technology. Available at http://www.ctt.bc.ca/edtech/framework.html.

Daniel, J. S. (1996). *Mega-Universities and Knowledge Media: Technology Strategies for Higher Education*. London: Kogan Page.

Gianini, P. (1998). Moving from Innovation to Transformation in the Community College. *Leadership Abstracts*. World Wide Web Edition 11 No. 9 (October).

Gilbert, S. W. (1998). AAHESGIT Listserv, Issue 195. See http://www.aahe.org/technology/aahesgit.htm.

Green, K. C. (1998, November). *The Campus Computing Project: The 1998 National Survey of Information Technology in Higher Education* [Online]. Encino, CA. Available URL http://www.campuscomputing.net/.

Hanna, D. E. (1998, March). Higher education in an era of digital competition: Emerging organizational models. *Journal of Asynchronous Learning Networks,* 2(1), 66-95.

Hardy, C. (1992). Managing the relationship: University relations with business and government. In Cutt, J., and Dobell, R. (Eds.), *Public Purse, Public Purpose: Autonomy and Accountability in the Groves of Academe*. Halifax & Ottawa: Institute for Research on Public Policy and the Canadian Comprehensive Auditing Foundation, pp. 193-218.

Kim, W. C., & Mauborgne, R. (1997). Fair process: Managing in the knowledge economy. *Harvard Business Review,* 75(4), 65-75.

Morrison, J. L. (1999). The role of technology in education today and tomorrow: An interview with Kenneth Green, Part II. *On the Horizon,* 7(1), 2-5.

Nedwek, B. (1999). Effective IT planning: Core characteristics. *Presentation to the Society for College and University Planning Winter Workshop, Information Technology Planning*, Hawaii, March 21-24.

Norris, D. M., & Poulton, N. L. (1991). *A Guide for New Planners*. Ann Arbor, MI: Society for College and University Planners.

Olcott, D. J. Jr. (1996). Aligning distance education practice and academic policy. *Continuing Higher Education Review*, 60(1), 27-41.

Ringle, M., & Updegrove, D. (1998). Is strategic planning for technology an oxymoron? *Cause/Effect*, 21(1), 18-23. Available URL http://www.educause.edu/ir/library/html/cem9814.html (Visited 1999, April 20).

Tamburri, R. (1999). Survival of the fittest. *University Affairs*, 8-12.

Chapter V

Information Management in Higher Education Administration: A Slow Drive on the Information Superhighway

Gunapala Edirisooriya
East Tennessee State University

INTRODUCTION

Society has entered a new information age and higher education administration remains far behind its counterparts in the business sector. Educational information management is being drastically underutilized by higher education administration. Databases are used exclusively for record keeping purposes as an end in itself. They are not being effectively used for information management. Thousands of human hours are wasted annually to complete various types of administrative paperwork without using the existing databases as sources of input.

This new information age is categorized by ongoing developments in multimedia and information technology that are opening new possibilities and forcing most people to restructure numerous activities in their lives, encompassing personal, professional, social, and institutional spheres. Rapid advancements in quality and versatility of products in information technology bring new challenges to every working environment. While the specialists in electronic technology keep upgrading the hardware, system and application software specialists continue to upgrade existing systems and create new systems and programs to increase access to new technology for the masses.

In the computer industry, entrepreneurs who recognized the potential of the market transformed an industry of "computers for computer wizards" into an industry where the computer was destined to become an essential household item. Nevertheless, a great majority of end-users are not up to par with the required repertoire of technical knowledge and skills to exploit the capabilities of available information technology. This is most certainly true in higher education. This case explores the underutilization of information technology in higher education administration and looks at whether higher education administration is ready for the new information age.

CASE QUESTIONS
- What are the problems with the current information management systems among higher education institutions?
- What type of restructuring might be necessary in higher education institutions in

order to find solutions to information management problems?
- What are the hurdles to be cleared in implementing a plan of action for the redesign of education information management systems?
- What is the role of end-users in the redesign process?

CASE NARRATIVE

Background

Generally, higher education administrative structure is based on the proliferation of administrative units centered on various functions. An unintended outcome of the growth of administrative progressivism concerns the building up of layers of super structures within organizations (Tyack & Hansot, 1982). This can be applied to both K-12 and post-secondary levels. Therefore, to understand higher education information management systems, one has to look at the evolution of various activities within these institutions.

There are three major administrative areas: student, finance, and personnel or human resources. These three areas present a major challenge in collecting, updating, and maintaining data in a way that is useful, timely, and efficient. They evolved as separate blocks in a centralized administration system. The collection of student records at various locations or units serves as an example of the current system. The admissions office admits students and collects the related data. Another unit, the registrar's office, collects records related to a student's program of study. The financial aid office handles matters related to financial aid, loans, pay plans, and so forth. Payments are handled by the cashier's office. Financial, human resources, and other divisions operate in a similar fashion. The budget office sets the budget. The comptroller's office controls expenses. The human resources office deals with hiring, promotion/demotion, firing, retirements, and benefits. Each of these offices collects, updates, and maintains data separately. Naturally, the redundancy of the system is guaranteed to generate errors (e.g., incompatible records) and leads to a waste of time, money, and resources.

For any higher education institution, one definite checkpoint is to examine a number of publications and look for consistency in faculty names, qualifications, titles, contact information, and so forth. For example, one could examine an institution's cumulative directory, a college directory, undergraduate catalog, and graduate catalog to see the extent of discrepancy among them. Consistency among such publications is hard to find because they are generated by various units and not by one database. The undergraduate admissions office is responsible for the content of the undergraduate catalog, while the graduate admissions office is responsible for the content of the graduate catalog. Nevertheless, the bulk of the data independently collected by each unit represents a common core. This administrative set up is prevalent among higher education settings.

There is abundant evidence concerning the ad-hoc manner in which information management systems evolved within higher education institutions. Incompatibility among unit-specific databases is one compelling source of evidence. For example, data fields have different lengths and different types. In a Human Resource System (HRS), the name of an employee can take three or four different fields (last, first, middle, suffix, etc.) and the total length of fields combined may run into 26-30 columns. In comparison, in a Student Information System (SIS), the combined length of fields of a faculty name can run into 24 or less columns. While name suffixes are included in HRS, they are excluded in SIS. Similarly, the field definitions of variables in Financial Record System (FRS) are incompatible with those in HRS or SIS in the case of common variables across the databases. Furthermore, in one database data files have been designed as flat files, while in another database one could find a hierarchical data structure.

What are the implications of this administrative set up on information management? Each unit must have developed or purchased an information management system to suit its individual needs. Across the nation, many higher education institutions bear witness to this evolutionary process. During the paper-and-pencil era of record keeping, separate units developed their own idiosyncratic ways of record keeping. Access to the records of one unit was limited to selected personnel in that particular area. When needed, each group supplied data to other units and to the top echelon of the administration. With the increasing demand for administrative compliance and accountability, educational institutions felt the need for the establishment of a separate unit for institutional data analysis and report preparation. (For a thorough discussion of the educational accountability issue, see Edirisooriya, 1999.) A separate unit emerged for that purpose with a myriad of titles: institutional research or effectiveness or planning or accountability or any combination of similar terms. Preparing reports on student evaluation of instruction, faculty workloads, and state and federal mandates are among the responsibilities of this unit.

For the end-user, FRS, SIS, or HRS offers very limited options: data entry and examining or printing of one screen of data at a time. When the end-user needs a subset of data drawn from those databases, they have to rely on the institutional research or effectiveness unit. Although higher education administration is quite willing to move forward from the paper-and-pencil era to the new information age, governance structure and the policy-making framework are deeply rooted in the early twentieth century mindset.

Problems with Current Educational Information Management Practices

The problems associated with current educational information management practices can be classified into two broad categories: human and institutional. These two broad categories are not mutually exclusive. The human aspect may include, among others, stress, frustration, anxiety, anger, and burnout. The institutional aspect may include, among others, loss of time, waste of money and other resources, inefficiency, underutilization of resources, and misallocation of funds and miscalculation of priorities. The following scenarios, which were created from anecdotal information that was gathered from several observations and eyewitness accounts across several campuses, are used to illustrate and describe a number of institutional procedures.

Scenario One:

A university student, Marisol, goes to the cashier's office to pay her bill for the coming semester. After waiting in a long queue, it is Marisol's turn to step up to the counter to greet the cashier, Patrice.

Marisol: This total is incorrect. I received some financial support and I am supposed to pay only half of this amount.
Patrice: You have to go the financial aid office to get the bill adjusted.
Marisol: I already went to the financial aid office and submitted all the paper work.
Patrice: When?
Marisol: Two days ago.

Patrice: It usually takes about three days to get those papers here. Until we get the papers we can't change the figures.

Marisol: Can't the financial aid office change my bill when they process my application, instead of this office making the changes after receiving the papers from the financial aid office?

Patrice: I wish we could do it like that. But, you see, they can't see our screen and we can't see their screen, (i.e., no access to each other's database).

Marisol: Okay, but one other thing. This total is incorrect, too. I dropped one course with three credit hours and added a course with four credit hours through the automated registration system this morning. So, the total should be a little bit higher than this.

Patrice: I see, for that you have to go to the registrar's office to get a new bill.

Marisol: So, there isn't any way I can pay this bill today?

Patrice: I don't see how you can! First, you have to go to the registrar's office to get a new bill. Then go to the financial aid office to check whether they have processed and forwarded your application to this office. If they haven't, you have to ask them to process it as soon as possible and send it to us.

Marisol: Tomorrow is the last day to pay bills without a penalty!

Patrice: There is plenty of time, you have until 4 o'clock tomorrow afternoon. I wish I could help you, but there is nothing I can do. I am sorry.

Marisol: Please one more thing. Can I pay for a parking decal?

Patrice: Sorry. There is a separate counter for parking decals. You have to go to counter number 13 for that.

Marisol: My goodness! How many offices and counters do I have to go to just to get a simple thing done? Don't you think this is crazy?

Patrice: You may be right. I am just doing what I am asked to do. There's nothing I can do about it.

Marisol's experience is not unusual either at her university or across many other higher education institutions. For different reasons, this is a helpless situation for both the student and cashier. The student experiences a lack of support with no forum available to bring the situation to the attention of administrators. The cashier may understand the predicament, but is powerless to change the situation because the information management system is not designed to handle this type of circumstance. Staff personnel like Patrice may also be faced with an additional dilemma. While they understand the difficulties that the students are faced with, they are cognizant of the fact that their livelihood is also dependent on the existing information management practices.

Scenario Two:

This situation illustrates problems related to the renewal of parking decals. The scenario combines mail and telephone communications. On the eve of a new academic year, some universities send notices to faculty and staff reminding them of the need to renew parking decals for the coming year. The notice includes a form to be completed and returned by faculty and staff if they wish to renew their parking decals. The form asks an applicant to provide her or his name, social security number, department's mailing address, and the mode of payment. Dana, a fairly new faculty member, complied with this routine for two or three years and then decided to ask some questions of Anthony, the person in charge of handling this matter in the administrative division of this university.

Dana: I get this form every year and it asks for the same information. Why do I have to waste my time writing the same information on a similar form every year?

Anthony: You need to renew your parking decal, right? Then, you have to fill out this form. No form, no parking decal—it's that simple.

Dana: Why do I have to fill this form out every year? You already have this information. It is the same that I have provided over the last few years.

Anthony: We don't have that information with us.

Dana: What do you mean? What do you do with the information collected last year?

Anthony: We don't keep the old forms.

Dana: What do you mean, you don't keep them? You collect all this information and throw them away and every year you start from scratch?

Anthony: Yes, we have a word-processed standard document. We get address labels from the data center and mail them every year. It's a fairly simple process.

Dana: It may look fairly simple to you, but it seems like a waste of university resources. Think about the time we all have to spend filling out these forms with information you already have and the amount of time you have to spend handling the papers.

Anthony: I don't know about that. This is the procedure.

Dana: If the university really wants a form for this for whatever reason, it can print all this information. The university already has this information in the HRS database. A simple program could be written to generate a form that already has the required information.

Anthony: We have being doing it this way for the last 17 years and this is the first time I have heard any complaint about it. But if you don't return the completed form, you won't get a parking decal for next year. I can tell you that much. So please, don't forget to complete and send that form to us.

This scenario explains a simple situation where the currently available data in the HRS database could be used to generate the forms with the required information, if a piece of paper is indeed needed for this purpose. Even this process is redundant and amounts to a waste of resources. Data on faculty and staff who intend to renew parking decals could be generated without wasting a single sheet of paper.

For the faculty, this is a frustrating experience. He understands how ineffective the operation is and does not understand why he should do extra work because of it. For forward-thinking academic and professional staff, this experience can also be quite frustrating, especially if no one else understands the inefficiency of the situation. Those who do want to improve existing practices are often viewed as troublemakers, even though a complacent attitude about change appears in direct opposition to the mission of higher education institutions.

Scenario Three:

The administrative division in charge of summer scheduling and budgeting, normally the office of the Vice President of Academic Affairs (VPAA), sends instructions to each of

Figure 1: Channels of Communication in Summer Budget Preparation

(Time) t_1	VPAA	→	Dean	→	Chair	→	Secretary
(Time) t_2	VPAA	←	Dean	←	Chair	←	Secretary

the deans of the colleges with a prototype of tables and forms to be prepared and submitted with specific instructions and deadlines. The dean's office of each college then relays this information to the department chairs and program coordinators. They in turn convey this information to their secretarial staff. When the materials are ready, they follow the same route in reverse order. This process is illustrated in Figure 1.

This process appears to be rather simple and straightforward, but there are many hurdles to overcome. There are two sets of documents to prepare: one set deals with estimates of instructional cost and the other with contractual agreements. Summer class schedules provide the primary basis for these two sets of documents. By this time, t_1, each departmental secretary had already entered at t_0 every course offered by her or his department into the SIS database. Then, they have to retract the same information twice to prepare Budget Request Forms and Summer Employment Contract Forms.

Secretaries are provided with prototypes of these forms, often with conflicting information. A familiar complaint is, "Last year we were asked to do it this way and this year it is different." Furthermore, departmental secretaries often receive conflicting instructions on how to resolve a simple problem when they contact different units or different personnel in the same unit in the administrative hierarchy, such as, "What do we put down as the starting day of these contracts?" A natural consequence of this situation is a lack of uniformity among contracts prepared by various departments.

Depending on what kind of training the secretaries have undergone and how they are instructed to enter the data, they may prepare Budget Request Forms in table format using a word processor or using a spreadsheet application. The preparation of contracts is even more difficult for departmental secretaries still doing this work using a typewriter. They have to use a set of printed forms (forms printed on carbon papers in blue, green, yellow, etc., which are glued together from one end—pre-photocopying era forms designed for various destinations once a contract is completed). Secretaries extract from the SIS the relevant data that were entered by the secretaries at t_0 (the same information used to prepare Budget Request Forms) and key in this information again on the contract forms. Included with the information to be keyed in by secretaries is the following: instructor's name, department, social security number, address, course ID, number of credit hours, begin and end dates, and amount of payment.

As Scenario Three illustrates, higher education administration information systems do not make full use of database technology. Secretaries often need to repeatedly key in the data for every form and report they have to complete, which defies the purpose of maintaining an electronic database system and leaves room for error and redundancy. When the data are entered into an electronic database, there must be a mechanism in place to produce output using the available input. These databases are designed and used for extremely narrow purposes and are heavily underutilized (Baxter, 1994).

Generally, the data center or the office of institutional research prepares reports routinely, as well as on demand, using each database separately. End-users then combine data from the reports and manually prepare other reports or forms. In other words, no attempt is made to merge databases electronically to produce various reports and forms. The human resources division sends a list of names of part-time faculty whose transcripts are not on file. The finance division sends a table listing each faculty's name, social security number, nine-month salary, a number of columns depicting amounts of remuneration per one credit hour, two credit hours, three credit hours, and so on. The office of continuing studies sends a list containing information regarding off-campus courses and rates of payment. Often, such reports provide overlapping information. Instead of establishing procedures for merging the existing databases to generate the required documents or forms, the administration argues that it is doing all it can to make the secretaries' jobs easier by providing data tables generated by separate databases. The procedures and problems explained in Scenario Three can be applied to the preparation of part-time contracts for regular semesters as well.

Another archaic feature of the current information management practices in higher education administration concerns the way in which various reports are produced by either the data center or by the office of institutional research. These units have mandates from the upper levels of the administration to generate periodic and on-demand reports. The middle or lower administrative units have to make requests for reports by completing and forwarding Job Request Forms either to the data center or the office of institutional research. These requests have to be made on an old-fashioned paper form requiring signatures through the chain of command. Quite often, these reports contain only raw data: workloads, financial transactions, enrollment figures, non-returning students, and employee leave data. Such reports rarely contain analytical data or evaluative summaries. Furthermore, data requests are honored only in printed form. Inevitably, pre-information age data management practices did not and do not entertain the idea of data sharing electronically, and as such there are often no mechanisms in place for electronic data sharing (i.e., no well-tested computer programs designed to generate a subset of data as needed, no well-tested electronic data transfer methods established, etc.).

Occasionally, when personnel in the middle or lower administrative levels request raw data in electronic form for analysis, traditional data managers find it difficult to honor such requests. In fact, data managers are often surprised at such requests, not being accustomed to providing raw data for analysis. Answers to such data requests vary depending on the type of data management personnel one is dealing with. Typical answers might include: We cannot share this data. They are highly confidential; you have to get permission from A, B, and C. For that, you have to fill out forms X, Y, and Z. Yes, we can send you the data for faculty who teach courses in your college. But, if you ask me to send the data for faculty in your college who teach courses across colleges, that's a whole different ball game. It might take awhile; or I can produce a subset of data you need, but I have no way of sending it to you electronically.

Scenario Four:

The following scenario illustrates a familiar dialog depicting the reluctance of administrators to share data.

Simon: These data are quite confidential. They contain personal and institutional information, which cannot be made public.

Taylor: I am not asking to make the data public. I simply want access to the raw data.

Simon: I can't do that. The moment they leave this office, we don't know what will happen to them, or where they will end up.

Taylor: I am the one who is getting these data. I can assure you no one else will have access to them.
Simon: That's easy to say, but you must understand that the more hands through which these data pass, the greater chance they fall into the wrong hands.
Taylor: I am aware of that. But to do my job efficiently, I need these data electronically.
Simon: I am sorry I can't do that. If you want, you can speak to my supervisor Haruko.

Taylor makes an appointment to speak to Simon's supervisor, Haruko.

Taylor: Simon asked me to speak to you about getting these data (Taylor explains briefly what it is that he needs). I can do a much more efficient job if I can get them in some electronic form.
Haruko: Didn't you ask Simon for this?
Taylor: Yes, but Simon is rather reluctant. That's why he suggested that I speak to you.
Haruko: If Simon didn't agree to this, I can't do anything about it. Simon has authority over the data and I do not want to go against his decision. However, we will be glad to do whatever we can to help you get your job done without accessing the data electronically. Please let me know.

This illustrates a typical dilemma faced by professional staff at the middle level of administration. How does this type of information management system work and what are the implications? Initially, in various departments, the secretaries enter the same data into the electronic databases (SIS, HRS, and FRS). Then, they key in the same data to produce various end-user documents. The databases are used for very narrow purposes, such as data entry or review of raw data. If the administration does not have the conceptual and technical understanding of how to merge various databases to generate reports and forms, then vast resources are wasted on the amount of time spent and efforts made to create, check, and revise various end-user documents. This process has an adverse impact on personnel both at an individual and institutional level within an organization, and because the higher echelon of the administration set information management policies, middle level administrators are left to struggle with the limitations or inadequacies of such policies in relation to performing their job responsibilities.

ANALYSIS

Some universities have entered into contractual agreements with private corporations to launch a change process to meet the challenges of the new information age. It is too early to comment on the impact of such partnerships on restructuring educational information management. Current evidence seems to indicate that initial efforts are being directed toward building the information technology infrastructure and issues related to upgrading hardware and software. Therefore, it would be unrealistic to assume that such partnerships will be able to bring about the kind of restructuring of educational information management processes advocated in this case. Furthermore, in the case of financially struggling institutions of higher education, the probability of establishing new information management systems is very low or nonexistent. As a result, every effort must be made to integrate the existing databases (SIS, HRS, and FRS). Such efforts can be divided into two groups: short term and long term.

There are several suggested short-term measures that could be taken to integrate existing databases, in terms of both technology measures, and personnel training and rewards. Technically, one of the first steps is to determine and introduce new data fields into the existing databases in order to collect the data needed for routine activities and educational accountability and accreditation purposes. There is also the need to facilitate and establish the electronic exchange of data as the standard method for exchanging data among various units.

In terms of people issues, it is important to identify personnel who have the professional knowledge and technical skills necessary to design algorithms that merge the existing databases and generate various types of reports and forms. Additionally, it is useful to design and conduct workshops and training sessions targeted to improving the professional and technical knowledge of faculty, administrators, and staff as part of a well-conceived plan to facilitate and improve educational information management practices. This would be most successful if the improvement of educational information management practices becomes an integral part of a continuous improvement strategic plan.

Perhaps the most important step would be to establish a reward mechanism to identify and encourage innovative methods to improve educational information management practices. This can be done by establishing an institution-wide task force to design, implement, monitor, and evaluate efficient information management practices to meet the challenges in the new information age. For this purpose, draw a body of dedicated individuals from the administration and faculty based on knowledge and skills in educational information management coupled with the appropriate representatives of the upper levels of the administration.

There are also several long-term measures that may be useful. For example, there needs to be a shift in the emphasis in hiring practices and policies when attempting to fill higher education administration positions. Traditionally, the top echelon of administration in higher education institutions was drawn from accomplished scholars, (especially in the liberal arts and the social sciences) with managerial and supervisory skills. This tradition is equally persistent at the middle administration level. Although there is some emphasis on technological skills in searches at the middle administration level, it is far below the standards needed for the new information age. Rarely are specialists in educational information management, data analysis, computer programming, or similar fields in the upper divisions of higher education administration. A widely held belief is that top level administrators do not have to be experts in information management, since they have a team of experts working at the next level below them. However, across many higher education institutions, the presence of much-needed expertise among such teams of experts is still lacking. It is time to conceptualize the need for professional and technical skills far beyond a familiarity with word processing and spreadsheets.

The formulation of policies designed to provide opportunities for personnel in higher education institutions to upgrade their technical knowledge base and skills is required. Those who are willing to work extra hard manage to keep up with the advancements in information technology. Their efforts should be encouraged, incentive schemes should be introduced, alternative personnel evaluation methods should be devised, and facilities and needed hardware and software should be provided. Additionally, professional degree programs designed to train personnel for higher education administration should be created and implemented.

The business sector, especially large corporations, looks for candidates with an MBA or equivalent combined with a solid background in professional and technical skills for administrative/managerial positions. Higher education institutions rarely think along those lines. Toward this end, well-established universities with the necessary resources should embark upon designing degree programs similar to a Masters of Business Administration for those who plan a career in higher education administration.

Policy makers in higher education must vigorously pursue a plan of action to change the culture of higher education administration in order to meet the needs of the new information age. Among those practices in need of immediate attention are enrollment-driven budgeting, crises-driven management, and inefficient and outdated administrative practices. The reevaluation and reorganization of the functions of higher education are necessary in light of the information technology opportunities that are becoming available every day.

CONCLUSION

Generally, the lack of knowledge and skill in information technology may vary among higher education institutions as well as within any given university or college (Morrissey, 1999). The lack of understanding of information technology can be found among faculty, administrators, and staff across disciplines and age groups. Personnel in the areas of science and technology generally possess a higher degree of understanding of information technology in comparison to their colleagues in other disciplines. However, in terms of seniority, junior personnel tend to be more comfortable in the use of information technology (Roschelle & Pea, 1999). While the need to upgrade the knowledge base and skill level in information technology in higher education administration is clearly evident, a perplexing question is whether policy makers have grasped the gravity of this problem.

In contrast, this need is well recognized in the business sector. As William Terrell (1999) points out, the harsh reality in the business world is that to be competitive in the marketplace through increased productivity, the business sector has to keep up with technology. Similarly, the survival of higher education institutions rests squarely on their ability to deliver the services to meet the standards imposed by the rapid advancements in information technology. One integral part of this adaptation process concerns the establishment of an integrated information management system. This should be among the top priorities of any higher education institution in the new information age.

At the individual employee level, a number of hurdles must be overcome. The perceptions and attitudes of higher education administrative personnel pose a problem. "I have no time to learn this stuff" is a familiar phrase among many faculty, administration, and staff. This may be a legitimate complaint as the current administrative policies do not accommodate or encourage individual efforts for improving professional knowledge and technical skills. However, the lack of knowledge of the basics of information technology among higher education personnel and their inclination to avoid incidents through which others may learn about such deficiencies is a major issue.

Issues of control, especially at the upper levels of administration, create formidable obstacles to change, and it can be observed that there is the tendency for higher education personnel to cling to what is familiar or comfortable.

At the institutional level, there are some deep-rooted hurdles encountered, such as inability or unwillingness to visualize and plan an overall information management system or partisan battles waged over safeguarding individual territories (FRS, SIS, and HRS). There is too much reliance on current practices and policies regarding data entry, access, retrieval, and analysis.

There are limitations and problems associated with the current databases. End-users can only perform data entry and view raw data one screen at a time. Options for the end-user to manipulate the data even on a single database are simply not there, let alone merging of different databases. (An extensive discussion of limitations of such practices can be found in Hansen & Hansen, 1995; Kroenke, 1995.)

The de facto rule is that data manipulations and access to raw data are the exclusive rights of those who are in charge of the data. At the same time, those in charge of the data are simply keeping the data. The data are not used to generate useful information for administrative purposes. The bureaucratic structures and procedures are based on current practices of data sharing and dissemination (completing Job Requests; sending reams of printed raw-data output based on FRS, SIS, and HRS from different branches; and special permission for access to raw data through the lines of command, etc.).

The time lag in the acculturation of information technology in an organization lies in its culture. By all accounts, institutional culture presents a formidable resistance to fundamental reforms (Cunningham & Gresso, 1993). Therefore, any ambitious plan to establish an integrated information management system in higher educational administration cannot afford to ignore cultural bottlenecks.

The need for establishing an integrated educational information management system in higher education administration is clearly evident. For the 21st century, higher education institutions must conceptualize a visionary mission and implement a plan of action to fully exploit the expanding opportunities stemming from the advancement in information technology.

The recognition of the demand to upgrade curricula and instructional technology—to prepare graduates with the necessary knowledge base and skills in information technology for the 21st century—by professional organizations, learned societies, and accrediting agencies is praiseworthy. The survival of the higher education system is contingent upon the upgrading of the knowledge base and skill-level in information technology among faculty, administrators, and staff. In addition, establishing educational information management systems and procedures on par with the advancement in information technology is mandatory. In the coming decade, the survival and competitiveness of many higher education institutions may rest squarely on this factor.

DISCUSSION QUESTIONS

1. Identify several quick-fix versus long-term solutions to problems in information management in higher education administration. What are the advantages and disadvantages to each?
2. If you were selected to serve on the committee for continuous improvement at your institution, how would you assess the information management problems and what steps would you take in developing a plan to solve those information management issues?
3. Should senior-level higher education administrators be expected to have expertise in

information technology and information management?
4. What considerations should be taken into account when designing a training program in information management for senior-level higher education administrators?

END NOTE

Opinions expressed in this chapter do not necessarily reflect the position, policies, or practices of East Tennessee State University.

REFERENCES

Baxter, B. M. (1994). *Lots of Data! No Information! Why Universities and Colleges Do Not Take Full Advantage of Their Information Systems*. Educational Resources Information Center, Document ID: ED368266.

Cunningham, W. C., & Gresso, D. W. (1993). *Cultural Leadership*. Needham Heights, MA: Allyn & Bacon.

Edirisooriya, G. (1999). Why we need to strengthen graduate training in educational administration. In Muth, R., & Martin, M. (Eds.). *Toward the Year 2000: Leadership for Quality Schools*. Lancaster, PA: Technomic Press.

Hansen, G. W., & Hansen, J. V. (1995). *Database Management and Design*. Englewood, NJ: Prentice-Hall.

Kroenke, D. M. (1995). *Database Processing: Fundamentals, Designs, and Implication*. Englewood, NJ: Prentice-Hall.

Morrissey, C. (1999). Enhancing Professional Education Through Virtual Knowledge Networks. Available from: http://horizon.unc.edu/TS/commentary/1999-07.asp

Roschelle J., & Pea, R. (1999). Trajectories from today's WWW to a powerful educational infrastructure. *Educational Researcher*, 28(5), 22-25 & 43.

Terrell, W. (August 04, 1999). IFETS-DISCUSS Digest—2 Aug 1999 to 3 Aug 1999. Available from: Automatic Digest Processor LISTSERV@LISTSERV.READADP.COM.

Tyack, D., & Hansot, E. (1982). *Managers of Virtue: Public School Leadership in America, 1820-1980*. New York: Basic Books.

Chapter VI

Development of a New University-Wide Course Management System

Ali Jafari
Indiana University Purdue University Indianapolis

INTRODUCTION

Distance learning is no longer a conceptual discussion, a buzzword, or a show-and-tell demonstration in a computer trade show. It is a multi-billion-dollar business moving its way up to the top of universities' lists of priorities. University and college administrators are now convinced that the Web and the Internet can and will change their traditional teaching practices into a semi-virtual and virtual operation. This is the arrival of a new paradigm where students and instructors make fewer trips to campuses to receive or deliver lectures.

A variety of computer tools and environments have been commercially developed and are being used to deliver distance learning content. Course management systems or course authoring tools are among the names used to refer to such software environments. Today there is a large selection of course management software packages on the market. This has created much debate over what brand of course management system a university should choose. Is WebCT better than Topclass? How does Domino Lotus compare to WebCT and BlackBoard? Many institutions have tried to compare and contrast different course management systems in order to make a decision. While some institutions have elected to use one or more off-the-shelf course management systems, others have developed their own software.

The selection or development of the "right" course management system for an educational institution is probably one of the most difficult decisions that information technology administrators have to make. It is not like deciding on the selection of Netscape versus Internet Explorer or WordPerfect versus Microsoft Word. It is substantially more complicated due to the fact that a course management environment should function as an enterprise system, able to link to or include many services and resources already in place in the university. This includes student registration, course offering catalogs, computing account IDs, personal Web servers, student information systems, and library resources, as well as file servers. Failure to link with these resources will create an expensive, difficult-to-use, and resource-intensive course management environment. A well-designed course management system should include or share resources with the existing services. Many information technology administrators may not yet understand the importance of a well-designed course management system, and often they have deployed systems without understanding the conceptual framework behind them, or defining the functional and technical requirements of the university.

This case study examines the development and implementation of the Oncourse project at Indiana University (Oncourse, 1999). Oncourse was designed, beta tested, and implemented at Indiana University Purdue University Indianapolis (IUPUI), a 28,000-student campus, and is currently in use at all eight campuses of Indiana University—serving around 100,000 students and 45,000 courses.

CASE QUESTIONS

- How does an institution decide whether or not to build or buy a university-wide distance learning system?
- Who is responsible for designing new distance learning technology systems within the university setting?
- What are the functional and technical requirements for a course management system that are necessary to support the teaching and learning needs of distance learning initiatives?

CASE NARRATIVE

Background

Founded in 1969, Indiana University Purdue University Indianapolis (IUPUI) is recognized as a leader in urban higher education, and is Indiana's third largest and most comprehensive university with more than 180 degree programs in 21 academic units. IUPUI has the largest weekend college in the nation. More than 3,200 students are enrolled in integrated credit classes on Friday nights, Saturdays and Sundays. One of the most sophisticated electronic libraries in the nation serves the IUPUI campus, offering cutting-edge information storage, retrieval, and distribution via technology.

Distance learning has been one of the top IUPUI university-wide initiatives. For the last 15 years, IUPUI has been actively involved in distance education using various print, video, and television networks to deliver course content. In 1996, IUPUI created an internal research laboratory called WebLab. The purpose of WebLab was to help the university respond to the technological opportunities presented by the Internet and World Wide Web. The WebLab is headed by a director holding a faculty position in the School of Engineering and Technology, and is staffed with research engineers and academic research fellows.

Assessing the Options

In 1997, the Community Learning Network, the university department responsible for continuing education and distance education, requested assistance from the WebLab to explore Internet-based solutions for distance education. At that time, WebLab conducted a study to evaluate off-the-shelf products and determine if the commercial products could meet current and emerging distance learning requirements. In 1997, a dozen course management systems were commercially available on the market. The WebLab study analyzed several off-the-shelf software packages that were available at that time, and provided an assessment of each product's limitations.

Generally, WebLab found that commercial course management programs were designed as stand-alone systems and were not capable of easy integration with the university legacy system and/or Student Information Systems. Due to the lack of integration capability with the university database system, manual creation of course accounts would have cost millions of dollars to support if used for the entire university. Additionally, many of the commercial software packages would not interact with the existing information technology services on campus, such as the University's file server, Web server, registration, and name directory database services. Replication of these services inside a course management system would increase unnecessary support costs in addition to the creation of various technical problems associated with database synchronization and updating.

Another issue was the problem of maintenance. The commercial packages required the manual creation of course templates and daily maintenance of course rosters, either by the course instructor or support staff, and therefore, would be a continual expense associated with the commercial stand-alone course management system. Additionally, commercial software packages were not capable, both technically and cost effectively, of handling a large number of courses and student accounts. This was a major problem since the university annually offered 45,000 course sections to over 100,000 students.

End-user issues were also considered. Several university departments, such as the Computer Technology Department, were actively involved in using advanced technology in distance learning, including streaming audio and video broadcast of live lectures and lectures available on CD-ROM. They felt strongly that the commercial software options did not meet the pedagogical and functional requirements for synchronous and asynchronous instruction. Additionally, there was the ease-of-use issue. None of the off-the-shelf software packages available met the ease-of-use requirements. All the software packages studied seemed to have been designed by engineers for engineers with the assumption that the end users (mainly faculty) would spend a day or more in training workshops and consultation to master the environment.

However, the WebLab team agreed that a more user-friendly, cost-effective solution needed to be found. Currently, there was a major problem with the lack of consistency across the university in user interface design and navigation schemes for existing distance learning applications. For instance, the courses offered by the School of Nursing were based on using the WebCT product while the School of Journalism used the TopClass product, and the Physics and Computer Science departments had made their own course management systems. Students taking courses from two or more schools from the same university were forced to learn two or more user interface environments. Additionally, the campus helpdesk responsible for providing technical assistance to the students needed to learn all the course management packages in use to be able to answer student technical and navigational questions. This was somewhat of an impossible task due to the size of the campus.

Designing a General-Purpose Web-Authoring Tool

After an unsuccessful attempt to find an appropriate off-the-shelf product, the WebLab decided to begin the development of its own distance learning authoring tool. Chemistry 101, a widely used freshman chemistry course, was selected to be redesigned for Web-based delivery (Schock, 1998). A group of technologists, librarians, and subject matter experts joined the WebLab research group to design and develop its first Web-based distance learning course.

After successfully developing Chemistry 101, the WebLab team began the design and development of a general-purpose Web-authoring tool that would address the needs of the Community Learning Network for producing distance learning courses. In July of 1997, the WebLab and the Community Learning Network explored the idea of developing a complimentary Web environment for all traditional and distance education courses at the university. Encouragement and support was received from the university Dean of Faculties to experiment with this idea, which was not yet being pursued by any other educational institutions (Jafari, 1999-1). The Community Learning Network, the Center for Teaching and Learning, the University Information Technology Services, the University Library, and the Office of the Registrar became involved in this research and development initiative. All of the offices, except the University Information Technology Services (the system-wide technology service responsibility for all the Indiana University campuses), were specific to the IUPUI.

This project and its product were named Oncourse. Although the original idea was to design the Oncourse system simply as a "cookie making machine" to produce Web sites automatically for university courses, the WebLab group conceptualized and designed a solution addressing wider teaching and learning needs. This evolved into the development of a comprehensive teaching and learning enterprise framework that offers a "one-stop" Web solution to all online teaching and learning needs.

From a technical perspective, the Oncourse Environment was designed as an "add on" to the university legacy system and Student Information System. It would create a personal homepage and a course Web site for every individual and every course section in the university. From a business perspective, the Oncourse Environment potentially offered millions of dollars in savings by neither creating duplicate database systems nor duplicating existing information technology services. Automatic Web site creation and maintenance would also offer significant savings. From a faculty perspective, Oncourse introduced a new and useful toolbox that could easily be learned and maintained without the need for most users to attend workshops or receive technical consultation.

In the spring semester of 1999, Oncourse went into full deployment at IUPUI. This included the dynamic creation of an Oncourse environment for every course section offered on the campus, a total of 6,041 course sections. By using the faculty and student data, every student and faculty member was given automatic dynamic access to their Oncourse Web site by using their university Network ID (the same ID used to access email accounts). This provided an opportunity for every faculty member to add course content to her or his existing course environment.

Although there were neither public announcements nor extensive promotional activity, Oncourse received high recognition among the students and faculty in a matter of days. On Sunday, January 10, a day before the first Monday of the new spring semester, more than 150 faculty members logged into their course Web sites and added content, such as greeting messages to students, syllabi, reading assignments, and so forth.

In the fall of 1999, the University Information Technology Services of Indiana University (http://www.indiana.edu/~uits/) offered the Oncourse service to all eight campuses of Indiana University. This provided the capability for all faculty members to create Web environments for their courses—making IU one of the very first universities with a totally automated and dynamic course management enterprise system. The Web address http://oncourse.iu.edu now provided the Oncourse front door access to every student and faculty member across the IU campuses.

The Oncourse System: How It Works
From a design perspective, every student and faculty member at the university owns an Oncourse Personal Profile, similar to a personal homepage that is dynamically generated

for every member of the university. Every member of the university may access his/her profile via a Web browser by entering his/her existing university computing ID, normally the same username and password used to check the university email (See Figure 1). For instance, once a student registers for a course, the course hyperlink appears on the student's Personal Profile page. Similarly, once a department identifies a course offering for an upcoming semester, the system automatically places a hyperlink on the instructor's Personal Profile page, pointing to that instructor's teaching assignments (see Figure 2). All of this happens automatically based on data entered and maintained by the university registrar. Every course Web site features a course template, which is used consistently for all university courses (see Figure 3). The course templates are preloaded with communication and collaboration tools including email, chat, threaded message forums, a class roster, a grade book, and online testing, as well as hundreds of online resources that are available through the university library.

The course instructor, by default, is given authoring privileges and assumes site administration responsibility. Faculty do not need to know any computing language. Word processing and Web surfing experience are sufficient skills to author and maintain a course Web site. The fully automatic and dynamic environment runs 24 hours a day with near-zero administrative maintenance. For instance, when a student drops a course, the Oncourse system will remove his/her access to the course and his/her name from the class roster. This is done automatically without any maintenance required by either the university technology administrator or the course instructor.

Due to universities' long history of supporting mainframe computing, many large universities still have hundreds of legacy technical and administrative staff working in their

Figure 1

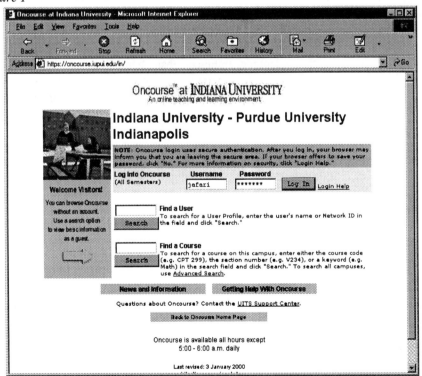

Figure 2

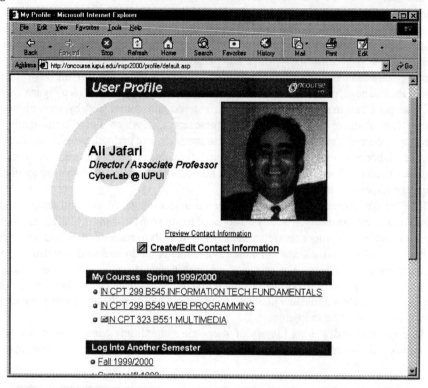

information technology department. Oncourse was designed to take advantage of existing information technology services in the university in order to provide a cost-effective and affordable solution. Each night at midnight, Oncourse acquires data from the university legacy system, including the student registration database, computing accounts IDs, drops and adds, and users status, and creates the Oncourse authentication and authorization table. These databases already exist and are maintained by various university departments without any additional cost.

Selling the Oncourse Concept

An interesting strategy was used to introduce and sell the Oncourse concept in the university. A conceptual story was written to introduce the Oncourse concept. The stories used scenarios that depicted examples of how a Web-based distance-learning enterprise system might operate. The purpose of the scenarios was to help nontechnical administrators and decision-makers understand better the needs for Web-based distance learning as an enterprise model rather than a stand-alone course management system. The exact copy of the Oncourse conceptual story follows:

The week before classes, Fall 1998
Professor Rodriques decides to put his course syllabus online. While he is comfortable using word processing, email, and a Web browser, he doesn't know HTML nor does he have the time to learn it. He uses his favorite Web browser to connect to http://oncourse.iu.edu/. He clicks on the logon screen and enters his

Figure 3

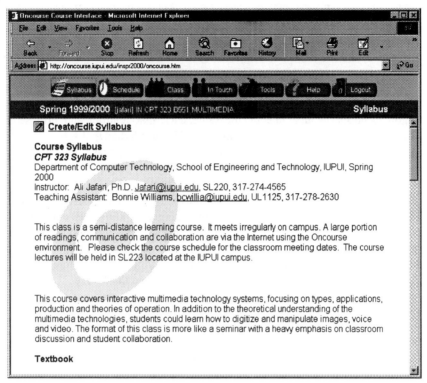

University Network User Name and Password. A welcome screen confirms that he is a faculty member in the XYZ Department, assigned to teach the fall semester class XYZ 499. He clicks on the XYZ 499 button; then he is asked to enter information about his XYZ 499 class. Instead of retyping the entire text of the syllabus he has prepared for his course, Professor Rodriques copies the information from his MS-Word document and pastes it in the appropriate fields. The information includes the course description, objectives, requirements, textbook, assignments, online reading, final project, and other elements. To his delight, Professor Rodriques realizes he does not need to enter students' names or user IDs anywhere to facilitate access to his course page or computer-mediated communication. Oncourse automatically and dynamically builds a roster, containing all the students' names, email addresses, and homepages. Professor Rodriques clicks on some check boxes to include a live chat room, a message board, and class mail. By clicking on the submit button, Professor Rodriques' class page or syllabus is automatically posted on the Oncourse Web server and is online before he goes to bed.

First day of classes, Fall 1998
Jennifer Wycoff, a student with the university, uses her home computer to visit the Oncourse site. Like Professor Rodriques, she uses her favorite Web browser to connect to http://oncourse.iu.edu/ and types in her Network ID, user name and password. The next screen displays Jennifer's courses. She clicks on XYZ 499

where she can access the course information provided by Professor Rodriques. Included in the information is a welcome message from Professor Rodriques. As part of the first class assignment, Jennifer is asked to take an online skill assessment. Jennifer may also take a few minutes to find out who else is registered, and she may chat with some of her classmates.

First day of classes, Fall 1998
Jennifer's dad, an adult student at the university, uses his laptop computer to logon to http://oncourse.iu.edu/, the same URL that Jennifer and Professor Rodriques have used. Although Adam Wycoff lives in Indianapolis, his new job requires him to make many business trips, sometimes overseas. This time he is in Australia, attending an important meeting. After logging onto the Oncourse site, Adam clicks on the Chemistry 101 button. Chemistry 101 is an online course designed for full delivery and access over the Internet with no face-to-face class meetings required. Like Jennifer, Adam will get to know his classmates, understand the course requirements, and take the first online assessment. Adam watches the first lecture via his laptop computer and spends a few minutes collaborating with his classmates and his chemistry professor. Before logging out, he sends mail messages to the course librarian and the course mentor.

Second day of classes, Fall 1998
Based on the students' responses to the online skill assessment, Professor Rodriques has decided to change the first XYZ 499 class assignment and post a new reading list. In addition, he wants to develop an online conference for the following Friday evening. Again, he points his Web browser to http://oncourse.iu.edu/ and enters his Network ID to logon to the system; he then clicks on the XYZ 499 link. Since Professor Rodriques is the faculty of record for XYZ 499, the Oncourse environment automatically gives him "edit" privileges to change, add, or delete any of the content and categories. Professor Rodriques successfully completes these tasks without any need to contact the university Support Center or the neighborhood kid who, in addition to mowing his lawn, is also his computer consultant.

Last week of classes, Fall 1998
Professor Rodriques is now convinced that a large portion of his class content and lecture could be delivered via the Web through the Oncourse environment. He is meeting with the chair of the XYZ department and the Dean of his school to discuss his idea to reduce his class contacts to only once a week while the rest of the course content will be delivered via the Web. In addition to the approvals needed to re-engineer the course curriculum and reduce the in-class contact, Professor Rodriques needs some funding to produce multimedia content to be purchased by the library as online resources for his class, including the digital version of his textbook.

The following years, 1999-2000
Now, all faculty from any IU campus can easily add their course syllabi and teaching content (more than 47,000 courses), as Professor Rodriques did in the

previous semester, from a single interface. Students from any IU campus or those enrolled in an IU certificate program will use their Network IDs to access course content and engage in communication with others in their learning communities.

This conceptual story helped to demonstrate how the new Web-based paradigm could be used by students and faculty, both for distance learning and traditional courses. The Oncourse conceptual story was published on the WebLab Web site and was distributed to university administrators and decision-making groups for their review and comments.

Additionally, two usability studies were conducted to evaluate the user interface design from both faculty and students' perspectives. In two separate usability tests, students and faculty were invited to participate in a laboratory testing of the Oncourse environment. The results of the usability tests were used to refine the human interface designs.

ANALYSIS

The Oncourse project provided a cost-effective enterprise solution for the automatic creation of a Web environment for all university courses. This was mainly due to the dynamic nature of the Oncourse architecture and design, which imported student registration data from the university database system as opposed to requiring manual input of data into a course management system. At the time of this investigation, all commercial course management systems required manual data entry and, therefore, routine maintenance as students add or drop courses. The dynamic and automatic features of Oncourse saved a great deal of operational cost.

Oncourse provided a consistent user interface design and course template for every course in the university. This provided a standard user interface system available across all the course Web sites. Students did not need to learn a new environment nor a new set of tools as they switched from one course to another or to courses from a different school or department.

Automatic creation of a Web environment for 100% of the university courses created a convenient and encouraging situation for faculty members to use the system, even those who were not sure about their instructional needs for a Web environment. Many faculty members had not been introduced yet to the capabilities and features of the Web in teaching. The automatic creation of a Web environment provided faculty members an opportunity to "get their feet wet" and begin to understand the pedagogical application of the World Wide Web in teaching and learning.

The automatic creation of a Web environment for every course provided students with virtual communication and collaboration opportunities. Even in situations where faculty members decided not to use the course Web environment, the students, on their own initiative, would often use the message boards and chat rooms to collaborate among themselves outside the classroom.

The methodology used for developing the Oncourse project was different from those that universities normally use to design and develop a new technology system. The traditional design practice is to assign the task to a committee or a task force or to hire an outside technology consultant, usually a vendor. Committee members define the conceptual requirements, review demos, and participate in vendors' presentations. The committee members, however, may not have any experience in system design or the architecture of information technology. Although there are many success stories and successful case studies using traditional procedures, equally as many experience failure.

The WebLab approach for the design and development of the Oncourse project also did not take a traditional approach. The WebLab team had extensive experience and knowledge in system design and system engineering for information systems, in addition to the full understanding of functional and technical requirements of a distributed distance-learning environment. Based on past experience, an understanding of user needs, and knowledge of system engineering, the WebLab designed the first prototype version of Oncourse and invited faculty and technology administrators to evaluate and comment on various aspects of usability and functional requirements.

The feedback received from end users and information technology administrators was used to refine the beta environment. The beta environment was made available to faculty members, both at IUPUI and at other universities, as an experimental trial. On a daily basis, feedback was received from faculty and student beta testers, and refinements were made in the system immediately (see Figure 4). By the end of the semester, there were more than 650 course accounts on the Oncourse system serving a total of 12,000 students. This not only provided very large-scale feedback information to the design team, it also provided the opportunity to test the server operation in a real-life situation. The beta environment proved to exceed reliability and usability expectations.

CONCLUSIONS

It is evident, due to the many pedagogical benefits of using the Web in teaching and learning, that over the next few years most higher education institutions will provide some sort of Web component for every course offered, not only for those courses offered as distance learning. Supplementing courses with a Web site is following the same evolution that email experienced. When email was introduced, at first it was offered only to a selected number of users, mostly administrators and faculty. Email was then extended to all

Figure 4

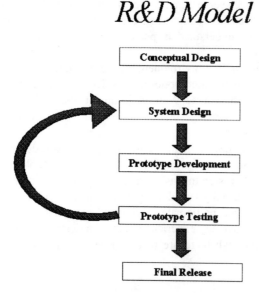

university members who requested the account, and before long, email accounts were created for everyone in the university as a default practice.

A course management environment should not be implemented as a stand-alone system. In order to provide full pedagogical, usability, and operational cost benefits, a course management system must be designed as an enterprise architecture. As an enterprise architecture, the course management system can link and interface with existing university database systems in addition to utilizing or including existing information technology services offered in the university.

DISCUSSION QUESTIONS

1. What are the advantages and shortcomings of a build versus buy approach for a course management system?
2. Why are the pros and cons of using an enterprise course management architecture rather than a stand-alone system?
3. What are the advantages and disadvantages of a fixed template for common use across a campus?
4. What features and capabilities are not yet conceptualized or offered in the commercial course management systems?

EPILOGUE

On February 5, 1998, the developers of the Oncourse Environment, under their new Laboratory organization named CyberLab (CyberLab, 1999), followed their Oncourse R&D project with the development of A New Global Environment for Learning—also known as Angel (Angel, 1999). Angel is intended to offer a new conceptual framework and enterprise technical architecture for teaching and learning needs in K-12, higher education, and training institutions. After six months of extensive university and K-12 beta testing, the Angel is expected to be commercially available around the publication date of this publication.

REFERENCES

Angel. (1999). *A New Global Environment for Learning*. [Online]. Available: http://angel.iupui.edu/ [1999, July 7].

CyberLab. (1999). *About the CyberLab, Formerly WebLab*. [Online]. Available: http://www.cyberlab.iupui.edu/ [1999, July 7].

Jafari, A. (1999-1). Putting everyone and every course on-line: The Oncourse project at Indiana University. *WebNet Journal*, 1(4), 43-49.

Jafari, A. (1999-2). The rise of a new paradigm shift in teaching and learning. *T.H.E. Journal*, 27 (3), 58-68.

Oncourse. (1999). *Oncourse Course Management Environment Developed at Indiana University*. [Online]. Available: http://oncourse.iu.edu/ [1999, July 7].

Schock, E. (1998). Only on the Internet; IUPUI offers first Net class to Chemistry 101 students. *The Indianapolis Star/The Indianapolis News*, February 16, 1998.

Chapter VII

The Selection and Implementation of a Web Course Tool at the University of Texas at Austin

Mark Lowry Decker and Morrie Schulman
University of Texas

Christopher Blandy
Human Code Inc.

INTRODUCTION

For the past 10 years, the University of Texas at Austin has pursued the goal of integrating information technology into instruction. Through the Center for Instructional Technologies and its parent organization, Academic Computing and Instructional Technology Services, the University has recently developed a centralized approach to Web course development by selecting and implementing a tool for voluntary use by the faculty. This case study illustrates some of the challenges encountered and the lessons learned in initiating such a plan, given the institutional and personnel constraints of a large, historically decentralized research university.

Educators from universities of all sizes realize that technological change has created a new reality for higher education both by intensifying the need for ongoing education and training and by creating tools that have changed the teaching and learning process. This study indicates that a small staff, even without overt institutional support, can have a large impact on this process by choosing an appropriate tool, actively promoting it, and conducting effective training.

CASE QUESTIONS
- What criteria should be used to select a Web course development tool from the multitude of available products?
- What factors should be considered when evaluating a Web course development tool for use at a large research university?
- Once a tool has been selected, how can interest in Web course delivery be generated among faculty members?
- What issues should be considered before a training program is designed and implemented for the faculty and staff who will be publishing online courses?

- How can the organization charged with selecting, implementing, and supporting this tool achieve its goals given personnel, budgetary, and institutional constraints?

CASE NARRATIVE

Background

The University of Texas at Austin (UT) has continually sought to incorporate information technology into instruction. As early as 1993 when two of the 125 Web servers worldwide were at the Austin campus, faculty members were using the Web to supplement instruction. The following year the award-winning World Lecture Hall (http://www.utexas.edu/lecture) began as "WWW for Instructional Use." Many of the early adopters who used this new resource served on key committees that had great influence on information technology at the University.

One such committee, the Faculty Computing Committee (FCC), developed a Vision Plan in 1989 that shaped the University's efforts. This original Vision Plan urged the development and funding of campus-wide academic computing facilities and services and recommended that the University identify key programs, projects, and individuals to integrate these facilities and services into research and instruction. Four basic components—information environments, access laboratories, information age classrooms, and infrastructure—were identified as essential elements. Later, the FCC submitted a revised plan, the 1995–2001 Vision Plan. The goal of this plan was to establish the University of Texas at Austin as a leader in the effective use of information technology in instruction, research, and service. To reach this goal, the University would be called upon to increase its investment in information technology and to forge new connections among its many academic and administrative units (Faculty Computer Committee, 1995).

Two other committees, the 1994 Multimedia Instruction Committee (MIC) and the 1997 Long-Range Planning for Information Technology Committee, had a large impact on the infusion of information technology into teaching and learning. From recommendations proposed by the MIC, then-Provost Mark Yudof brought together three smaller entities in 1996 to form the core of a new Center for Instructional Technologies (CIT) to champion the development of innovative instructional technologies on campus. The new organization was part of the restructuring of the Computation Center—founded in 1961—into Academic Computing and Instructional Technology Services (ACITS).

ACITS' representatives on the Long-Range Planning Committee, along with those from Administrative Computing, the Office of Telecommunications Services, the General Libraries, the MIC, the Telecommunication/Distance Learning Committee and High Performance Computing, were instrumental in issuing the 1997 report *Information Technology in Higher Education*. This detailed work attempted to coordinate information technology efforts at the University of Texas and suggested that goals and supporting policies for technology-enhanced learning and online course delivery be developed. The report led to a survey of how major universities were using the WWW in instruction (Schulman, 1997) and culminated in the decision to charge the CIT with selecting a viable World Wide Web course development tool for the University community.

Since its inception, the CIT has grown to incorporate multimedia, information and Web-based design, instructional design, distance education, and expert programming staff devoted to research and development of emerging technologies. The CIT offers services and facilities that promote, support, and integrate digital technologies in learning, teaching, and research. Originally staffed by four individuals, the Center has grown to 15 full-time employees and has an annual budget of about $550,000 (Culp, 1999).

The Role of the Center for Instructional Technologies

The Center for Instructional Technologies (CIT) was charged with selecting and implementing a Web course development tool for the University. Traditionally, faculty members had received little direction about how to accomplish online delivery of their courses. Even without a top-down directive, individual faculty members and departments had already incorporated the Web in their instruction successfully. Many had discovered various software packages (Web Course in a Box, FirstClass, LearningSpace, and HTML editors) to assist their efforts to deliver course materials online. Staff at the CIT realized early in the process that a centralized approach to delivering online instruction needed to enable the faculty to maintain complete control over the content and scope of their courses and allow them to use familiar editing tools. They also understood that they were a small organization dealing with a huge research institution whose faculty valued their independence.

The task of selecting a Web course tool fell upon one of the CIT's components, the Office of Distance Education, because the motivation for considering a Web course development tool was based in part on delivering learning at a distance.

Sheldon Eckland-Olson, the new provost at the University of Texas at Austin, helped refocus the CIT's efforts to embrace what he termed "local distance learning." Within this new paradigm, the CIT grew from supporting distance education to enabling local online course development through the use of tools originally envisioned primarily for distance education.

A review of available Web course tools in late 1997 found a large number of products that could be used to deliver entire courses online or to supplement resident courses (Schulman, 1997). In March of 1998, the CIT director appointed five staff members to serve on a Web Tool Selection Committee in order to select a tool for use by faculty and for long-term support by ACITS staff. The committee added representatives from the Engineering Department, which had been active in distance education efforts.

While the committee had its initial sessions, Penn State University launched its World Campus and the University of Texas System initiated the UT TeleCampus. During its deliberations, the *Chronicle of Higher Education* reported on the Instructional Enhancement Initiative that mandated a WWW page for nearly every undergraduate course at UCLA. External pressures such as these pushed the selection and implementation process forward at a rapid pace.

Web Tool Selection

The Web Tool Selection Committee followed rating criteria published by the British Columbia Standing Committee on Educational Technology (SCOET) (http://www.ctt.bc.ca/landonline). Products selected for review were Interactive Learning Network, LearningSpace, TopClass, Virtual U, WebCT, and Web Course in a Box. FirstClass was also reviewed on the basis of potential applications in distance learning. A subset of SCOET's criteria for analyzing Web tools was adapted for use in the committee's testing. Selection criteria included student and authoring ease-of-use, communication tools, course creation and uploading tools, course management tools, testing and assessment tools, and capacity for customization. Finally, the committee applied selection criteria on the basis of the ability of ACITS to provide a reasonable level of support with existing staff.

In the process of reviewing, discussing, and comparing notes on Web course tools, the selection committee gained valuable understanding of the range of tools available, as well as projected requirements for technical support. As committee members acquired increased understanding of each of the Web course tools' capabilities and limitations, a refined set of criteria began to emerge. In addition to providing a large variety of features, the tool needed to be platform-independent, easy to use, have a two-year track record, provide prompt technical support, be customizable, be maintained and supported by the CIT's limited staff, and have an interface that allowed faculty members to create their own look and feel.

Increasingly, committee members concluded that unless a Web course tool met the prime requirement of ease-of-use, then the goal of reaching mainstream faculty—beyond early adopters—would be missed. The issue of what faculty to support was of fundamental importance, but pragmatic considerations related to staff support provided the answer. ACITS staff had to be able to support selected products, with minimal additional training and staff reassignment.

Web course tools are evolving rapidly. The committee's requirement that Web course tools demonstrate a track record of at least two years effectively eliminated recently developed products from consideration. The maturity criterion, which was identical to that used in *PC Week*'s August 1997 report on its multimedia course-authoring contest, helped narrow the number of products to a more manageable level. Although this requirement may have eliminated newer, innovative products, it helped to ensure the selection of a viable company that could provide ongoing support. One Web course tool in particular, Interactive Learning Network (ILN) (currently marketed as Blackboard), would likely have been among the committee's recommendations had the product been in existence for a longer period of time. Future versions of these tools will undoubtedly bring improvements in ease of use, user interface, and feature sets. The committee determined that it would be important to revisit the available options as they develop and continue to improve.

After telephone and electronic interviews with vendors and institutional adopters of each product, the Web Tools Selection Committee narrowed the list of products to Web Course in a Box, TopClass and WebCT. Of the products that met the majority of the committee's selection criteria, Web Course in a Box proved easiest to use, WebCT sported the richest and most fully developed features, and TopClass demonstrated a balance between ease of use and a complete feature set.

Products that did not meet the committee's criteria were eliminated on the basis of corporate track record (Virtual U, Interactive Learning Network) and expectations that existing staff would not be able to provide adequate support (LearningSpace). While none of the products recommended were judged entirely self-operational, projected support requirements were among the most important criteria applied in selecting appropriate Web course tools for recommendation. Cost, support, and staffing requirements led to the decision not to include LearningSpace as a recommended tool, but the committee suggested it remain in the product list for future reviews because it was in current use at several UT Austin departments and research sites. Similarly, Web Course in a Box was chosen for limited support because it was being used in one department. It was simple to use and it was offered at no cost at the time. Although FirstClass was judged to be a mature collaborative tool, it was eliminated on the basis of not qualifying as a true Web course application.

TopClass was eliminated because it was more costly, appeared to provide less technical support, was used less widely, and was incompatible with existing software.

The selection committee chose to implement WebCT. It had the most features and good technical support. WebCT's availability for both Windows NT and UNIX was also an important factor. Once the committee chose WebCT, the process of installing hardware and software, assigning staff members to support roles, and establishing a marketing and training plan began. The Office of Distance Education, under the direction of the CIT's instructional design expert, took the lead in this implementation process.

One of the goals of the selection committee was to choose a product that could be incorporated into ACITS' existing UNIX servers, one of which was available for immediate dedicated use. With the help of ACITS' UNIX Group, an IP address and domain name were designated (webct.cc.utexas.edu) and assigned to the server that was part of the University's central Web service cluster. A UNIX administrator performed the software installation and CIT staff members tested the configuration and took over basic server administration.

Initially, five CIT staff members, each of whom had other duties, were assigned to administer the WebCT server and provide training for faculty members. These staff members consisted of an instructional designer who led the process, a systems analyst who would provide training support, a computer programmer who would administer the server and develop initial training materials, and two multimedia specialists for additional faculty consulting support.

Once the server had been successfully configured, the marketing and training plans were developed. The initial marketing strategy included recruitment of interested faculty members who had an affiliation with distance education. They were recruited through brown bag lunch sessions and targeted mailing lists. "Spotlight" links on the University's Web pages were also used to promote WebCT and invite as many interested faculty members as possible to participate in the training sessions.

Designing a Training Program

At first, the CIT began to develop their own complete training curriculum. They attempted to develop a multimedia presentation that would serve to familiarize the faculty with the product's features, but quickly realized that the amount of time and energy required of the two staff members assigned to this task would not be balanced by the benefits of such a presentation. They decided to use existing tutorial content developed and supplied by the authors of WebCT.

To establish a base level of prerequisite knowledge, the training program designers developed a short overview of WebCT highlighting its interface and basic tool set; these features would be important for the participants to understand in order to successfully use the product. They encouraged the participants to look over the elements of the overview prior to attending an introductory workshop. As reinforcement, one of the components of the automated sign-up process was a question asking whether the participant had visited the overview Web page.

Sessions began in August 1998, consisting of a PowerPoint presentation and staff-developed training modules that used WebCT during a hands-on portion of training. The training program provided participant faculty members with a template containing basic tools and pre-loaded student accounts.

This initial effort was challenging because the goal was to enable faculty to get their courses online in time for the fall semester. The CIT had only slightly more than a month to develop the overall training scheme, recruit "students" for the training sessions, and provide adequate support for any necessary follow-up consulting and training. Considering these obstacles, initial response to both the product and the training was very positive.

However, it became increasingly clear that numerous faculty members required additional support beyond what was offered in the initial training sessions. This was due in part to the fact that the attendees were not required to have any prerequisite knowledge. In addition, the CIT realized that the training content had a tendency to fluctuate from session to session. They realized that more consistency was needed in the training curriculum for the future.

In addition to the faculty training program, in the spring of 1999, WebCT was used for a team-taught course by members of the CIT in hopes that it would eventually serve as a model. However, they failed to fully show the instructors of that course the features of WebCT. In addition, the instructors did not designate a WebCT administrator for the course. The end result was that some of the instructors became disenchanted with the product. In fall 1999, the training designers developed a similar course for delivery. The nature of this course, Introduction to Interactive Media, lent itself well to the WebCT environment. In order to ensure successful implementation of the course in the fall semester, the CIT staff took on the role of administrator. Knowing that they had done so, the instructors of the course were more receptive to utilizing the tool.

ANALYSIS

Evaluating the Performance of the Center for Instructional Technology

Participants filled out a survey at the end of a training session. Originally designed for hard copy, the survey was later released online. By using WebCT, the results were easily compiled, automatically graphed, and easy to analyze. The survey posed several questions about the session using a Likert scale so that statistics could be generated. These statistics then enabled a determination of the effectiveness of the training curriculum and helped the CIT adapt materials to better accommodate the faculty's needs. The survey results revealed that many faculty desired and needed basic HTML training and an introduction to Web-based instructional design concepts, in addition to the WebCT-specific training sessions. This was reinforced by the trainers' observations.

Although the efforts to integrate WebCT into the University community were largely successful, there were many things that could have been done better. For instance, a clear definition of how the tool was to be used—whether to put courses totally online (distance education) or to supplement existing courses (local distance education)—would have allowed a more accurate prioritization of evaluation criteria. In addition, the course development tool selection probably should not have occurred until an evaluation team more representative of the various faculty constituencies could be organized. An academic approach with field-testing similar to that used at the University of Maryland (http://sunil.umd.edu/webct/) was planned but never initiated due to time and money constraints. More staff training and preparation prior to implementation would have saved valuable time during the initial "crunch" period faced before the beginning of the fall 1998 semester. For instance, the initial training efforts would likely have been more successful if vendor-supplied training materials had been incorporated at the outset. Additionally, the CIT may have generated more interest by creating model courses that demonstrate the features of WebCT.

From an organizational perspective, it would have been helpful if marketing the tool had been initiated from an administrative level as opposed to a staff level as it was in this case. Since the University did not mandate the adoption of WebCT, the CIT was solely responsible for involving the faculty in the use of WebCT for course development. Perhaps a more centralized approach to providing this service, including a mandate from the highest levels of administration, would have allowed for more funding, a more broad-based selection committee, and faster faculty acceptance of the chosen product.

The Effect on Teaching and Learning

In the absence of a clear institutional policy regarding instructional use of the Web, it is remarkable that so many faculty and students took advantage of the selected tool. Anecdotal evidence indicates users were satisfied and that the product facilitated learning. Quantitative studies are underway to determine the degree of student and faculty satisfaction with WebCT and to determine the relationships between product use and student performance.

Most faculty who attended training sessions used WebCT to create a basic Web presence for their classes. Course pages consisted primarily of a password-protected site containing a syllabus, course materials, communication tools (bulletin boards, chat rooms and/or email), an interactive calendar and a gradebook. Some instructors added more tools and greater functionality as they became more comfortable with the package or realized that many features are based on solid pedagogical principles that can have a positive impact on learning. In either case, students benefited by having greater access to course materials, more opportunities to communicate with their instructors and other students, and more learning resources.

As expected, faculty on the two extremes of the computer experience—those already using information technology in their courses (early adopters) and those who have previously resisted the urge to migrate any course materials into an information technology framework—appeared to have the most difficulty becoming comfortable with the tool. Many of the early adopters seemed satisfied with their existing information technology resources and were unwilling either to take the time to learn a new tool or to consider any potential benefits. A number of those with limited computer experience never developed their course accounts beyond what was created as part of the training process.

Those with limited experience, perhaps the majority of faculty, responded well to the implemented training approach. Overt departmental support, a dedicated teaching assistant, and staff support produced courses which were the most robust and successful and most likely to be used in subsequent semesters.

Sight- and hearing-impaired instructors had limited success using the tool for instruction. Future versions of this software are expected to be more receptive to their needs and the needs of disabled students.

CONCLUSIONS

The efforts and recommendations of scores of committee members for integrating technology into the instructional scheme at the University of Texas at Austin are beginning to bear fruit. Despite challenges, UT Austin's Center for Instructional Technologies was able to successfully implement, market, and train faculty on the Web course development tool that was chosen. After one year, 120 instructors had used the product in their courses, over 4000 student accounts had been created, more than 200 faculty and staff members had received formal training, and countless others had viewed a custom-made online overview and tutorial. Feedback from the training session evaluations was consistently positive and reflected the fact that the faculty members were satisfied with the training they had received and were prepared to continue self-directed development.

Another measure of the success of the program is demonstrated by the interest in WebCT by various departmental and some non-academic units of the University. For example, the Office of Human Resources is adopting WebCT to provide compliance training for the University's 20,000 faculty and staff. In addition, WebCT was featured in the Pharmacy Department's annual international Teaching Academy.

A recent draft report submitted by the Technology Enhanced Learning Committee suggests that the University adopt "a centralized but flexible and open approach to technology evaluation and implementation and ongoing support" (Technology Enhanced Learning Committee, 1999). The CIT's experience in selecting and implementing a Web course development tool supports this conclusion. Although the selection committee did have an open approach during the selection process, their inability to engage other key players affected the legitimacy of their final choice. In particular, they had to work after the selection process to convince nonparticipants that they had made the correct choice. Fortunately, their implementation of WebCT, though not error-free, was flexible enough to allow them to reexamine the training methods and tools they initially used. The revamped training, incorporating existing training materials, helped them to use existing staff more efficiently and to deliver more consistent training. This, in turn, made it easier for the staff to attentively support the faculty using WebCT.

The CIT does not profess complete satisfaction with the process, but they are very satisfied with the outcome. After finding the right tool to deliver distance learning, they aggressively pursued willing innovators, adapted their approach to suit the locally focused climate, trained those willing to learn, and aggressively marketed the product.

The number of available Web course tools continues to grow at a rapid rate. The latest list of products evaluated by the SCOET (http://www.ctt.bc.ca/landonline) has more than doubled in size since the selection committee's original review. Even more are listed in a recent comparison by Marshall University (http://multimedia.marshall.edu/cit/webct/com-pare/comparison.html). This adds difficulty both for those selecting a Web course tool for the first time and those reviewing new products after an initial selection. Although the committee pledged to continually monitor new products, budgetary and personnel constraints have limited this process. Selecting and implementing a Web course development tool is a time-consuming venture that is as much art as science.

DISCUSSION QUESTIONS

1. As the training and support progressed, the CIT realized that faculty had to allocate significant time to develop and maintain online courses, even with the timesaving features of a course development tool. Given that there is an increasing expectation that faculty should put elements of their course online, how should institutions address these time-related issues?

2. As universities move more courses to an online environment, how should they prepare faculty and support staff for the necessary changes in instructional design? At what point should the organization address those issues?

3. What role should university administrators have in promoting the use and implementation of instructional technology?

REFERENCES

Center for Instructional Technologies. (1999). *About the Center for Instructional Technologies.* [Online]. Available: http://www.utexas.edu/cc/cit/about/history.html [1999, August 10].

Comparison of Online Course Delivery Software Products. [Online]. Available: http://multimedia.marshall.edu/cit/webct/compare/comparison.html [1999, August 10].

Culp, G. (1999). Establishment of a Center for Instructional Technology. *Syllabus,* June.

Faculty Computer Committee. (1989). *The Original Vision Plan.* [Online]. Available: http://www.utexas.edu/computer/fcc/The_Original_Vision_Plan.html [1999, August 10].

Faculty Computer Committee. (1995). *The New Vision Plan.* [Online]. Available: http://www.utexas.edu/computer/fcc/The_New_Vision_Plan.html [1999, August 10].

Internet-based training tools run close race. *PC Week.* August 18, 1997. [Online]. Available: http://www8.zdnet.com/pcweek/reviews/0818/18chart.html [1999, August 10].

Hazan, S. *Evaluation and Selection of Web Course Management Tools.* [Online]. Available: http://sunil.umd.edu/webct/ [1999, August 10].

Landon, B. *Comparison of Online Education Applications.* [Online]. Available: http://www.ctt.bc.ca/landonline [1999, August 10].

Long-Range Planning for Information Technology Steering Committee. (1997*). High Priority Recommendations.* [Online]. Available: http://www.utexas.edu/computer/lrp/ch1_rec.htm [1999, August 10].

Morgan, M. (1999). World lecture hall. *Current ACITS,* April. [Online]. Available: http://www.utexas.edu/cc/newsletter/apr99/index.html [1999, August 10].

Multimedia Instruction Committee. (1995). *Technology Integrated Learning Environments: Executive Summary and Summary of Recommendations.* [Online]. Available: http://www.utexas.edu/computer/mic/executive_summary.html [1999, August 10].

Schulman, M. (1997). *Survey of WWW Courses.* [Online]. Available: http://uts.cc.utexas.edu/~disted/survey.html [1999, August 10].

Schulman, M. (1997). *Web Course Development Tools.* [Online]. Available: http://uts.cc.utexas.edu/~disted/webtool2.html [1999, August 10].

Technology-Enhanced Learning Committee. (1999). *Infrastructure Issues in Technology-Enhanced Learning* (DRAFT). July.

Web Course Tool Selection Committee. (1998). *Web Course Tool Selection Committee Report.* [Online]. Available: http://www.utexas.edu/cc/cit/tools/index.html [1999, August 10].

Section II

Impact on People
and Culture

Chapter VIII

Access to Internet-Based Instruction for People with Disabilities

Sheryl Burgstahler
University of Washington

INTRODUCTION

Internet-based instruction promises to make learning accessible to almost everyone, everywhere, at any time. Internet use, however, raises a number of issues. One of them is equitable access. The Americans with Disabilities Act (ADA) of 1990 requires that those making programs and services available to the public provide the same programs and services to people with disabilities that they provide to people without disabilities.

Increased access is commonly given as a key justification for offering educational programs through a distance learning format. For the most part, when this argument is made, proponents are focusing on students unable to participate because of geography. Rarely is the argument made for students unable to participate because of disabilities.

Providing access to students with disabilities can be considered from several angles. Making assurances that individuals with disabilities can participate in distance learning courses is an ethical issue (Woodbury, 1998); some say it is just the right thing to do. It can also be seen as a legal issue. The ADA requires that people with disabilities be provided equal access to public programs and services. According to this law, no otherwise qualified individuals with disabilities shall, solely by reason of their disabilities, be excluded from the participation in, be denied the benefits of, or be subjected to discrimination in these programs. When people think of the ADA they often think of elevators in buildings, reserved spaces in parking lots, and lifts on buses. However, the ADA accessibility requirements also apply to educational opportunities, and more specifically, to programs offered on the Internet. As the United States Department of Justice clarifies:

> Covered entities that use the Internet for communications regarding their programs, goods, or services must be prepared to offer those communications through accessible means as well (ADA, 1997).

Specifically, if a qualified person with a disability enrolls in a distance learning course offered via the Internet, the course must be made available to the student.

But, what is required to assure that a distance learning class taught over the Internet complies with the ADA? This chapter discusses access issues, presents design guidelines, and provides an example of an accessible course at the University of Washington. The chapter explores the feasibility of offering this course online and of making it accessible to potential instructors and students with a wide range of abilities and disabilities. The field of universal design provides a framework for the discussion of the case.

Offering a course via the Internet presents unique challenges to the course developer. This case addresses a few of these challenges. It considers content that is typically taught onsite with printed materials, videotapes, lectures, demonstrations, discussions, and field experiences and explores the feasibility of offering it in a distance learning format using the Internet.

CASE QUESTIONS

- What are the challenges for making a distance learning course accessible to individuals with a wide range of disabilities, and how can these challenges be overcome?
- How are accommodations needed for people with disabilities in an online course different as compared to those needed in a comparable on-site class?
- What benefits do people without disabilities gain when an Internet-based course is designed to be accessible to individuals with disabilities?

UNIVERSAL DESIGN

Designing a product or service involves the consideration of a myriad of factors that include aesthetics, engineering options, environmental issues, safety concerns, and cost. One issue that designers often overlook is "universal design." Universal design is defined by the Center for Universal Design at North Carolina State University as "the design of products and environments to be usable by all people, to the greatest extent possible, without the need for adaptation or specialized design." At this center a group of architects, product designers, engineers and environmental design researchers collaborated to establish a set of principles of universal design to provide guidance in the design of environments, communications, and products (Connell et al., 1997). General principles include a design that: is useful and marketable to people with diverse abilities; accommodates a wide range of individual preferences and abilities; communicates necessary information effectively to the user, regardless of ambient conditions or the user's sensory abilities; can be used efficiently and comfortably, and with a minimum of fatigue; provides an appropriate size and space for approach, reach, manipulation, and use regardless of user's body size, posture, or mobility.

When designers apply these principles, their products meet the needs of potential users with a wide variety of characteristics. Disability is just one of many characteristics that an individual might possess. For example, one person could be tall, 15 years old, a poor reader, and blind. All of these characteristics, including the person's blindness, should be considered when developing a product that might be used. In the case of distance learning, a goal should be to create a learning environment that allows a person who happens to have a characteristic that is termed a "disability" to access the content of the course and fully participate in class activities.

When universal design principles are applied to the design of Web pages, people using a wide range of adaptive technology can access them (e.g., Burgstahler, 1998; Burgstahler, Comden, & Fraser, 1997; Dixon, 1996; Kautzman, 1998; Resmer, 1997; Waddell & Thomason, 1998). Adaptive technology includes special hardware and software that allow individuals with a wide range of disabilities to make productive use of computers (Closing the Gap, 1999).

The World Wide Web Consortium (W3C), an industry group that was founded in 1994 to develop common protocols that enhance interoperability and guide the evolution of the Web, has taken a leadership role in this area. The W3C is committed to promoting the full potential of the Internet to assure a high degree of usability by people with disabilities. As stated by Tim Bernes-Lee, W3C Director and inventor of the World Wide Web, "The power of the Web is in its universality. Access by everyone regardless of disability is an essential aspect." The Web Accessibility Initiative (WAI) coordinates W3C's efforts with organizations worldwide to promote accessibility (Randall, 1999). Its Web Content Accessibility Guidelines (Chisholm, Vanderheiden, & Jacobs, 1999) tell how to design Web pages that are accessible to people with a wide variety of disabilities.

The WAI guidelines address two general themes: ensuring graceful transformation, and making content understandable and navigable. Pages that transform gracefully remain accessible despite constraints imposed by physical, sensory, and cognitive limitations; work constraints; and technological barriers. Content can be made easy to understand and navigate by using clear and simple language and providing simple mechanisms for navigating within and between pages. The 14 WAI Web page accessibility guidelines are listed below.

1. Provide equivalent alternatives to auditory and visual content.
2. Don't rely on color alone.
3. Use markup and style sheets, and do so properly.
4. Clarify natural language usage.
5. Create tables that transform gracefully.
6. Ensure that pages featuring new technologies transform gracefully.
7. Ensure user control of time-sensitive content changes.
8. Ensure direct accessibility of embedded user interfaces.
9. Design for device-independence.
10. Use interim solutions.
11. Use W3C technologies and guidelines.
12. Provide context and orientation information.
13. Provide clear navigation mechanisms.
14. Ensure that documents are clear and simple.

To create pages that are accessible, Web page developers must either avoid certain kinds of data types and features, or create alternative methods for carrying out the functions or accessing the content provided through the inaccessible feature or format. Some of the specific guidelines are discussed below.

Using W3C technologies (e.g., standard HTML) is recommended because W3C technologies include "built-in" accessibility features. W3C specifications are developed in an open, consensus process and undergo early review to ensure that accessibility issues are considered. Many non-W3C formats (e.g., PDF, Shockwave) require viewing with plug-ins or stand-alone applications that cannot be viewed or navigated with some types of adaptive technology. Where it is not possible to use an accessible technology, an alternative version of the content should be provided. However, Web page designers should resort to separate, accessible pages only when other solutions fail. Maintaining a separate page is time consuming. Alternative pages tend to be updated less frequently than "primary" pages and, therefore, often provide outdated information to the site visitors using them.

Some people cannot access images, movies, and audio clips because of sensory impairments. Providing equivalent alternatives to auditory and visual content assures access to people with sensory disabilities. For example, a blind person cannot see a graphic image, although a screen reader and voice synthesizer can read text. It is necessary to provide the content presented in a graphic in a form that a blind person can access. The simplest way to do this is to provide text that describes the content presented in the graphic. The voice output system can then read the text. For example, if a Web page displays an image of a globe, the Web developer could insert a text description of the globe (through an ALT attribute of the image element). Or, if more detail is required, a text alternative to the globe image could be provided on the screen or accessed via a hyperlink. Similarly, audio clips should be captioned or transcribed so that site visitors who are deaf can access the content. Besides individuals with disabilities, people who are using older technology that cannot access multimedia will benefit when alternative formats for information are provided.

Using clear and simple language promotes effective communication and ensures that site visitors with a diverse set of characteristics can understand documents. Providing clear and consistent orientation information, navigation bars, and other navigation mechanisms increases the likelihood that a site visitor will find the information they are looking for on a Web page. Following these guidelines benefits all site visitors, but especially people with cognitive or visual disabilities.

Since some visitors cannot perceive color differences, it is important to make sure that information conveyed with color is also available without color. Following this guideline benefits people using monochrome monitors as well as those with visual impairments.

Some people with learning or visual disabilities are unable to read moving text because they cannot read fast enough. Screen readers for people who are blind are unable to read moving text. For some people, movement can also cause such a distraction that the rest of the page becomes unreadable. People with physical disabilities might not be able to move quickly or accurately enough to interact with moving objects. It is important to ensure that the user can pause or stop objects on pages that are moving, blinking, or scrolling.

Web developers should also design for device-independence. Device-independent access means that a person may interact with Web pages using a wide variety of input and output devices (e.g., mouse, keyboard, voice). If, for example, a selection can only be made with a mouse or other pointing device, someone who is using speech input or a keyboard alone will not be able to activate the function. Following this guideline benefits people with a variety of system configurations.

Web pages for a distance learning class should be tested with a variety of monitors, computer platforms, and Web browsers. One of the test browsers should be text-only, such as Lynx. If a Web page makes sense with Lynx, then most people with sensory impairments can read it, too. Another good accessibility test is to determine if all functions at a Web site can be accessed using a keyboard alone. A Web site can also be tested for accessibility using "Bobby." Bobby, created at the Center for Applied Special Technology, is an HTML validator program that tests for accessibility and identifies nonstandard and incorrect HTML coding.[1]

If universal design principles are employed in Web page development, people with characteristics besides disabilities will also benefit from the design. They include people working under environmental constraints such as in noisy or noiseless environments; people whose hands or eyes are occupied with other activities; people for whom English is a second language; people using older, outdated computer equipment; and individuals using mono-chrome monitors.

A COURSE IN ADAPTIVE COMPUTER TECHNOLOGY
Adaptive Computer Technology

Along with the lightning-speed development of computer and Internet technologies has been a rapid development of adaptive technology. Because the adaptive technology on a student's computer may provide all or most of the accommodation needed to access materials on the Internet, an instructor of a Web-based course may not even know that a student in the class has a disability. Below are a few examples of access challenges faced by students and instructors in the distance learning course discussed below. These include visual impairments, specific learning disabilities, mobility impairments, and hearing impairments.

For example, a student who has limited vision, but is not totally blind, can use special software to enlarge all screen images. The student may see only a small portion of a Web page at a time, and consequently might get lost when Web pages are cluttered with too much text and too many images, and when the page layout is inconsistent from page to page. The standard size of course printed materials may also be inaccessible. Students who are blind can use screen reading software and speech synthesizers to read text presented on the screen.

Some students with specific learning disabilities that impact the ability to read, write, and process information often need books on audio tape and extended time to complete assignments. For some, speech output or screen enlargement systems similar to those used by people with visual impairments help them read text presented on computer screens. People with learning disabilities often have difficulty understanding Web sites when the information is cluttered and unorganized, and when the screen layout changes from one page to another.

There are a wide range of mobility impairments; for example, some students have no functional hand use access computers with alternative keyboards, speech recognition, and other input devices that provide access to all of the Internet-based course materials and navigational tools. Some mobility impairments result in a reduction of fine motor skills that makes it difficult to select buttons on the screen when they are very small.

Most Internet resources are accessible to people with hearing impairments because they do not require the ability to hear. As the Internet incorporates more multi-media features, however, barriers are being erected. When Web sites include audio output without providing text captioning or transcription for those who cannot hear the sounds, this group of individuals is denied access to the information. Course videotapes that are not captioned are also inaccessible to individuals who are deaf.

The Course

Adaptive Computer Technology (Burgstahler, 1995, 1997) is a course designed for teachers, parents, service providers, and computer lab managers. It is offered for three college credits in both rehabilitative medicine and education through the University of Washington in Seattle. The course surveys the field of adaptive technology as it impacts the lives of people with disabilities, including applications to employment, education, and recreation. Topics include legal issues, special hardware and software for accessing information technology, computer applications, resources, and implementation strategies.

The first time the course was offered via the Internet, the instructors were from the University of Washington and New York's Rochester Institute of Technology. They had co-presented at conferences and in workshops before, when it was possible for them to be in the same place at the same time. The distance learning course was developed collaboratively via electronic mail. The co-instructors "met" regularly to discuss the progress of the course, but never in person. One of the instructors is blind. His computer is equipped with screen reader software and a speech synthesizer. Basically, this system reads with a synthesized voice whatever text appears on the screen, such as text found on the Internet. He uses a text-only browser to navigate the World Wide Web. He cannot interpret graphics unless text alternatives are provided. For example, his speech synthesizer will simply say "image map" at the place where an image map would be displayed to someone using a multi-media Web browser. Printed materials, videotapes, and other visual materials create access challenges for this instructor.

In an on-site offering of this course, students would come together in a common physical location on a regular schedule. For the distance learning course offering, there is no meeting "place." This means that finding an accessible classroom to accommodate students with disabilities is not required. However, course materials and methods must be made accessible to students with disabilities. The instructional tools for this course are printed materials, a videotape, electronic mail, an electronic distribution list, and the World Wide Web.

Most correspondence with prospective students is carried out via electronic mail. If printed correspondence is necessary with a visually impaired individual, materials are enlarged on a photocopy machine, or standard university services are used to produce the documents on tape, on disk, or in Braille. A TTY is available for telephone communication with prospective students who are deaf.

Printed Materials

This distance learning course is supported with a textbook and other printed materials. Printed media create a challenge for individuals who are blind or who have specific learning disabilities that affect their ability to read (e.g., dyslexia). For them, the textbook is available in recorded form from Recordings for the Blind and Dyslexic. The publisher of the handouts that accompany the videotape used in the course, DO-IT (Disabilities, Opportunities, Internetworking and Technology) provides these materials in standard print, Braille, large print, and electronic formats.

Videotape

A videotape which overviews adaptive technology options, facility access, and accessible Web page design is a required course material purchased by the students. The videotape is open captioned for hearing-impaired students. "Open" captioning means that transcriptions of the spoken words appear on the screen at all times. The tape is also available with audio description for individuals who are blind. Audio-described videotapes include an extra voice to describe key visual content. Audio-described versions of the videotape used in this course are available through DO-IT at no additional cost to the students. To make this option available, DO-IT contracted WGBH/Descriptive Video Service to add an extra audio track that describes visual material.

Internet Resources

A prerequisite to the course is for students to have access to electronic mail. They can use any software that supports email on the Internet. Therefore, access issues related to electronic mail that students with disabilities might face have already been resolved before enrolling in the course. Their own computer systems provide whatever accommodations they need in this area.

Communication between individual students and course administration staff, the instructor, and other students takes place using electronic mail. All students are placed on an electronic distribution list managed by ListProcessor software on a Unix host computer. The ListProcessor software distributes the syllabus and other course materials to the students. Lessons, along with reading and videotape viewing assignments, are distributed every few days to the course distribution list. The students read and respond to the electronic messages over a period of approximately 10 weeks. Full-class discussions also take place via the class distribution list. To keep communications lively, for every lesson each student is required to contribute at least one message to the list. Small group discussions break off from full class discussions as students discover common interests.

Guest speakers often join in class discussions. They are placed on the distribution list for a period of about two weeks. One of the regular guest speakers is the course textbook author, who is blind.

All assignments are turned in to the instructor via electronic mail. The first assignment is to distribute a short biography to the rest of the class via the course distribution list. Three "papers" are required. They involve writing on a topic related to the course content using and referencing Internet resources, visiting a local program and evaluating computer access issues for people with disabilities, and making recommendations regarding disability-related accommodations for a particular facility.

Students must take the final exam before the six-month ending date of the course. When they are ready, students request the exam from the instructor via electronic mail. Then it is sent to them via email. They are allowed to access printed and electronic resources while completing this "open book" test. Students have several days to complete the essay exam and return it by electronic mail.

Once distributed, course lessons are archived on the course World Wide Web site for reference by the students and instructors. This Web site also hosts the course "library." Links to other resources provide students with thousands of pages of useful resources for in-depth study and provide launch pads for research. The course Web pages are designed in such a way that people using a wide range of adaptive technologies can access them and care is taken to refer students to sites that are accessible.

Potential students and instructors in an Internet-based distance learning class may have visual, hearing, mobility, speech, and learning disabilities that impact their participation in the class. Planning for access as the course is being developed is much easier than creating accommodation strategies once a student with a disability enrolls. In the distance learning course described in this chapter, simple steps were taken to assure that the course was accessible to those with a wide range of abilities and disabilities. It was found that people without disabilities also benefit when universal design is considered in the course development process.

ANALYSIS

Challenges and Solutions

Some distance learning courses use textbooks and other printed materials to support online instruction. Students who are blind or who have specific learning disabilities that affect their ability to read printed information may require alternative formats. Making the text of printed materials available online may provide the best solution.

Ideally, if a videotape is one of the course materials, captioning should be provided for those who have hearing impairments and audio description provided for those who are blind. If the publisher does not make these access options available, the distance learning program should have a system in place to accommodate students who have sensory impairments. For example, the institution could hire someone local to describe the visual material to a blind student or to sign audio material for a student who is deaf. Or, they could work with the publisher to provide, in accessible format, a transcription of the content. Since these accommodations may be difficult to implement on short notice, it is best that an institution think carefully about access issues and procedures before videotapes are distributed as part of a distance learning program.

Text-based resources such as Usenet discussion groups, electronic mail and distribution lists create no special barriers for students with disabilities. Individuals who have visual impairments or reading disabilities can use their own adapted systems to access course content with these tools. World Wide Web pages, if universal design guidelines are followed in their development, are highly accessible to individuals with disabilities. In the distance learning course described, a conscious choice was made to use simple software tools— electronic mail, distribution lists, and the World Wide Web. When it comes to people with a wide range of disabilities, generally speaking, the simpler the software, the easier it is for them to access. For example, text-based information is easier to access by people with sensory impairments than multi-media materials. And, real-time chat systems are difficult or impossible to use by individuals for whom input and output methods are slow, whereas simple electronic mail is completely accessible. As tools to be used in a distance learning course are selected, they should be tested to assure that people with disabilities can participate in the course offerings.

On-Site Versus Online Accommodations

In a traditional course, assuring facility access for individuals with mobility impairments is required. Providing an accessible classroom and parking is not an issue when a distance learning format is used.

One of the most vocal students in the class described in this case was a student who has Cerebral Palsy and cannot speak in the traditional way. In an on-site course he would use a computer-based voice synthesizer to speak; composing responses can be time-consuming. With his adapted computer input system he was able to fully participate in all class discussions and activities offered in the distance learning format.

In an on-site class, note-takers for lectures are sometimes used by individuals with mobility, visual, or hearing impairments. In some cases lectures are recorded. Because, in most cases, distance learning materials provided via the Internet can be repeatedly accessed and because adaptive technology allows individuals to do their own writing at their own speed, these types of accommodations are not required when a distance learning format is used.

Sometimes students with learning disabilities require more time to complete coursework. Assigning work with flexible deadlines is often easier in a distance learning format than in on-site instruction and helps assure the successful participation of individuals with specific learning disabilities.

Students or instructors who are deaf may require interpreters to facilitate communication in on-site courses. However, they do not need interpreters in online classes as long as course materials do not require the ability to hear.

Access issues regarding videotape and television presentations and printed materials are the same regardless of how the course is taught. Individuals who have disabilities that affect their ability to read printed materials (e.g., dyslexia, blindness, poor vision) may require alternative formats, including electronic, Braille, audio tape, and large print. Access challenges created by videotapes for individuals who are deaf or blind can be overcome with captioning and audio description. Planning ahead is better than dealing with a request from a student in a course, and is particularly important when the course is taught in a distance learning format. For example, if a videotape is shown in an on-site class, a deaf student's interpreter is present to translate the information presented. However, in a distance learning class, providing access to a videotape remotely is problematic. Creating a transcription or hiring an interpreter in a timely manner can be expensive and time-consuming.

Electronic resources, whether used in a distance learning course or on-site class, should be designed with universal access in mind. If universal design principles are followed in the creation of Internet-based course materials, special accommodations for individuals with disabilities are minimized.

Benefits of Accessible Design to People Without Disabilities

People without disabilities may have situational limitations that are similar to the limitations imposed by disabilities. For example, those for whom English is a second language experience reading challenges similar to those experienced by people with specific learning disabilities. Individuals using monochrome monitors face challenges like those who are colorblind. People who need to work in a dark environment, those needing to watch the road while driving a car, and individuals who cannot access graphics due to computer system limitations are in a similar situation as those who are blind. A noisy work environment or older, outdated computer equipment that prohibits use of audio introduces constraints similar to those faced by individuals who have hearing impairments. A noiseless environment also imposes limitations like those faced by people who are deaf. People whose hands are occupied with other activities face challenges similar to those who cannot use their hands due to mobility impairments.

Using clear and simple language and navigational mechanisms on Web pages benefits people with visual and learning disabilities, but also helps people whose first language differs from the language in which the course is delivered, including those who communicate primarily in sign language. Captions provided on Web pages or videotapes benefit people who are deaf, work in noisy or noiseless surroundings, or for people whom English is a second language.

Besides those who are blind, students and instructors using older computers or slow Internet connections or who have turned off support for images on their browsers in order to maximize access speed may be left out when multi-media features do not provide text alternatives for the content. Similarly, people operating computers in the dark and those who cannot view the screen because they must attend to other things benefit from speech output systems designed for people who are blind. Providing multiple formats of information address differences in learning styles. Text equivalents can also help all users find pages more quickly, since search robots can use the text when indexing the pages.

People who use computers with small screens benefit from features employed to accommodate individuals with poor vision. Making sure that information conveyed with color is also available without color benefits those who cannot perceive color because of colorblindness or simply because of system limitations such as monochrome monitors.

If universal design principles are used in creating a distance learning class, it will be accessible to any student who enrolls and any instructor who is hired to teach it. Distance learning course developers should consider all of the potential characteristics of instructors and students and of the environments within which they work. Considering disability-related access issues during the design process may take extra time and thought, but this process often leads to better products for everyone. For example, taped books, originally created for individuals who are blind, are now used by people in automobiles and with young children.

CONCLUSIONS

In the twenty-first century the ability to compete will be closely tied to access to information. Much of this access will be via the Internet. If a person with a disability does not have access, that person cannot compete—not because of the disability, but because of lack of access. Educators may not be able to change the characteristic of blindness, but they can make information accessible to people who possess this characteristic.

The Internet is a powerful, flexible, and efficient instructional tool. Of the potential instructors who might teach a distance learning course and of the students such offerings might attract, some may have disabilities. Technology has the potential to level the playing field for everyone, but this potential will be realized only if everyone has access. What steps can be taken to narrow the digital divide?

Providing a course using the Internet can enhance accessibility for people with disabilities. Electronic text materials are generally highly accessible to those with disabilities. Media conversion and other customized accommodations are minimized since participants already have access to computers when they enter the class. Whatever adaptive technologies they use facilitate the accommodations. For example, a blind student does not need the electronic lessons produced in Braille or on tape; the student's existing computer output method provides this accommodation. Similarly, a student with a hearing impairment does not require interpreters or amplification systems since lectures and discussions occur online. The inability to speak, hear, see, or move is not a limitation in electronic communication when accessible materials are provided.

Following accessibility guidelines that address disability-related issues makes course content more available to all students and instructors, whatever constraints they may be operating under. Design decisions made to benefit participants with disabilities often result in improved access for people who have little experience with computers, for those using older technology, for individuals for whom English is a second language, and for participants who are in a situation where their eyes, ears, or hands are busy or interfered with.

The necessity for special accommodations for individuals with disabilities can be reduced when simple universal design principles are applied beginning at the earliest stages of development. Some solutions are hard to implement, but developers cannot claim they are unable to do some simple modifications. If accessibility is addressed during the design phase of development process, solutions are generally inexpensive and simple to implement. Individuals with disabilities should be involved in the design and evaluation phases of distance learning software and course development.

Few Web pages are designed with access in mind, not because it is difficult or because there are no guidelines, but simply because Web page developers simply do not think about the access problems they are creating for people with disabilities, or they do not think it is important enough to justify the effort. On the part of multimedia developers, the National Council on Disabilities (1998) reports a general lack of awareness about disability access issues, but a willingness to comply with accessibility guidelines once the issues are explained. Efforts should be made to increase the awareness of universal design guidelines.

Designed correctly, distance learning options create learning opportunities for students with disabilities. Designed poorly, they erect new barriers to equal participation in academics and careers. We must strive to find the elusive balance between the technical, educational, and access goals for distance learning. Employing universal design principles can bring us closer to making learning accessible to everyone, everywhere, at any time.

DISCUSSION QUESTIONS

1. What are the ethical and legal issues related to providing access to distance learning classes for instructors and students with disabilities?
2. How would you, as a distance learning course developer, respond to concerns by administrators of the added costs involved in making distance learning courses accessible to students and instructors with disabilities?
3. What are the benefits of employing universal design principles rather than focusing only on disability issues?
4. In your institution or company, who should be responsible for assuring that distance learning programs are accessible to individuals with disabilities?
5. Published evaluations of distance learning software rarely mention accessibility as a criterion for selection. What can be done to get universal access considered in software development and selection?

REFERENCES

Americans with Disabilities Act of 1990, 104 STAT. 327. Available http://www.usdoj.gov/crt/ada/statute.html.

ADA accessibility requirements apply to Internet Web pages. (1996). *The Law Reporter,* 10(6), 1053-1084.

Burgstahler, S. E. (1995). Distance learning and the information highway. *The Journal of Rehabilitation Administration,* 19(4), 271-276.

Burgstahler, S. E. (1997). Teaching on the Net: What's the difference? *T. H. E. Journal,* 24(9), 61-4.

Burgstahler, S. E. (1998). Universal access. *Journal of Telecommunications in Higher Education* 2(1), 18-22.

Burgstahler, S.E., Comden, D., & Fraser, B. (1997). Universal access: Designing and evaluating Web sites for accessibility. *CHOICE: Current Reviews for Academic Libraries,* 34 Supplement, 19-22.

Chisholm, W., Vanderheiden, G., & Jacobs, I. (Eds.) (1999). Web content accessibility guidelines. World Wide Web Consortium, Web Accessibility Initiative. Available http://www.w3.org/TR/WAI-WEBCONTENT.

Closing the Gap 1999 resource directory. (1999). *Closing the Gap,* 17(6), 41-185.

Connell, B.R., Jones, M., Mace, R., Mueller, J., Mullick, A., Ostroff, E., Sanford, J., Steinfeld, E., Story, M., & Vanderheiden, G. (1997). *The Principles of Universal Design*. Raleigh, NC: North Carolina State University, Center for Universal Design. Available http://www.design.ncsu.edu/cud/pubs/udprinciples.html.

Dixon, J.M. (1996). Leveling the road ahead: Guidelines for the creation of WWW pages accessible to blind and visually handicapped users. *Library Hi Tech,* 14(1), 65-68.

Kautzman, A.M. (1998). Virtuous, virtual access: Making Web pages accessible to people with disabilities. *SEARCHER: The Magazine for Database Professionals.* 6(6), 42-45, 48-49.

National Council on Disabilities (1998). Access to multimedia technology by people with sensory disabilities. Washington, DC. Available http://www.ncd.gov

Randall, L. (199). March 25, W3C proposes guidelines on Web accessibility. *Newsbytes.* Available http://www.newsbytes.com/pubNews/128454.html.

Resmer, M. (1997). Universal access to information resources technology. *Syllabus,* 10(6), 12-14.

Waddell, C.D., & Thomason, K.L. (1998, November). Is your site ADA-compliant ...or a lawsuit-in-waiting? *The Internet Lawyer*. Available http://www.internetlawyer.com/ada.htm.

Woodbury, M. (1998). Defining Web ethics. *Science and Engineering Ethics,* 4, 203-212.

RESOURCES

For more information about universal design and access to distance learning for people with disabilities, consult the following Web pages.

Americans with Disabilities Act Information on the Web
http://www.usdoj.gov/crt/ada/

Center for Applied Special Technology (CAST)
http://www.cast.org/bobby

The Center for Universal Design
http://www.design.ncsu.edu/cud

Disabilities, Opportunities, Internetworking, and Technology (DO-IT)
http://www.washington.edu/doit

Equal Access to Software and Information (EASI)
http://www.rit.edu/~easi

National Center for Accessible Media (NCAM)
www.wgbh.org/ncam

Recordings for the Blind and Dyslexic
http://www.rfbd.org/

The Trace Research and Development Center
http://www.tracecenter.org

U.S. Department of Justice ADA Home Page
http://www.usdoj.gov/crt/ada

Web Accessibility Initiative, World Wide Web Consortium
http://www.w3.org/WAI/

WebABLE
http://www.webable.com

WGBH/Descriptive Video Service
http://www.wgbh.org/wgbh/access/dvs/

ACKNOWLEDGMENT

This chapter is based upon work supported by the National Science Foundation under grant number 9800324. Any opinions, findings, and conclusions or recommendations expressed in this material are those of the author and do not necessarily reflect the views of the National Science Foundation.

ENDNOTES

1. Bobby is located at http://www.cast.org/bobby.

Chapter IX

Social Impacts of Computer-Mediated Communication on Strategic Change Processes

Dubravka Cecez-Kecmanovic and Andy Busuttil
University of Western Sydney Hawkesbury

INTRODUCTION

Communication in the workplace has been revolutionized by workers having individual access to networked computers. Computer-Mediated Communication (CMC) enables staff members to interact electronically and actively participate in a group or organization-wide debate from their desk. Email, video-conferencing, groupware, and intranet-based systems are all examples of CMC technologies. Universities have been early adopters of CMC because of a number of factors, including easy individual access to a networked computer and readily available software. This has also meant that universities have been amongst the first to experience the socio-organizational effects of these media of communication.

This case is about a University, named Uni-X, which adopted and appropriated CMC to support a University-wide consultative process to inform its future strategic directions. Strategic change was required in response to a number of external political and economic factors. The President and the Executive Committee decided to use the consultative process both to increase staff awareness of the circumstances being faced by the University and to engage them in an exploratory process leading to the decisions that were to be made. The CMC system used was intended to provide equal access to information by all staff, to enable a University-wide electronic forum for discussion, and to support the coordination of a multitude of the other in-vivo tasks arising from the process.

The case enables examination of (at least) three controversial issues of CMC deployment: equality of access, equality of participation, and democratizing potential. Equality of access means that all the participants have an equal opportunity to access the communication network and information resources in the system. Equality of access has to be distinguished from the equality of participation, which denotes equal opportunity to contribute to the discussion, both to affect and be affected by the opinion of others. CMC's democratizing potential is an even more complex issue that refers to CMC's contribution to the openness and transparency of organizational processes and to consensus-based participatory decision-making. Understanding the use and appropriation of CMC by individuals as members of different groups and as members of the Uni-X University, together with understanding the uniqueness of their specific local contexts, is a prerequisite for exploring the richness of social impacts, and why and how they emerged.

CASE QUESTIONS

- In what ways can technology be used to enhance communication in a large educational institution?
- What makes using technology-enhanced communication appealing?
- What effect does technology-enhanced communication have on social interactions?

CASE NARRATIVE

Background

The Uni-X University is situated in a semi-rural area on the outskirts of a large metropolitan center. It was originally established in 1891 as a single purpose college and evolved over the ensuing years to become a part of a greater university network in 1989. It has an enrollment of about 6,000 students. The staff body comprises approximately 250 academic staff distributed over five faculties and approximately 420 general staff members, including administrative staff, technical and scientific officers, and field and maintenance staff.

Confronted with long-term budget cuts, increased competition, and other economic, political, and social challenges, Uni-X embarked on a strategic change process in 1997. This organization-wide restructuring was the first carried out as an explicitly designed consultative process. Substantial workloads severely restricted the time available for staff to meet face-to-face. The use of CMC was, therefore, considered the only way to achieve such broad-based contributions. This was indeed a realistic option as all staff had access to the Uni-X electronic network, and they were generally proficient in the use of this form of electronic communication. A CMC system based on email and the intranet was deployed to enable organization-wide communication, equal access, and broad participation.

The University and Computer-Mediated Communications

In 1997, the Uni-X President released a paper entitled "Strategic Issues and Actions," and shortly after that, the Uni-X Executive Committee published five additional papers that dealt with the university's future. The papers addressed teaching and learning, research and consulting, funding and income generation, the structure and management of Uni-X, and the organizational culture. The papers were distributed on email using the "Uni-X–All" listserve containing addresses of all Uni-X members. The President and other members of the Executive Committee invited all the staff to respond to the strategic papers by providing comments and feedback on the issues raised by the papers. Staff members were invited to send their messages either directly to the Executive Committee or to a facilitator, who published them in batches via Uni-X-All. Individual staff could not publish on Uni-X-All without approval, and initial staff response was far below the expectations of the Executive Committee.

Further opportunity for the members of Uni-X to express their views and opinions was provided through the "Staff Survey – Critical Issues" administered via both email and hard copy (also available for downloading from the Uni-X intranet). Members had the option of answering the questions either individually or in groups. The facilitators involved in the consultative process analyzed, categorized, and summarized the responses, and published the results via email and the intranet.

The strategic papers, several public discussions, and the survey provided a rich source of knowledge and critical-thinking that served as the basis for a Planning Conference held in mid-1997. At this Conference, approximately 10% of Uni-X staff, selected by the Executive Committee, addressed all the major issues concerning the structure and function of the University. The report from the Conference, including a summary of the discussions and recommendations, was again made available via email and intranet.

A month after the Conference, the President released a draft document "Uni-X Restructure." In it he proposed a redesign of the academic and the administrative (including the Executive Committee) structure, a new staffing and resource allocation model, and planning-based accountability and quality improvement in all areas. Members of Uni-X were invited to send written submissions by email in response to this document by September 30th. As a result, the use of email intensified: 67 email discussions were posted, 48 by individuals and 19 by faculties, schools, and other groups. At this stage, the intranet began to be used more widely, initially due to the overburdening of email.

The final, revised version of the "Uni-X Restructure" released five weeks later contained some changes that the President accepted from "publicly recorded and disseminated views from the consultative process" (as stated in the document). An implementation plan was also attached detailing the basic strategy for structural and functional changes outlined in the document. This included the setting up of four "domain-specific" implementation teams (each reporting to a senior executive staff member), a definition of their membership and the tasks required of them, an implementation timetable, and the role of various supporting committees. The central Implementation Team, chaired by the President, was to direct, monitor, and coordinate the whole process. The Joint Union-University Consultative Committee was also involved in the implementation planning process on a regular basis. The task and design of the implementation planning phase were quite complex, as was the structure of the committees, teams, and associated groups. In addition, the timing was critical as the process coincided with the end of the academic year.

The four implementation teams were established with the mandate to produce working solutions in the areas of: 1) Teaching and Learning, 2) Research and Consulting, 3) Administrative Services, and 4) Information Services and Systems. Participants in the implementation teams and various attached groups worked under great pressure to resolve critical issues (such as the new academic structure) and to produce negotiated solutions. Most teams used email intensively to discuss issues and create drafts of documents (documents normally had many versions). Each team rushed to publish their latest version of a document on the intranet in order to make it available across the University and to other teams in particular. The CMC system, including both email and the intranet, played a vital role in this phase of the consultative process as it enabled and supported intensive, parallel work of many teams and groups, often involving interrelated problems.

CMC was based on the University-wide communication network and included an email system with "Uni-X-All" facility enabling distribution of messages to all members of the university. Participants in the consultative process sent their messages, discussion papers, official documents, announcements, and so forth to a coordinator who posted them on Uni-X-All. In addition the coordinator updated an intranet repository. This repository contained messages and documents organized according to the type of document and the stage of the consultative process. While the coordinator was responsible for managing and updating email and the intranet, he did not have a censorship role.

Computer-Mediated Communications: Local Contexts

There were two levels of CMC use. At a group level, CMC supported interaction of individuals within a group and between the groups. At the University level, CMC enabled institution-wide, public interaction between individuals and groups.

Every individual staff member regularly got all the messages and documents (via Uni-X-All). There were sometimes several per day. Moreover, most of the schools (academic departments), administrative units (finance and human resources), and support services units (library, computing center, and student services) had dedicated meetings resulting in a group submission posted on CMC. However, the way different individuals and groups appropriated CMC for their own engagement in the consultative process varied enormously throughout the University. The three typical local contexts that became apparent in this study are illustrated below.

First is the "Authoritarian and Bureaucratic Group Context." Several groups in the Uni-X University exhibited a hierarchical and bureaucratic management model and an authoritarian local culture (found more often in administrative and support services groups). A group leader defined, directed, and controlled the work of group members. The characteristics of the local context and the modes of use of the CMC found in this type of context are presented in Figure 1.

During the consultative process members of these groups were typically asked to meet with their leader or manager to discuss proposals, issues, and concerns. The manager would then interpret and represent the group's position by way of Group submission to higher levels via CMC. Thus CMC was appropriated to fit the existing management model and values (Mode 1A, Figure 1).

Figure 1: Authoritarian and Bureaucratic Local Context and the Modes of Use of CMC

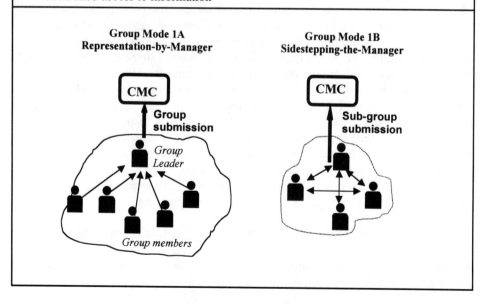

Characteristics of the local context
- Rigid hierarchical structure and authority of power
- Authoritarian and bureaucratic style of management: group leader (manager) directs and controls the work of members (subordinates)
- Subordination and obedience to the leader demanded
- Members dependent on their leader
- Controlled access to information

Group Mode 1A
Representation-by-Manager

CMC

Group submission

Group Leader

Group members

Group Mode 1B
Sidestepping-the-Manager

CMC

Sub-group submission

Despite open access to all information in the consultative process and repeated invitation by the Executive Committee to all staff to participate, members of such groups tended to feel disempowered and voiceless. Their perception of their lower status and pressure to conform to their manager's views appeared to make them feel peripheralized. They perceived the role of CMC as assisting their manager and his/her coercive use of power. In their views, CMC reinforced their manager's power position and the existing interaction patterns in their group.

In a few cases, however, some members of a group got together without their manager and submitted their contribution by email. They perceived CMC as an opportunity to avoid their manager and escape the inhibiting forces within their unit (Mode 1B, Figure 1). Although these examples demonstrate a potentially emancipating use of CMC, the fact that the members acted outside the accepted interaction patterns indicates that the provision of an open communication platform, like CMC, may not have been enough to change the local culture.

Second is the "Close-Knit Group Context." Some groups, mostly academic, revealed a very strong local culture, characterized by a particular value system, goals, and professional standards, believed to be distinct from the rest of the University (see Figure 2). Members of such groups felt a strong identification with their group (often coinciding with profession-identification) and were committed to the betterment of their group and the protection of their own interests. Other groups for them were competitors in their fight for University resources. They perceived the University as the bureaucracy, interfering in their business and constraining their academic freedom. All they wanted was "to be left alone to do their own thing."

Internally, their members nurtured free and open dialogue, democratic and participatory management style, and consensus-based decision-making. Members of the smaller close-knit groups openly discussed all the relevant issues (often using their group email) and would normally formulate their group position or response quickly and submit it via CMC (Group Mode 2A, Figure 2). Larger close-knit groups, often consisting of several factions or subgroups (Group Mode 2B, Figure 2), would also submit their consolidated group response, but would spend more time and effort in negotiations. Irrespective of the size, though, close-knit groups tended to perceive the consultative process as a new threat to their autonomy, as an intrusion into their own business and their professional responsibility. They perceived the CMC not as an opportunity for a University-wide debate and engagement with the broader community, but as a means to protect their group's interests and promote their values more effectively.

The third is "Open, democratic group context." Some groups exhibited an open, democratic, and participatory local culture, encouraging loyalties toward both the group and the University (Figure 3). They not only engaged in the consensual processes within the group, but also actively promoted and battled for participatory and democratic ideals within the University. Most of the active participants (apart from members of the Executive Committee) in the consultative process came from these groups. The availability of information and the transparency of the consultative process achieved through the CMC made them feel empowered and better prepared to take a critical approach.

These groups used the CMC according to their ideals of an open and democratic process. They used the full potential of CMC to engage in the University debate, to hear from others, and to be heard. They felt "well informed" and were able to "form their opinion and make a decision quickly." They experienced many benefits reported in the literature: equality of access, softening of status-related barriers, and a decrease in their physical and emotional distance from the Executive Committee and from other fellow members.

A different view of the use of CMC is presented at the University level. The focus here is on the University-wide pattern of interaction. Interestingly the pattern of interaction supported and enabled by CMC did not remain the same throughout the consultative process but evolved from a typical hierarchical top-down to more lateral and collaborative interaction.

Computer-Mediated Communications: Organizational Contexts

At the very beginning stages, the consultative process was conducted as a top down, hierarchical interaction process, characterised by the vertical flow of information from the Executive Committee to the members (see Figure 4).

The use of the electronic media by the Executive Committee to disseminate information was perceived by some staff members as an exercise of the authority of power. The feedback from the community was nevertheless triggered as each member of the University and all the departments and administrative and other units were invited to respond. A public two-way vertical communication had been established (Organizational Mode 1, Figure 4) and intensified during the September discussion about the President's "Uni-X University

Figure 2: Close-Knit Group Local Context and the Modes of Use of CMC

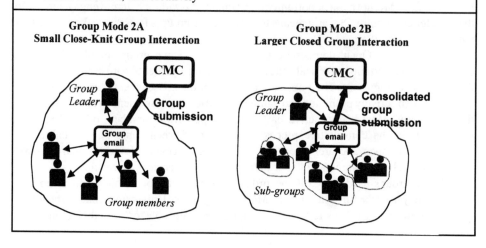

Characteristics of the local context

- Democratic and participatory management style and consensus-based decision-making
- A strong sense of community, collective responsibility, and high commitment and loyalty to the group in contrast to their alienation from and mistrust towards the University
- Mutual interdependence within the group; feeling of physical and emotional closeness
- The University perceived as the bureaucracy, constraining their autonomy, academic freedom, and creativity

Group Mode 2A
Small Close-Knit Group Interaction

CMC

Group Leader

Group submission

Group email

Group members

Group Mode 2B
Larger Closed Group Interaction

CMC

Group Leader

Consolidated group submission

Group email

Sub-groups

Restructure" draft document. The CMC was instrumental in achieving the two-way communication between the Executive Committee and the Uni-X members. Some members found it democratizing and contributing to a more participatory form of decision-making. Others, less enthusiastic, found the interactions "controlled and carefully managed by the center," "diminishing the origins of potential resistance and taking control of them, appropriating them."

Although it technically enabled interaction among all staff members, the CMC was perceived by staff as a means for two-way communication between them and the Executive Committee, not as a dialogue among the members. This mode of use of the CMC reiterated the vertical flow of information typical of bureaucratic and hierarchical organizations.

The turning point in the use of the CMC was when the interaction context became collaborative (with the intranet). There was an agreement at the beginning of the implementation planning process that documents might be published electronically in draft form as they were created or changed, without necessarily being officially approved. Despite the strict policy (consistently applied prior to this point) that required presidential approval of any official document, the major implementation team (chaired by the President) admitted that the sheer volume of documents in circulation and the dynamics of their creation and refinement made the policy unrealistic. Instead, implementation teams were encouraged to

Figure 3: Open, Democratic Local Context and the Mode of Use of CMC

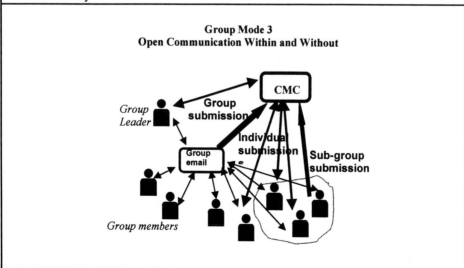

Characteristics of the local context
- Democratic and participatory management style
- Open and tolerant local culture encouraging both loyalties toward the group and the University
- Active engagement in the consensual decision-making and collaboration within the group, as well as in the promotion and affirmation of participatory and democratic ideals within the University
- Information and knowledge shared within the group and a broader University community

Group Mode 3
Open Communication Within and Without

CMC

Group Leader
Group submission

Group email

Individual submission

Sub-group submission

Group members

share their draft documents via CMC, so that others could learn about them and check if there were any contradictions, inconsistencies, or other problems; possible solutions; proposed policies, procedures; or so forth. The culture of sharing ideas and proposals with others and collaborating on the critical issues was gradually developing (Figure 5).

Compared to the previous phase, the mode of use of CMC had changed: various teams and groups used it more and more for lateral communication, knowledge sharing, and collaboration. The process of creation and refinement of documents within an implementation team and for interaction with other teams, groups, and individuals via CMC was accepted as a knowledge legitimization process. Interestingly, the participants in this process found themselves in control of what was established as organizational knowledge despite the fact that it was contingent upon the President's final approval.

ANALYSIS

Many researchers from a number of fields have developed a keen interest in the social effects of CMC. Well-known social psychologists Sproull and Kiesler (1991a,b; 1992), for instance, expressed the view that the ideals of open communication and equality of access, freedom of speech and participatory, democratic decision-making, seem to be consistent with the assumptions behind the design of CMC technologies. They wrote:

> In a democracy, people believe that everyone should be included on equal terms in communication; no one should be excluded from the free exchange of information. Independent decision-makers expressing themselves lead to more

Figure 4: Hierarchical, two-way interaction context and the mode of use of CMC

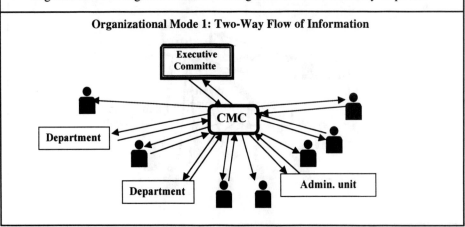

minds contributing to problem-solving and innovation. New communication technology is surprisingly consistent with Western images of democracy (Sproull and Kiesler, 1991b, p. 13).

They found CMC, and especially email, instrumental in fostering democracy in organizations. In a series of controlled experiments with groups of students using CMC, Dubrovsky et al. (1991), Sproull and Kiesler (1991b), and Kiesler and Sproull (1992) provide evidence that electronically mediated communications reduce social inequalities by softening the status-related barriers and decreasing the informational and emotional distance between the center and peripheral employees. Similar effects have been reported by Neilson (1997) who found that Lotus Notes "democratizes information access rendering traditional structures meaningless" (p. 41).

However, other research studies have tended to contravene these findings. Bikson et al. (1989), for instance, did not find CMC effective in diminishing social barriers:

Electronic links—they claim—primarily enhance existing interaction patterns rather than creating new ones (Bikson et al., 1989, p. 102).

Child and Loveridge (1990) explain that, because these systems are designed to support existing power structures and hierarchies, they facilitate the continuation of existing relationships and interaction patterns, and maintain status barriers and power distance. Rice (1990) also found that CMC systems tend to enforce rather than reduce status-related

Figure 5: Collaborative Interaction Context and the Mode of Use of CMC

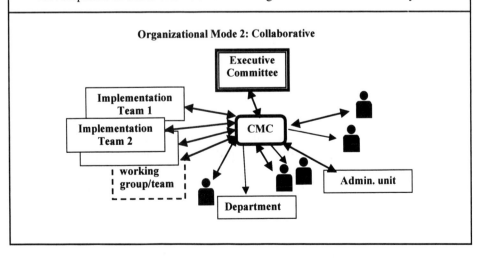

differences. In their study of CMC in everyday work situations, Adrianson and Hjelmquist (1991) found that equal participation and the lowering of status related differences are not necessarily the effects of CMC.

Numerous other studies have contributed to the controversy over whether social effects such as equality of access, freedom of speech, and the lowering of social barriers, as well as the capability to democratize organizational processes, are inherent features of CMC (Mantovani, 1994) or are, perhaps, due to some other factors. Searching for social effects of technologies, though, seems to be fundamentally problematic:

> It is apparent that some degree of technological determinism is implicit in searching first for the social effects of the new communication technology rather than the multiple ways in which individuals, social groups, and organizations control cognitive artifacts, so as to adapt them to the uniqueness of social contexts (Mantovani, 1994, p. 47).

These controversial research results, it appears, cannot be explained without a deeper understanding of the social contexts within which actors interpret and appropriate a particular technology. Central to this issue, therefore, is the need to understand the subtle interplay between the actors, the technology, and social context.

From a purely technical point of view, since all Uni-X members had access to the University network, CMC provided equal access to information distributed via email and in the intranet repository. It therefore also potentially provided an equal opportunity to contribute to the discussion. The Executive Committee itself articulated the belief that CMC would enable broad participation and increase the transparency of the consultative process.

What is of significant interest is that the CMC system was perceived, interpreted, and used differently depending on the social typology of the work groups. Hierarchical, authoritarian types of groups, for instance, appeared to use CMC as an instrument to reinforce the existing power positions. In close-knit groups CMC tended to advance the group's interests and position in the University's political struggle. More democratic groups found CMC naturally served their open, cooperative, and consensus-based mode of work.

This case confirmed that widely contrasting social impacts of CMC can be found not only between organizations, but within a single organization as well (Robey and Boudreau, 1999). The reasons for this, therefore, appear to lie in the characteristics of local contexts. CMC tended to fit into the framework of the particular social context and local culture, thus reproducing the existing power relations, management structures, interaction patterns, beliefs, and value systems. This can be explained from the theoretical perspective of organizational culture (Martin, 1992). According to the differentiation perspective of organizational culture, technology may acquire different significance and meaning depending on the local cultures in the organization (Orlikowski and Gash, 1994; Robey and Boudreau, 1999).

On the other hand, the CMC helped some individuals escape existing hierarchical structures and bureaucratic relationships (Group Mode 1B) and have their voice heard. They recognized the emancipating potential of CMC and appropriated it apparently against the norms within their group. Staff from other groups, who previously did not interact with others in such a public way as via Uni-X-All, did so for the first time. However fragmentary and inconsistent, these events indicate that CMC may provide the opportunity to facilitate and assist change.

More evident change, however, evolved at the University level. The shift from the hierarchical, two-way interaction via CMC (Organizational Mode 1) at the beginning of the consultation to the collaborative and lateral interaction (Organizational Mode 2) towards the end was a significant change that requires further explanation. It should be noted that this change was not brought about through equal contribution by all the groups. As a matter of fact, the implementation teams and associated working groups, formed in the last implementation stage of the consultative process, contributed most to the increase in CMC use. CMC became more vital for these teams and groups to work effectively. The use of CMC in this stage changed the way members shared and created knowledge. New proposals and documents were posted via CMC and shared with others as soon as they were created, without prior approval by the President. Communication channels and mechanisms of organizational knowledge creation and sharing (provided by CMC) seemed to become more open and less controlled. It can therefore be concluded that CMC at the University level was instrumental in fostering more open and democratic interactions, knowledge creation, and decision-making.

It is interesting to note that while in some cases the use of CMC supported the preservation of the status quo, in other cases it served as an agent of change. A theoretical perspective of organizational politics may be useful to help explain this apparent contradiction (Bacharach et al., 1996). In particular, Foucault's (1979) concept of disciplinary power may help to explain how CMC preserved the status quo and reinforced existing relationships and power structures. According to this theory, individuals and groups exhibit self-control. They discipline themselves in order to conform to the established norms and "normal" ways of doing things. As a result, those in power positions do not have to exercise power over their subordinates. As disciplinary power is so embedded in social structures and social relations, the provision of technical capabilities for open access to information and debate via CMC could not easily change its force. The mechanism of autoregulation within authoritarian and hierarchical groups prevented their members from using the opportunities provided by CMC.

Another view of organizational politics focuses on conflicting interest groups pursuing more or less incompatible goals (Bacharach et al., 1996). Tensions arising from intergroup conflicts and misalignment of their goals and actions can be transformed into new energy and can create change. This phenomenon can be recognized in the intensified use of CMC in the implementation stage of the consultative process. Tensions and latent conflict between some groups (including academic and administrative) and between the staff and the Executive Committee were sources of strategic initiatives and changes. The use of CMC to announce documents prior to the President's approval was one such example. The intensive work going on in implementation teams and groups, internal and external conflicts, the large number of documents generated daily, and practical limitations in resolving many conflicting issues by consulting with the Executive Committee, created pressure to change the norm. In this example CMC appeared as both an enabler of evolving social changes (changes of the nature of work and intensity of interactions) and as a vehicle for transforming the way organizational knowledge was created and legitimated.

CONCLUSIONS

The presented case demonstrated varieties and subtleties of the use and appropriation of CMC within organizational and group contexts. The examination of particular contexts and specific patterns of CMC use help in understanding the complex interplay between the actors and the technology. It also revealed multiple contextual factors that affected how actors perceived and interpreted the purpose and role of CMC, and how they appropriated it to their unique needs, interests, goals, and values.

In conclusion, it should be emphasized that this case represents a real-life deployment of CMC and its roles and social consequences within a context of organizational strategic planning. Its outcomes were consistent with those of other recent studies that have identified contradictory social consequences arising from the use of information technology within organizations. As indicated by Robey and Boudreau (1999), these contradictions cannot be explained through the use of simple and neat theoretical models:

> Instead of simple imperatives, researchers and practitioners have acknowledged the value of viewing information technology as an ingredient in a more complex process of social change, in which forces for transformation are frequently offset by forces for persistence (p. 182).

DISCUSSION QUESTIONS

1. Why is it important to understand a social context, local culture and institutional characteristics in the study of the role and impacts of information technologies?
2. Compare characteristics of social contexts presented in the case with some that you are familiar with. Explore the use of any tool for electronic communication, such as email, intranet, computer conferencing, Lotus Notes, etc., and compare the consequences. '
3. Contradictory social impacts of the use of CMC in this case are explained from several theoretical perspectives. Do you agree with these arguments? Can you offer counter arguments? Discuss other possible theoretical approaches that may shed light on the contradictions found.

REFERENCES

Adrianson, L., & Hjelmquist, E. (1991). Group processes in face-to-face and computer-mediated communication, *Behavior and Information Technology*, 10(4), 281-296.

Bacharach, S.B., Bamberger, P., & Sonnenstuhl, W.J. (1996). The organization transformation process: The micropolitics of dissonance reduction and the alignment of logics of action. *Admin. Sci. Quarterly*, 41, 477-506.

Bikson, T.K., Eveland, J.D., & Gutek, B.A. (1989.) Flexible interactive technologies for multi person tasks: Current problems and future prospects. Olson, M .H. (Ed.), *Technological Support for Work Group Collaboration*. Hillsdale, NJ: Erlboum.

Child, J., & Loveridge, R. (1990). *Information Technology in European Services – Towards a Microelectronic Future*. Oxford: Blackwell.

Dubrovsky, V.J., Kiesler, S., & Sethna, B.N. (1991). The equalization phenomenon: status effects in computer-mediated and face-to-face decision-making groups. *Human-Computer Interaction*, 6, 119-146.

Foucault, M. (1979). *Discipline and Punish*. New York: Vintage Books.

Kiesler, S., & Sproull, L. (1992). group decision making and communication technology. *Organizational Behavior and Human Decision Making Processes*, 52, 96-123.

Mantovani, G. (1994). Is computer-mediated communication intrinsically apt to enhance democracy in organizations? *Human Relations*, 47(1), 45-62.

Martin, J. (1992). *Cultures in Organization: Three Perspectives*. Oxford UK: Oxford University Press.

Neilson, R. (1997). *Collaborative Technologies*. Hershey: Idea Group Publishing.

Orlikowski, W. J., & Gash, D.C. (1994). Technological frames: making sense of information technology in organizations. *ACM Trans. Inform. Systems*, 12, 174-207.

Rice, R.E. (1990). Computer-mediated communication systems network data: Theoretical concerns and empirical examples. *International Journal of Man-Machine Studies*, 32, 627-647.

Robey, D., & Boudreau, M-C. (1999). Accounting for the contradictory organizational consequences of information technology: Theoretical directions and methodological implications. *Information Systems Research*, 10(2), 167-185.

Sproull, L., & Kiesler, S. (1991a). Computers, networks and work. *Scientific American*, 265(3), 84-91.

Sproull, L., & Kiesler, S. (1991b). *Connections: New Ways of Working in the Networked Organization*. Cambridge, MA: MIT Press.

Chapter X

Implementing Relational Database Systems: Implications for Administrative Cultures and Information Resource Management

Andreea M. Serban
Santa Barbara City College

Gregory A. Malone
Cabrillo College

INTRODUCTION

Traditionally, administrative computing has been the main, or often only, unit in a campus developing and maintaining the basic operating systems of an institution (McKinney et al., 1987). Information resources have been confined to an infrastructure, such as a mainframe computer or minicomputers, which processes registration, financial aid, and other services (Van Dusen, 1997). The advent of increasingly sophisticated software and hardware tools has challenged the centralization of the control and manipulation of information resources. Crow and Rariden (1993) describe an ideal information resource management model as follows:

> Powerful software tools are available that can essentially eliminate the technical expertise necessary to process either university-wide data or off-campus re-search databases. ... Students, faculty, and administrators will be able to ask and answer their own data-related questions from their desks without the assistance or intervention of a computer center's staff (p. 467).

To date, no institution has achieved this ideal (Van Dusen, 1997). However, colleges and universities are making progress toward it. This chapter describes the experiences of two institutions, University of Redlands and Cabrillo College, as they implement similar relational database systems. It describes the effects of the implementation process on the institutional administrative cultures, and the implications for information resource management.

CASE QUESTIONS

- What factors drive an institution to replace its existing administrative information system (AIS)?

- What are the elements and phases of the implementation process?
- What are the expected benefits of implementing a new AIS? What are the potential risks?
- When replacing an existing AIS, in what ways should an institution consider changing the organizational structure that was supported by the original system?

CASE NARRATIVE

Background

Founded in 1907, the University of Redlands (UOR) is a private institution, located 60 miles east of Los Angeles. The organizational structure of the University includes the Board of Trustees, the President and Vice Presidents for Finance and Administration, and Academic Affairs. The University has two colleges—the College of Arts and Sciences (CAS) and the Alfred North Whitehead College of Lifelong Learning (ANWC). CAS offers more than 25 majors in liberal arts and programs of study in professional and pre-professional fields to over 1,500 residential students. ANWC offers undergraduate and graduate programs to more than 2,200 students. The University has a main campus and five adult learning regional centers throughout Southern California. The structure and size of the University have fostered a climate of high-quality, personalized education for both traditional-aged students and adult learners.

Cabrillo College is one of the 107 California community colleges and enrolls almost 14,000 students on three campuses. The main campus conducts most of the classes and all of the administrative business. The organizational structure includes a Governing Board with decision-making authority over all site functions, the President, and Vice Presidents of Business Services, Instruction, and Student Services. The Cabrillo community college district is a supportive environment characterized by extensive collegiality in both instructional and administrative areas.

Cabrillo College is a union organization in both the academic and nonacademic domains. In this aspect, it differs sharply from most private institutions of higher education, including UOR. Whereas private schools generally allow and even encourage employees to contribute extra time, this is not an option for a unionized organization. Union employees are required to work no more than eight hours per day unless prior approval is granted. One result of this has been that there are often longer implementation times when urgent and intensive project efforts are required.

The operations of the two colleges share some commonalities. The registration, student billing, and financial aid processes are located in the main campuses. However, UOR's adult college is decentralized. Each regional center conducts recruitment and admissions, academic advisement, enrollment services, and degree audit and graduation checks. Additionally, Cabrillo has two small branches in nearby cities.

History

Both institutions have relied on traditional administrative computing environments with the Information Technology Services (ITS) at UOR and the Computing Resources (CR) at Cabrillo to manage the structure, processing, and reporting of institutional information through mainframe and minicomputer systems. In 1987, UOR acquired and installed the Information Associates' (IA) suite of administrative software to support most of its administrative information processing needs. The implementation of IA was completed in 1990. However, some offices never fully converted to IA and continued to maintain their own systems. The IA suite was an example of a "monolithic software model" (Mignerey, 1996, p. 40) in which applications were developed to support university-wide (as opposed to department-level) processes. This system required heavy-duty maintenance. Any change involved ITS staff rewriting Cobol programs or modifying data dictionaries. The system also required nightly batch maintenance. Similarly, Cabrillo's legacy Santa Rosa system required 18 months of data conversion and programming when an upgrade was loaded.

Prior to 1993, UOR's system was heavily modified to accommodate the operational needs and processes of the University. The level of modification was so extensive that upgrades to newer versions required extensive programming. Functional users had very limited input and access to the management of institutional information. The communication between functional users and the ITS staff was weak. This setting led to duplication of efforts among different offices. Reporting and data retrieval were difficult and the reliability of data questionable. Many routine tasks required manual operation due to the lack of integration among the existing systems. All these issues increased the frustration of functional users and hampered the effectiveness and efficiency of the University's operations.

Two other major factors contributed to the decision to convert to a new system at UOR. In 1993, Systems & Computing Technology (SCT) bought IA and announced that it would not support development of new IA versions. By 1993, UOR was aware of the need to address the Year 2000 compliance of its systems and IA was not compliant. In early 1993, UOR's senior administrative management, under the leadership of the Vice President for Finance and Administration, decided that it had to evaluate its administrative computing needs and address issues such as ITS structure and role, data ownership and management, and core administrative processes.

At Cabrillo, Hewlett-Packard declared the main information system in use at the time obsolete as of 1998. Support for the equipment ceased and it was announced that it would not be made Year 2000 ready. In October 1996, Cabrillo's Technology Committee met for a retreat to study and evaluate the existing condition of the administrative information systems. This group included teachers, bargaining unit representatives, power users from departments, and the vice presidents of the college. Difficulties encountered with the existing information systems provided incentive to conduct a meeting to generate recommendations to solve these problems. The retreat resulted in the following recommendation:

> Cabrillo College must implement a new Student Support/Administrative Information System (SS/AIS) to overcome the paralysis caused by our current software and hardware. The schedule for replacing the current systems is being driven by software and hardware incompatibilities with the year 2000 and current system inability to provide comprehensive SS/AIS information to the College Community (Cabrillo College, 1997a).

Conversion Strategy

UOR's strategy was captured in the acronym that became associated with the evaluation process: ACORN—Administrative Conversion: Operational Redesign and INnovation. As in process reengineering models (e.g., Davenport, 1993), this process encompassed a strategic vision, organizational processes, people, and technology. Although the emphasis was on operational processes, a strategic focus guided the administrative conversion. The focus was multifold: to align operational processes with the University's strategic priorities; to restructure the ITS in order to meet the computing needs of the

University and improve its efficiency and effectiveness; and to create an organizational culture of change.

From an organizational perspective, the conversion had several goals: to establish a service-oriented culture; to create an environment proactive and adaptable to technological changes; to adopt a cross-functional team approach in managing operational processes; to improve organizational processes through better use of technology; to improve communication and collaboration between ITS and functional users; and to change the role of ITS from the gatekeeper of information to the facilitator of information processing and management.

The planners of the conversion process recognized that the keys to a successful implementation and to organizational change are the individuals affected by the process. The process incorporated the goals to establish and support leadership of the functional users, to provide incentives and resources for learning, and to increase the ability of all level users to manage and utilize information.

On the technology side, several priorities guided the process: to select and implement a system that best meets the needs of the institution and has broad capabilities; to create an integrated information environment; to implement process automation; to provide easy access to authorized users; to allow real-time interaction of information from various administrative units; and to provide a comprehensive source for accurate and timely data reporting.

Cabrillo embraced a similar strategy. The mission of the implementation project was to improve Cabrillo's service to students, faculty, staff, and the college community through the implementation of integrated information systems for student support, curriculum, finance, and human resources, and the concurrent improvement of operational processes. The goals of the project included: elimination of duplicate efforts and redundant systems; automation of manual processes; increased employee effectiveness; and availability of timely, reliable information. Strategies to achieve those goals included: communicating frequently with those involved with and affected by the project; providing appropriate project information to those who need it; providing appropriate training and documentation to team members; identifying and allocating the resources required for success; taking advantage of each application's flexibility to eliminate the need for programming modifications to the software; adopting and following a project plan; and knowing when to change the plan.

Both institutions sought a single vendor that could provide an integrated information system that met the following requirements. It could be: implemented without vendor customization; accommodate site-specific modifications through non-programming solutions such as rules; be designed to retain local modifications as new software releases are implemented; and have the ability to support all core institutional operations.

Pre-Implementation

At UOR, the first step in the conversion process was the evaluation of the University's administrative computing needs. In February 1993, UOR selected the Higher Education Technology and Operations Practice of KPMG Peat Marwick to conduct this evaluation. Its purposes were to:

> Determine which functions might be supported by an automated system; ... obtain from functional users information required of the system; establish a benchmark against which software packages can be qualified and initially evaluated; and provide the level of detail necessary to identify the software package(s) which most reasonably "fit" Redlands' needs (KPMG, 1993, p. 7).

The evaluation found that the existing systems met 35 percent of the administrative computing needs, partially met 24 percent, and did not meet 41 percent. The main reasons cited for the existence of the unmet needs were: poor implementation, planning, and execution of the IA; poor training; lack of functionality; and weak vendor and ITS support. The report concluded that the unmet needs negatively influenced UOR's administrative operations through an abundance of manual work, "work around" procedures, redundant maintenance of data, and strain on employees (KPMG, 1993). KPMG recommended that:

> UOR should undertake a long-term administrative systems upgrade project to focus on: investigating and implementing client/server technology; fostering increased systems integration with off-the-shelf vendor applications; allowing fewer or no modifications to vendor-supplied software; and decentralizing certain computer support services (KPMG, 1993, p. 3).

UOR faced the clear need for converting to a new system but it had to determine which system best met its needs, how the conversion could best be conducted, by whom, and with what resources. For the next year, UOR studied and discussed the results of the evaluation in order to establish the most appropriate course of action. During the summer of 1994, UOR developed a request for proposals to acquire a new administrative information system.

Before engaging in vendor selection, UOR had to decide who would lead the conversion. Due to the weak relationship between the ITS and the user community at the time, UOR's senior management decided that the conversion process would be better coordinated and conducted by a group especially dedicated to this purpose. In February 1995, the President's Cabinet established the Project Office, composed of three employees of UOR, to coordinate all aspects of the conversion project. The President's Cabinet appointed the Vice President for Finance and Administration as the senior manager (Program Sponsor) in charge of the conversion project to work directly with the Project Office. In order to ensure the continuity of the conversion process without disruptions due to possible turnover, UOR converted two of the Project Office positions from full-time employees to contract positions for the duration of the project.

UOR committed to acquire and provide the financial and human resources needed for the conversion process. In 1995, UOR applied for and obtained a bond issue which covered, along with some other major projects, most of the costs associated with the conversion: consulting, software, hardware, training, personnel, and administrative costs (see Table 1 for costs).

With the leadership of the project established and the financial resources secured, the next step was the selection of a vendor. The KPMG evaluation clarified the general requirements of a new system in terms of system integration, user control, usage, transaction and document processing, inquiry capabilities, correspondence control, query and report-

Table 1: Total Costs of the UOR Conversion Project

Conversion Project Costs	Dollars	Percent
Personnel, Administrative and Consultant Costs	$1,441,683	46%
Training/Travel of ITS and Project Office Staff	77,367	3%
Software	760,380	25%
Equipment (workstations, printers, minicomputers)	793,959	26%
Total Conversion Project	**$3,073,389**	**100%**

ing, security, and interface with other systems. In addition, the system had to address the major functional areas of the University: admissions, registration, financial aid, student housing, alumni development, human resources, and financial management.

The Project Office, in collaboration with the managers of the major functional areas and ITS, reviewed the vendor proposals. Narrowing down the qualified vendors was easy at the time, since there were not many choices available. The finalists were two major vendors: SCT with its product Banner, and Datatel with its products Colleague (Student, Financial, and Core Demographics systems) and Benefactor (Alumni Development system). During July and August 1995, the two companies conducted demonstrations of their products at UOR. These demonstrations combined general overviews of the products with specific demonstrations developed in response to "business cases" developed by UOR and submitted to the two vendors in advance. The business cases exemplified some of the processes that UOR's functional users employed routinely. In addition, during the summer of 1995, the Project Office, functional area and ITS managers conducted visits to colleges and universities already using these products and to each company's corporate headquarters. UOR considered the potential of each of the prospective vendors as a business partner for at least five years. Consequently, UOR selected Datatel for all functional areas except for Human Resources. The perceived weakness of Datatel's Human Resource module led to the selection of a different vendor (ProBusiness) for Human Resources.

Cabrillo College staff approached the search for a new information system as a collaborative effort with meetings and on-site visits resulting in: multiple vendor demonstrations; advice of an outside consultant regarding major providers of SS/AIS appropriate for use in California community colleges; and reviews of current SS/AIS requirements and requests for proposals utilized at other community colleges in California.

Cabrillo's staff attended vendor demonstrations of SCT Banner, Datatel Colleague, and Buzzio. Additional meetings with the Higher Education and Technology Operations at KPMG Peat Marwick confirmed that the major SS/AIS packages available had been identified. Based upon responses to the requests for proposals, site visits, and positive customer feedback, Cabrillo selected Datatel's Colleague software. Several California community colleges had selected Colleague during the same period. The significance of this migration of multiple sites to the Colleague product resulted in Datatel producing some specific data modifications for California colleges. Such a notable modification is the "California Gold" version of the Human Resources module that deals with retirement programs unique to California.

During October 1997, Cabrillo College continued to evaluate Datatel Colleague to ensure a close fit with its needs. The College organized a four-day series of demonstrations to address the needs of the various departments, with half-day sessions provided for each department. Numerous representatives from Cabrillo and three other colleges attended these meetings. Cabrillo provided an additional full-day session to present information for instructional areas and to answer some of the concerns of the business services department. A representative from a neighboring college attended this session. Cabrillo staff met with Datatel representatives and discussed optional modules needed, number of concurrent user licenses necessary, and pricing structure. These sessions addressed most of the concerns of the College community and reinforced the impressions of the staff that this was a complete, flexible, and configurable solution.

At the December 1, 1997, Governing Board meeting, the Board adopted the action item for the Vice President of Business Services to execute a contract to purchase Datatel's

Table 2: Estimated Costs of the Cabrillo College Conversion Project (Cabrillo College, 1997b)

Conversion Project Costs	Dollars	Percent
Personnel, Administrative and Consultant Costs	$302,500	26%
Training/Travel of ITS and Project Office Staff	85,000	7%
Software	630,000	55%
Equipment (workstations, printers, minicomputers)	139,000	12%
Total Conversion Project	**$1,156,500**	**100%**

administrative information system. Cabrillo estimated the total cost of the project at $1,156,500 (see Table 2 for estimated costs). This estimate included the software, data conversion, travel expenses, training, consulting, utility software tools, hardware replacements, and hardware and software support.

On December 22, 1997, Cabrillo College purchased Datatel's Colleague to replace its legacy systems for financial management, human resources management, and student, faculty, and curriculum management. The College targeted the replacement of these systems and conversion of data from Spring 1998 to Summer 2000 (see Table 3 for implementation timetable). In 15 months, Cabrillo progressed from the realization that something needed to change to the purchase decision of the appropriate system.

Implementation

At UOR, the implementation of the new system lasted almost two years (September 1996-August 1998; see Table 4) and involved 75 individuals from various administrative units.

Table 3: Cabrillo Implementation Timeline

System/Modules	Full Start Date
Core System	
Demographics	August 1998
Scheduling	August 1999
Facilities Profile, Communications Management	October 1999
Finance System	
General Ledger, Accounts Payable, Purchasing	August 1998
Budget Management	March 1999
Auxiliary Funds—General Ledger, Accounts Payable, Purchasing; Decentralized Account Management Lookup	July 1999
Human Resource System	
Personnel	May 1999
Student System	
Faculty Information, Curriculum Management	August 1999
Admission/Recruiting, Accounts Receivable, Registration, Academic Records, Degree Audit, Advising, Counseling (Education Plans)	October 1999
Financial Aid	March 2000
Web Registration	April 2000

One of the most important aspects of the conversion process at UOR was the transfer of information ownership from ITS to the administrative units (for example, the Registrar's office became the owner of modules such as registration and degree audit/advisement). This resulted in a change in the role of the ITS from manager of the information to facilitator of data input, processing, and reporting. Such a transition meant addressing several critical issues:

- Establishing a system of continuous communication between ITS and administrative units, on one hand, and among administrative units, on the other
- Rethinking the operations of computing services and their relationships with administrative units
- Ensuring that operational processes are clearly defined and understood and the effects of the system integration on overlapping areas are continuously monitored and communicated between administrative units/functional areas
- Training of an initial group of end-users on both the use of the Datatel systems and personal computer software, who would then train users within their units
- Defining and establishing levels of data access for various clients of the Datatel system
- Establishing mechanisms for ensuring data integrity
- Developing policies and procedures for access to and use of the information
- Determining mechanisms of data manipulation, analysis, interpretation, and reporting

Table 4: ACORN Chronology

1993	February: UOR hires KPMG Peat Marwick's Higher Education Division to evaluate the administrative computing needs. September: KPMG completes the evaluation of administrative computing needs.
1994	UOR develops request for proposals to acquire a new administrative system.
1995	February: Project Office established to conduct and oversee the conversion project. July-August: On-site demonstrations by Datatel and SCT and visits to colleges and universities using the products of the two companies. October: Contract with Datatel finalized. November: Equipment purchased.
1996	Installation of equipment and software. Initial training of selected functional users and contract employees of the Project Office. Functional analysis and implementation begin.
1997	Training of selected functional users, functional analysis and implementation continue. Units start full use: July: Finance (General Ledger and Accounts Payable/Purchasing). August: Benefactor. November: CAS Admissions. December: ANWC Admissions.
1998	Implementation continues. January: Human Resources (with a different vendor – ProBusiness). February: Financial Aid. April: Housing. July: Finance (Budget Management, Fixed Assets, Inventory, Physical Plant, Pooled Investment). August: Billing and Registration and Student Systems. September: Implementation completed, Project Office closed.

In light of these principles, the implementation process evolved around several distinctive features. Individuals from all functional areas were involved in the implementation process. Two functional user-based teams were formed at the outset of the implementation, the System Implementation Managers and the Implementation Team. The System Implementation Managers were the managers of the main functional areas: the Controller for the Finance Area, the Registrar for the Student Area, the Director of Alumni Development for the Alumni/Development Area, and a Human Resources Analyst for the Human Resource Area. The Implementation Team included, along with the System Implementation Managers, the designated module leaders. Each of the four major systems (Student, Finance, and Alumni Development with Datatel and Human Resources with ProBusiness) included a number of modules that reflect various processes within the major functional areas (see Table 5 for the structure of systems and modules within systems).

The two functional user teams were the champions of their systems and modules. The Project Office and functional user teams agreed that a technical group composed of ITS staff and two of the Project Office staff was also needed. This group would deal with the installation and testing of the new software systems and the conversion of the data from the old to the new systems. These four groups represented the driving forces throughout the implementation process.

Based on KPMG's recommendations, the UOR's Program Sponsor and implementation groups decided to engage in a functional analysis of all university processes concurrent with the implementation of the new systems.

Functional analysis is a holistic methodical approach to establishing a new vision for providing services and fully exploiting the functional capabilities of the new software. Functional analysis will result in processes designed to meet UOR's objectives and tasks defined to complete the conversion project (Caudle, 1996, p. 25).

Table 5: Structure of the Integrated Systems

System	Modules
Student (Datatel Colleague)	Financial Aid, Accounts Receivable, Communications Management, Registrar, Degree Audit/Advisement, Student Affairs/Housing, Demographics, Admissions
Financial (Datatel Colleague)	General Ledger, Budget, Accounts Payable, Cash Receipts
Alumni Development (Datatel Benefactor)	Major Prospects, Activities and Events, Individual Information, Organizational Information, Campaign Management, Correspondence Control, Gift and Pledge Processing
Human Resources (ProBusiness and Datatel Colleague)	Personnel, Payroll
Core Demographics (Datatel Colleague)	Person Demographics, Corporation Demographics, Facilities, Correspondence Control, Parameter Definition

The analysis was accomplished by creating work groups that focused on various processes. The work groups addressed specific and cross-functional processes, established communication between administrative units, and provided decision-making for process streamlining to be more service oriented. A KPMG consultant acted as facilitator for each functional analysis meeting.

At both institutions, the implementation tasks were divided into three major phases to help organize the workflow and activities (Caudle, 1996). This was based on the design of the Datatel systems, which included the creation of three separate environments: the "education" environment where functional users could learn the systems; the "test" environment that contained the same data as the actual production database but where functional users could try various processes and procedures without the risk of corrupting the data; and the "live" environment that represents the actual production database. In the initial phase of the implementation, only the first two environments were available. The "live" accounts were created at the final stage of the implementation of each of the systems. The creation of the "live" environments meant the completion of the implementation for a particular system. The three phases represent the implementation sequence for each of the major systems:

Phase I – Planning, Analysis, and Learning – "Getting Understanding"
This phase included tasks performed in the "Education" account that allow the implementation team leaders to gain an understanding of their modules. Tasks associated with this phase included: analysis of current tasks and procedures; preparation for vendor training; module training for technical staff, decision makers, and internal trainers; design of code tables for the new system; test of reports; translation of current procedures to the new software; consultation with software vendor; planning data conversion; and conversion data mapping.

Phase II – Decision Making Phase – "Getting Crazy"
During this phase, the implementation team for each system and module formalized decisions and procedures. Tasks were performed in the "test" account. Tasks associated with this phase included: writing test plans; setting up codes and parameters in the test account; testing codes and parameters; creating test data manually; creating print programs for standard forms and/or order forms; writing and testing conversion programs; testing processes; determining and writing procedures; writing specifications for reports; and preparing manual or converted end-user training data in the "test" account.

Phase III – Going "Live" – "Getting Real"
In the last phase, final decisions made in the test account were duplicated in the "live" account. Tasks associated with this phase included: document procedures; training end-users; setting up security in live account; setting up codes and parameters in live account; testing reports; manually creating the live data files not being converted; duplicating reports from the "test" to the "live" account; running data conversion in the "live" account; cleaning up data; and going "live"!

During the implementation at UOR, there were multiple issues that the Project Office, functional user teams, and technical group had to address. They had to decide in what order the four systems and their modules should be implemented. The four groups decided to start the implementation with the easiest system—the Finance system. The assumptions driving this decision were twofold: the experience gained with the implementation of this system would facilitate an easier transition to the more complicated systems, and the first system had to be implemented successfully to increase the enthusiasm for and trust in the conversion. During the two-year scheduled implementation timeframe, the University experienced only a one-and-a-half-month delay that did not involve any major adverse consequence to the University operations (University of Redlands, 1998).

Cabrillo decided to implement each of the four major applications that comprise the Colleague software. The scope of this implementation, by design, did not include every module within each application. For example, Cabrillo did not implement the Alumni Development module (Benefactor) because the College's Foundation that conducts alumni development activities was using stand-alone software that did not require integration with the student and financial systems. As at UOR, Cabrillo organized the implementation into a number of teams and committees with responsibilities for implementing or overseeing a particular aspect of the project (see Table 6). The organization into teams was intended to make the process of implementation more manageable.

At both institutions, the teams were not intended to be static, but instead to accommodate new conditions and events as they occurred. Compared to UOR, the senior management of Cabrillo was more directly involved in the implementation process. At UOR, the senior management oversaw the major decisions but left the details and management of the implementation to the Project Office.

Table 6: Cabrillo College: Organization for Implementation

Team	Responsibilities	Membership	Escalation
Steering Committee	General Implementation Guidelines & Policies – Final Adjudication of Unresolved Problems	President, Vice Presidents, Director Computing Resources	None
Implementation Oversight Committee	Data Standards Technical/Security Scheduling General Guidelines & Policies	Implementation Manager Application Team Leader Application System Administrators Technical Services Representatives	Steering Committee
Core Development Team	Shared Codes Team	Application Team Leaders Analysts Instruction	Implementation Oversight Committee
Teams: Colleague Applications	Finance Student Human Resources	Application Team Leader Application System Administrators Representatives from Each Module Area Technical Services Representative	Implementation Oversight Committee
Module Teams: One Per Module or Module Office	Various	Department Manager Decision Makers Selected Others	Application Team

At Cabrillo, the sequence of implementation of systems and their modules was similar to that at UOR. The Finance System was implemented first, live production being achieved in a record four months. As at UOR, the implementation sequence was driven by the degree of complexity of each of the systems. Furthermore, Cabrillo's project management benefited from the expertise gained by two of the UOR's Project Office members with the prior implementation of Datatel's products.

ANALYSIS

Both institutions recognized that the implementation of a new administrative system is a very complex task. From the President and the senior management to administrative departments, the project was viewed as a truly significant undertaking that would include pain and suffering in order to achieve potentially remarkable results. The implementation at both institutions demonstrated that this project was expensive, difficult, and required a great deal of effort on the part of employees who had to accept change and assume additional concurrent work tasks. A related effect has been the realization, across job roles, of the amount of information needed and work done by others. A positive synergy has resulted from this sharing of information about workflow.

Additional challenges presented by the implementation project included the balancing of the difficult conflicts between valuable change and historical process ("the old way"). The outcomes required compromise, rethinking, and reengineering of how business was conducted. In some cases, this required a change in process that improved service. The benefits of discarding isolated separate systems in favor of an integrated data system brought about a new thinking and a greater willingness to accept change.

The cumbersome interface of the Colleague system was one of the implementation challenges. If the software creates difficulty to the performance of the job or even makes itself felt as a challenge, then the software is not providing a reasonable service to the user.

> Something as banal as printing a computer file can be a debilitating exercise that resembles voodoo more than respectable human behavior (Negroponte, 1995, p. 92).

It is not surprising to see a very powerful relational database system with an awkward front-end interface. Most information management systems have evolved from the data processing model based on mainframe computing that required finite programming to run the interface. Unfortunately, this has generated a credibility problem for users who expect to see the more popular graphical user interface as represented by the Microsoft Windows interface. Some assume that an interface that is awkward represents software that is not as capable as packages with graphical features. More importantly, the issue of navigation to specific screen locations is a critical issue. The ability to find the proper location and appropriate function for completing the task at hand is paramount to software productivity. The Datatel software combines these forces by providing a very rigid system as the interface while allowing users to define some elements such as "validation codes" as values represented by mnemonic codes and abbreviations.

At both institutions, the predominant theme of the implementation has been boundary crossing. The implementation of a relational database and its applications providing integrated data throughout the institutional infrastructure has led to cross-departmental discussions of workflow, shared decision-making, and an increased understanding of how processes in one area affect and are affected by those in another. The implementation has been methodical due primarily to effective project management, and effective staff and team involvement and leadership. Further, by making sure the implementation was at the user level, it resulted in a higher degree of success.

Before the conversion, at UOR, there were 100 users of the mainframe-based systems. Currently, there are 230 users. Throughout the conversion process, the University purchased, installed and networked 250 personal computers and 21 printers, conducted a total of 1,800 hours of group discussions, and provided on-site training that covered system modules for all 230 users. The relational nature of the new system has increased the awareness of the various administrative units and system users of the necessity of updating and maintaining the data in an accurate and timely manner. The implementation of the new system has reduced organizational barriers by increasing communication between the various administrative units.

In spite of successful implementation processes at both institutions, the elimination of all "shadow" systems and discouragement of duplicate or add-on systems are still goals to be achieved. Another difficult task has been helping users understand the required changes due to the implementation of the new system. Long-range use of data and its effect on administrative units, data confidentiality, and storage requiring constant updating of system processes to take advantage of the newest technologies, and continuous training of users are just some examples of challenges that both institutions still need to tackle.

In spite of the differences in structure, size, and mission, the two institutions and their respective implementations of the Datatel software share significant similarities. This is in part a function of the software manufacturer's philosophy and in part due to recommendations of the consultants hired to facilitate the implementation. The software requires many user-defined values and codes leading to extensive input from the client. These values and codes "personalize" and customize the implementation at each site. Cooperative decision-making is essentially built-in to the product due to the interaction and some overlap between the major systems and their modules.

The amount of work, time, and staff resources required always seems to be more than is available, yet somehow deadlines are met and progress is achieved. The initial efforts were crucial as they set the stage for all that followed. Progress tracking and adequate celebration of success were important to the continuity of the project. The project manager at Cabrillo and the Project Office at UOR provided critical information to the Governing Board and the President's Cabinet, respectively. Their reports were instrumental in sustaining the effort and flow of project activity as well as providing benchmarks to those inside and outside the project implementation.

At both institutions, the projects could not have been accomplished without the expertise and assistance of the project consultants. As overall project manager and resource to all functional committees, a competent consultant provides direction, leadership, and technical expertise regarding a very sophisticated management information system and the requirements to successfully implement it. A senior manager at Cabrillo College stated that an important factor was bringing in outside help in the form of a skilled project manager, who was also one of the Project Office staff at UOR. The outside help brings 'out-of-the-box' thinking to the project. Cabrillo College chose this path for its implementation. Although at UOR existing employees managed the implementation, the University benefited from the expertise of KPMG that facilitated the process through the initial evaluation of administrative computing needs and the functional analysis.

At both sites, the senior management provided support and encouragement as needed to facilitate workflow and meet deadlines. The involvement of executive management at Cabrillo College in all critical decision-making phases of the project was essential and supportive. At UOR, the Project Sponsor and Project Office informed the President's Cabinet of all steps taken and decisions made in collaboration with the implementation teams.

Cabrillo reached its vendor selection decision in a shorter period than UOR mainly because of the interaction it had with numerous similar institutions in California that had already decided to implement the same system. There was also an existing contract between the Community College District and Datatel. UOR, on the other hand, had to make this decision from the perspective of its unique needs.

The two institutions had similar implementation teams. The organization of the implementation teams was a consequence of the structure of the software and of the main functional areas that exist in most higher education institutions, regardless of size and mission.

There are also important differences between the two sites in terms of goals and costs of the projects. UOR used the conversion to the new system as an opportunity to thoroughly analyze all operational processes of the University by engaging in a functional analysis and redefining the role and structure of its ITS staff. The former endeavor led to higher project costs and much more time invested in cross-functional meetings and discussions. The latter goal increased the complexity and scope of the project.

Without a doubt, the most important achievement of the implementation for both institutions was the synergy created between the administrative units and the significant progress made towards transforming the organizational cultures to embrace change as a normal and permanent process.

CONCLUSIONS

As Mignerey (1996) suggests:

> For all of its problems, there is little if any doubt that distributed computing is the computing environment of the future. As solutions are found to some very difficult technological problems, more and more traditional computing applications will migrate to the distributed client/server model (p. 45).

Cabrillo and UOR have confirmed Mignerey's prediction. Although information technology is advancing rapidly, the market of integrated information systems for higher education has remained fairly stable in terms of major vendors and systems available. The choices available in 1999 are not much different from those available in 1995. The difference is mainly in the quality and sophistication of the products rather than in their number. Thus, it is safe to assume that had the two institutions engaged in the selection process in 1999, it is likely that their final choices would be similar to those they decided upon in 1995 and 1997, respectively.

The experience of Cabrillo College and University of Redlands with the implementation of the Datatel products suggests the following factors and steps be considered by institutions planning for or contemplating similar projects:

1.   Evaluate the need for change to a new system.
2.   Determine the goals of change.

3. Analyze resources—are there sufficient budget, staffing, and time resources available?
4. Make a careful determination of the match between 1, 2, and 3 and resolve differences.
5. Do not try to do it all yourself—outside consultants are valuable for many reasons (objective point of view; "outside the box" thinking; expertise from similar sites; not a long-term expense).
6. Choose consultants who have expertise and support local "capacity-building," not dependency.
7. Dedicate some personnel exclusively for the implementation project.
8. Factor at least 30% over initial budget.
9. Ensure very broad user input to conversion and design processes.
10. Emphasize service orientation and campus-wide communication and collaboration.
11. Involve executive management to lend credibility and support to the efforts needed.
12. Have a clear decision-making strategy for all aspects of the project.
13. Network heavily with other schools, especially those with the same implementation projects, which are showing success.
14. Be flexible—allow timelines to shift.
15. Obtain everything in writing from the vendor. Vague promises or statements will not suffice.
16. Place a priority on training and preparation of staff.
17. Collaboratively solve problems and seek solutions. Communicate with all those involved.
18. Celebrate successes.

The implementation of such projects is not an endeavor to approach casually. It is a major series of significant events requiring a great deal of preparation to accomplish successfully. Decision-makers at institutions faced with a project of this magnitude are advised to collect as much information as possible about the nature of the process before implementation.

DISCUSSION QUESTIONS

1. How does an institution determine the magnitude of change required by the conversion to a new Administrative Information System (AIS)?
2. What are some of the critical factors in successfully implementing an AIS ?
3. How does an institution address resistance to change?
4. How does an institution evaluate the outcomes of implementing an AIS?
5. In what ways was the implementation in this case successful?
6. What was the role of senior leadership in the process?

REFERENCES

Cabrillo College. (1997a). *Presentation to the Board of Trustees.* October 6, 1997.
Cabrillo College. (1997b). *Presentation to the Board of Trustees.* December 1, 1997.
Caudle, P. (1996). *Administrative System Conversion Implementation Plan.* University of Redlands. January 11.
Crow, G. B., and Rariden, R. L. (1993). Advancing the academic information infrastructure. *Journal of Research on Computing in Education,* 25(4), 464-72.

Davenport, T. H. (1993). *Process Innovation: Reengineering Work Through Information Technology*. Cambridge, MA: Harvard Business School Press.

KPMG Peat Marwick. (1993). *Evaluation of Administrative Computing Needs*. University of Redlands. September.

McKinney, R.L., Schott, J. S., Teeter, D.J., and Mannering, L.W. (1987). Data Administration and Management. E. M. Staman (Ed.), *Managing Information in Higher Education, New Directions for Institutional Research*, No. 55. San Francisco, CA: Jossey-Bass Publishers.

Mignerey, L.J. (1996). Client/server conversions: Balancing benefits and risks. *CAUSE/EFFECT*, 19(3), 40-45.

Negroponte, N.P. (1995). *Being Digital*. New York, NY: Alfred A. Knopf, Inc.

University of Redlands. (1998). *Presentation to the Board of Trustees*. September 8.

Van Dusen, G.C. (1997). The virtual campus—technology and reform in higher education. *ASHE-ERIC Higher Education Report 25, No. 5*. Washington, DC: The George Washington University, Graduate School of Education and Human Development.

ADDITIONAL RESOURCES

There are numerous publications and useful Web resources that can provide further insights into similar projects undertaken by other higher education institutions. Listed below are just a few:

- *CAUSE/EFFECT* is a practitioner's journal for college and university managers and users of information resources – information, technology, and services – published quarterly by EDUCAUSE: http://www.educause.edu/pub/ce/cause-effect.html.
- A site of resources related to managing computer technology in higher education: http://www.temple.edu/admin/other.htm.
- *Technology Tools for Today's Campuses*. James L. Morrison (Editor): http://horizon.unc.edu/projects/monograph/CD/.
- On the Horizon: http://horizon.unc.edu/horizon/.

ENDNOTE

The authors would like to thank the following individuals for their invaluable insights and support that enabled the completion of this project:

From University of Redlands: Mr. Philip Doolittle, Vice President for Finance and Administration; Ms. Georgianne Carlson, Associate Vice President for Finance and Administration; Ms. Patricia Caudle, Controller; Mr. Hamid Etesamnia, Director of Integrated Technology; Mr. Cory Nomura, Director of Administrative Services; Ms. Betty Porter, Senior Software Analyst; Mr. Steve Garcia, Senior Software Analyst; Mr. Matthew Riley, System Manager; Ms. Nancy Svenson, Associate Dean of Admissions for Operations.

From Cabrillo College: Ms. Pegi Ard, Vice President for Business Services; Ms. Tess Hunt, Manager Business Services; Ms. Marcy Wieland, Technology Computer Systems Coordinator; Cabrillo Project Consultant and Project Manager Mr. Darren Rose of Rose & Tuck, LLD.; Sue Hass, Manager, Computing Resources; Project Consultant and former member of the Project Office at University of Redlands: Mr. Mark Tuck, also of Rose & Tuck, LLD.

Chapter XI

The Politics of Information Management

Lisa Petrides, Sharon Khanuja-Dhall and Pablo Reguerin
Teachers College, Columbia University

INTRODUCTION

Developing, sharing, and working with information in today's environment is not an easy task. With today's technological advancements, the management of information appears to be deceivingly easier. However, building and maintaining an infrastructure for information management involves complex issues, such as group consensus, access and privileges, well-defined duties, and power redistribution. Furthermore, higher education institutions are continuously faced with the need to balance the politics of information sharing across departments, whether the administration operates in a centralized or decentralized manner.

The need to develop, share, and manage information in a more effective and efficient manner has been proven to require a challenging shift in the norms and behavior of higher education institutions as well. This shift does not have as much to do with the actual use of technology as it does with the cultural environment of the institution. Davenport notes:

> Information cultures determine how much those involved value information, share it across organizational boundaries, disclose it internally and externally, and capitalize on it (Davenport, 1997, p. 35).

Depending on the history, people, and cultural environment, each organization faces its own dilemmas around the task of compiling and sharing information.

This case details one institution's attempts, at a departmental level, to develop an information system for planning and decision-making. It looks at the department's effort to manage and track students and to design a management tool that would help departmental faculty to function more effectively. It examines the challenges faced in managing information and the behaviors that drive new information management processes with the increased use of technology.

CASE QUESTIONS

- Whose responsibility is it to lead information systems integration in higher education? Who will or will not benefit from this?
- How do certain behaviors and group norms help or hinder the effective design and implementation of information systems?
- How can decentralized organizations negotiate and balance the competing demands and goals of the institution?

CASE NARRATIVE

Background

Midwestern University (MU) has an enrollment of approximately 15,000 students. Since it was founded, the mission of MU has been to provide world-class leadership in teaching and research. Within MU there are 15 academic departments and several administrative units. University administration had historically taken a very centralized approach to program enrollment, recruitment, financial aid, and general administration of student-related matters. However, more recently, top-level administration has encouraged individual departments to take more local control of their planning, ranging from student administration to budget setting. The push for local or departmental control has not been accompanied by the requisite development of reliable information systems necessary for both short- and long-term planning. This decentralized approach has placed departments at a distinct disadvantage due to increasing levels of accountability at the department level.

Historically, information such as student enrollments and financial aid allocation flowed downward from central administration offices to the departmental level. The upward flow of information consisted of a set of checks and balances associated with departmental graduation requirements. In addition, data that were specific to the department level did not flow upward (e.g., faculty advising lists and student progress reports). Administrative divisions were centrally managed with multiple databases tracking data in functional units. For example, enrollment data were maintained and controlled by admissions, but the graduate studies office controlled doctoral student data. Many of these systems were run with old and outdated software, and the university struggled with the lack of a coordinated information system that managed all data collected throughout the university. This resulted in issues of data integrity, redundancy, and accuracy, with a low level of trust concerning the interpretation of data.

Enrollment data were maintained at the university level. These data were available to assist the department in knowing how many students were enrolled during a particular semester. However, it could take three to four weeks to obtain data from the central student information system, and field definitions were seldom defined. Additionally, because students were not centrally tracked through the various stages of doctoral completion, it was difficult if not impossible to ascertain the types of classes, services, and faculty commitment that students required with any degree of certainty. Departments relied on anecdotal information to conduct planning, and this became a standard and acceptable practice by default. Additionally, many faculty suspected that there were dozens of students who slipped through the cracks in the process somewhere along the line and might have been precipitously close to dropping out.

There was also a high level of dissatisfaction among MU students with regard to information management. Students were frustrated with the number of repetitive steps and processes involved in their educational experience. For example, students needed to register for classes at the registrar's office. However, depending on the class students wanted to register for, they may have needed to receive departmental signatures prior to registration and then go to an entirely different office to make tuition payments. Because of the amount of time spent in completing these tasks, students' frustration level only increased when the data across these areas could not be shared.

The Arts and Humanities (A&H) department has approximately 200 doctoral graduate students, 200 graduate master students, and 300 undergraduates enrolled. Unlike the master and undergraduate students, who have structured two- and four-year programs, doctoral students went through several different stages of enrollment; first as graduate students enrolled in classes, then as doctoral candidates once they passed comprehensive exams, followed by a period of time during which they took independent dissertation-related methods courses and dissertation writing seminars. This multi-stage process was very complicated to track and the department had been unable to determine with much accuracy at what stage in the matriculation process their 200-plus doctoral students were at any given time.

This had many implications for departmental planning. The opportunities and challenges presented by a more decentralized structure of decision-making needed to be supported by reliable information. In conjunction with this challenge, the department began to conduct long-term planning for doctoral course offerings and faculty dissertation loads. This affected planning for core courses, research seminars, and dissertation writing workshops.

Additionally, there were implications for faculty workload since work with doctoral students could be a very time-consuming process at various stages of their degree. In fact, the proposal and final writing stage for doctoral students working on their dissertations often required a large investment of faculty time, mainly consisting of reading draft chapters and supplying timely feedback.

The Politics of Information Sharing

With the University's push to a decentralized model of operation, departmental accountability and ownership of doctoral student data were becoming a priority. The need for the department to track and assess doctoral student status was crucial to both the doctoral students' and departments' success. Members of the department decided that they needed to do something about the situation. They agreed to tackle their first goal – how to improve access to student information.

In an attempt to address this issue effectively, a needs assessment was conducted. This consisted of determining what type of information was required about doctoral students in order to do more short- and long-term planning. During the planning process, the department faculty realized they did not even know how many doctoral students had continuous enrollment over the past two semesters, let alone how many students were projected to graduate that year. There were larger issues of completion and attrition that faculty wondered about but seemed afraid to find out. Simple questions were unable to be answered, such as: how long do doctoral students take to complete the program, how many students have completed their coursework but not yet taken their comprehensive exams, how many students need to take a dissertation writing seminar the next semester, and how much financial aid support do students need to graduate.

Not only were there student-related questions without answers, but there were also issues of faculty workload. There were 25 full-time faculty members in the A&H department. Seven of them were untenured but on the tenure track. It had been brought to the Dean's attention in promotion and tenure reviews that the junior faculty might have a disproportionate amount of the doctoral student load. However, when asked, the department chair was only able to answer the question based on general estimates and hearsay. There were no reliable data regarding faculty workload issues. This lack of information regarding doctoral students and faculty workload only made stronger the department's chair request that the information management of the department be improved upon.

The departmental culture was one in which information was heavily protected. Traditionally, the sharing of information had been the source of political disputes. Faculty neither felt that they gained anything by sharing information about doctoral workload, nor did they see the need to. In this case, senior faculty members typically had a lighter doctoral student workload than junior members and wanted to avoid workload reallocation. However, junior faculty who had a heavy workload struggled to obtain and share doctoral student information with other faculty. In this case, these issues only added to the closed nature of sharing information in the department, since information sharing behavior was neither recognized nor rewarded.

> Whether we like it or not, information politics involves competing interests, dissension, petty squabbles over scare resources (Davenport, 1997, p. 78).

A First Step

Two years earlier, the department chair had instructed his administrative assistant to begin to collect and maintain departmental doctoral student data using a Lotus spreadsheet. These data were kept independently of the university-wide information systems. Numerous challenges associated with creating, sharing, and updating the spreadsheet files were faced. The historical operation of the department was heavily reliant on another office's data, and faculty's self-management of their doctoral students led to information that was not readily available at the departmental level. Furthermore, it was very difficult for the administrative assistant to consolidate the information from the disparate systems and faculty members. Specifically, the data that were to be compiled included information such as: the number of credits for students currently enrolled, their year in the program, their comprehensive exam completion status, their faculty member adviser, and the amount of time students had left to finish their coursework.

As indicated, this information was not centrally located and each system varied in type and form. Within the department, some data were in hardcopy only, filed in a file cabinet or in handwritten notebooks that faculty used for personal tracking of their students. Some of the information was not even documented or available in an accessible system. With so many varying types of systems and the data being scattered throughout the department, the effort to consolidate the information into a spreadsheet was difficult. In order to create a workable tool, the scope of the data collection effort was limited only to departmental doctoral student information.

Once the information was collected and consolidated into the spreadsheet, reports were summarily disregarded by faculty. When looking closely at why the spreadsheet failed, several items were identified. For example, there was the limitation that spreadsheets impose on data – data must be depicted in columns and rows, and the ability to crosscut data is limited. For example, a header row contained student year, faculty adviser, and the number of years that student had been enrolled. The spreadsheet had 50 columns across and more than 200 rows down. Because a spreadsheet cannot be queried, the only way to find or organize the information was by sorting the entire spreadsheet. This became cumbersome because, if a multiple column sort was conducted, Lotus would sort one column at a time, independent of the other columns, with the end result being a sorted list of all students not just the category desired. The administrative assistant tried to counteract this by taking a portion of the complete spreadsheet and cutting and pasting it into another file. This resulted in multiple spreadsheets with information that needed to be updated in eight or nine different files. Even if the person responsible for doing this kept track of the updates, it would be extremely inefficient, redundant, and prone to error.

The inability to develop special views of the data and custom reports was a limiting factor with the spreadsheet. This querying limitation only increased the lack of support and use for reliable information. A second, and more obvious challenge, was the administrative assistant's lack of sophistication and training around the software itself.

The Web-Based Relational Database Project

Despite the initial failure, the chair of the department asked two technologically minded faculty members, both untenured, to write a proposal for building a relational Web-based database that would consolidate and centralize data from several different areas of the university, including other administrative offices outside the immediate department. They submitted a proposal to build a Web-based, password-protected database that would be accessible to all faculty. The proposed system would be easy to use; they estimated that it would take approximately two hours to train a computer-knowledgeable individual to use the system. The data would reside in one file, and reports could be created automatically. They would provide two-hour training for the administrative assistant, a two-page list of instructions of how to import data and produce reports, and a one-page list of instructions for faculty members on how to access and use the database via the Web. They estimated that it would take them eight months to complete the project. The department chair gave them $7,000 the next week to begin their work.

The design team was led by the two faculty members. An outside consultant who specialized in database design was hired to join the team. Because the Web-based technology was somewhat new to the department, a consultant specializing in Web development was also brought on to help create the proposal and pilot system.

In creating a proposal that would define the scope of the project, the resources required, and the required information for the database, the two faculty members divided the project into three main phases – planning, design, and implementation. This provided them with a framework that gave measurable and clear checkpoints that were dependent on departmental faculty approval.

The planning stage first involved a requirement study that consisted of identifying a comprehensive list of the department's information needs. This also required looking at external data requirements and the systems that data would come from. The additional data that would be gathered from across the university included data from the Student Information System (SIS) managed by the Registrar's Office, the Doctoral Student Database (DSD) managed by the Graduate Studies Office, and the Student Payment System (SPS) managed by the Student Accounting Office. Student data for each of these systems were to be consolidated into the A&H relational Web-based database, along with additional data that were collected at the departmental level only (e.g., faculty advisers and dissertation chairs).

The two faculty leaders conducted interviews with each of the faculty and prioritized requests from the departmental members and the chair. The need for new data that had not been collected previously by any office was also identified. The compilation of all the requested data came from approximately 20 different subsystems both manual and electronic. As described earlier, these systems ranged from word processing to handwritten notebooks.

The next phase required designing the relationships between the data elements and tables. The database consultant helped to incorporate a database design that was able to depict the relationships between each of the different data tables with relative ease. This provided an initial understanding of system complexity by focusing on the relationships between data, data types, and source. This exercise was essential in proactively understanding how the new system would

Diagram 1: Sample Relational Table

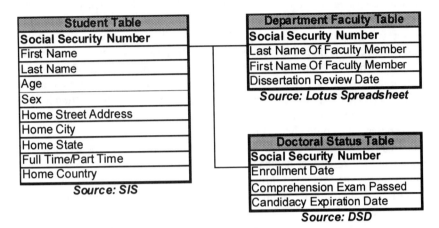

Student Table
Social Security Number
First Name
Last Name
Age
Sex
Home Street Address
Home City
Home State
Full Time/Part Time
Home Country

Source: SIS

Department Faculty Table
Social Security Number
Last Name Of Faculty Member
First Name Of Faculty Member
Dissertation Review Date

Source: Lotus Spreadsheet

Doctoral Status Table
Social Security Number
Enrollment Date
Comprehension Exam Passed
Candidacy Expiration Date

Source: DSD

be queried and what information would be collected in the new system. Diagram 1 shows a relational schematic of how a few tables in the database would be linked by student social security number, a primary and unique key across each table.

The diagram illustrates the relationship between the new tables to be created and the source of the data. The design team determined that approximately 32 tables with 500 data elements would be required in the new Web-based system. This included information such as: demographics, address, first enrolled, last attended, dissertation chair, whether students attended school full time or part time, and when their doctoral candidacy expired.

The issue of data maintenance was raised as a main concern in the design phase, and the team recommended a system manager to keep the data integrity at an optimal level. The team selected software tools based on the data complexity and faculty interviews. Having a clear understanding of the faculty requirements concerning doctoral student information, explicitly outlining the data relationships, and assessing the current mix of systems and interfaces, the team was able to confidently select effective software tools for implementation. The main goal surrounding the selection process was to identify a user-friendly and intuitive front-end that would provide faculty with ease and functionality for sharing and accessing data.

The last phase, implementation, consisted of running a pilot with faculty, training the faculty, and receiving sign-off approval from the chair to operationalize the entire system. In piloting the system the two faculty members demonstrated the capability of the new system at a faculty meeting and also provided one-on-one demos. Based on these demos, faculty members requested even more features and functionality from the system. Not only did the team implement the requested functionality, but they also incorporated an automated feedback form that would allow new feature requests to be delivered to the core development team on an ongoing basis. For example, if a faculty member identified a new feature she or he wanted, the faculty member could complete an online form that would forward the request to the right development team member. In addition, a response could then be provided back to the faculty member indicating when and if the proposed feature would be integrated. Up to this point, the core team thought the support for the system was mostly positive and energetic.

As faculty members started to use the pilot, problems began to surface. In order for the information system to become embedded as an integral part of the department's planning and decision-making processes, faculty needed to verify data and recommend reports for use. However, faculty started to resist requests for updated information, such as confirmation of their status on all of their doctoral committees. Because these data were not centrally maintained, the current information was anecdotal and was sometimes passed on incorrectly by word of mouth. When faculty were pressed to provide a list of their doctoral advisees, they either did not have the time or could not figure out how to look at the existing list online. Some faculty went so far as to have their secretaries print out dozens of pages of student information so that they could check it manually.

When there were finally enough data in the pilot to begin to produce reports with calculations from the relational database, such as faculty workload, enthusiasm for the project started to fade and issues of information sharing, politics, and resistance to change became visible. Additionally, the administrative assistant quit during this time leaving no trained replacement.

At this point, support and participation levels were quite low. When faculty members complained that they still did not understand how to use the Web-based system, additional one-on-one training was offered. Some faculty thought the system was too complicated and reverted back to their old paper systems of tracking, while others simply did not participate, saying that the system was cumbersome. Unlike the planning and design phases, faculty members began to show non-supportive and unresponsive behavior to the pilot system. In fact, the few faculty members who did use the system were still collecting and managing their individual information and only checking the system as a secondary source, even though this system was easily accessible from their homes or offices and globally available on the Web.

Information that was once individually owned and managed became visible to the entire department. Historically, faculty were not used to working together collectively to solve department-wide problems. Furthermore, as the two untenured junior faculty members were the main drivers behind the proposal, senior faculty were most vocal in their resistance to the system, which meant that a full-scale implementation looked doubtful. As Green indicates, this lack of support is critical in technology and higher education integration:

> [...] failing to recognize and promote faculty who invest in technology in their scholarly and instructional activities sends a chilling message about the real departmental and institutional commitment to the integration of technology in instruction and scholarship (Green, 1999, p. 8).

ANALYSIS

What would a successful implementation of the Web-based system have looked like? Would it have changed the department's attitudes, changed the behaviors around information sharing, or improved the overall experience for doctoral students? These questions have gone unanswered because of the complex interrelations of technology, people, and information-related change.

Although the department chair and faculty members initially decided to move forward in improving doctoral student information availability, two very different attempts, both resulted in failure. The spreadsheet and the Web-based database were functionally different, yet both failed around similar issues: group buy-in, information ownership, data collection, and an inability to change the working norms and culture.

In both cases, garnering initial buy-in did not seem to be difficult. The faculty and the department chair wanted to increase access to student information. Everyone agreed that the use of technology could provide the department an advantage in planning and meeting goals and objectives. However, when faculty members were asked for information or asked to change their working patterns, few cooperated. There was a discrepancy between what agreement or buy-in meant, specifically between what was said and what was practiced. The faculty agreed, in theory, that the use of technology was needed to increase access to student information. However, it could be argued that the buy-in was not present when the ideas required change in work and behavior patterns. Furthermore, the responsibility for design and collection was handed-off to individuals in the group with junior status. Even though they had more technical expertise, their junior status may have dissuaded senior faculty from embracing the project, and in fact, the two junior faculty members were neither recognized nor rewarded for their efforts. Morgan notes:

> When a high-status group interacts with a low-status group, or when groups with very different occupational attitudes are placed in a relation of dependence, organizations can become plagued by a kind of subculture conflict (Morgan, 1986, p. 137).

In the design process, the faculty were challenged by setting standards and specifying criteria in order to define data fields. This process worried some faculty. For example, the ability to measure doctoral student workloads may have raised a discussion around redistributing work. The image that some faculty portrayed of being overloaded could have been proved or disproved. Obviously, some faculty might have benefited and others might have faced unease and additional work. The data collection and information ownership activities were difficult because of the underlying norms and behavior of the department.

> Different norms, beliefs, and attitudes to time, efficiency, or service can combine to create all kinds of contradictions and dysfunctions. These can be extremely difficult to tackle in a rational manner because they are intertwined with all kinds of deep-seated personal issues that in effect define the human beings involved (Morgan, 1986, p. 137).

The complete list of recommendations and requirements for implementing the system across the entire department was never fully realized. For example, a "system owner" who had skills in information management was recommended. However, the chair and fellow faculty members did not think that such a person was necessary or needed. An appreciation of the technological skills required to maintain the system was not present. In an attempt to leverage other technologically driven functions of the university, the faculty team tried to involve the director of Information Systems (IS) at the university to help drive the implementation as a pilot project to gain support. Despite the system being well received by the director, the IS department was unable to support the effort because of costs and other in-house responsibilities.

Furthermore, the chair and faculty members wanted to hand off the maintenance of the system to an administrative assistant even though the skill sets required and recommended by the core team did not match. Secondly, despite the $7,000 grant allocated to this initial effort during the proposal stage, the estimated cost to roll out the system across the department was closer to $150,000. The faculty team came up with these estimates based on the work done in the design and implementation phase. Specifically, the technical development work, the expected database size and volume, and the maintenance of the new Web-based technologies drove up the team's estimate. As the continuation of the project became extremely expensive, the department chair did not approve the roll-out plan.

One of the most challenging issues was the working norms and culture of the department concerning issues of data ownership and sharing. This department was resistant to technology in practice and was not open to sharing information, let alone integrating their respective information processes. The culture at the department level was not one that was open to sharing information. This was especially apparent when faculty did not support the need to share workload profiles nor discuss doctoral information with other faculty members. This attests to the importance of not moving forward until there is evidence of real commitment from other stakeholders.

Lastly, and perhaps most importantly, the data and information availability that the system provided were not culturally aligned to the individualistic, competitive, and non-sharing environment at the department. These are known to be major factors in the failure of information system project design and implementation (Lyytinen and Hitschheim, 1987), and which ultimately contributed to the system implementation not being rolled out across the entire department. As Senge illustrates:

> New insights fail to get put into practice because they conflict deeply with internal images of how the world works, images that limit us to familiar ways of thinking and acting (Senge, 1990, p. 174).

CONCLUSIONS

Prior to the onset of information-related initiatives, whether it is a new system, a push for new behaviors in managing information, or training faculty members with new tools, higher education institutions must examine information-sharing behaviors. In order to begin this examination, it is critical to understand the people who will drive, implement, and sustain the change. Similar to the resistance towards the implementation of the Web-based system in this case, if change is to occur, new systems and structures that can drive information-related change (e.g., rewarding people for sharing information) must be examined. As higher education institutions strive to improve access to information and integrate new technologies, it is clear that the information environment (including the people and their behaviors) is a critical deciding factor while striving for and designing new information management processes for decision-making.

In summary, improving the use of information technology in higher education cannot be the task of a single department, professor, or person. There are critical success factors that must be addressed concerning ownership, politics, and information sharing, despite the traditional challenges of information technology costs and maintenance. A national campus computing survey indicated that 62 percent of all higher education institutions have a strategic plan for information technology, yet there are still many difficulties associated with the norms and behaviors of an organization's culture during implementation (Green, 1999). Therefore, when embarking on the infusion of information technology into a higher education setting, the possible non-technical challenges must be considered. Notes Morgan:

> When we choose a technical system (whether in the form of an organizational structure, job design, particular technology) it always has human consequences, and vice versa (Morgan, 1986, p. 38).

This is important to realize so that a department or organization is not faced with trying to design a technical solution for a non-technical problem.

In this case, the problems encountered in required data collection were not technical in nature, but rather a result of a pre-established set of norms among the faculty. Distinguishing these issues, where visible, is important for the design and implementation of information systems in higher education. Says Davenport:

> Information and knowledge are quintessentially human creations and we will never be good at managing them unless we give people a primary role (Davenport, 1997, p. 3).

This primary role is not merely a leadership position on a committee that approves a technology or makes new information polices in higher education. Instead it is the central role in which people, their behaviors, their information sharing attitudes, and the environment of an institution are examined, understood, and incorporated into the information-related change.

DISCUSSION QUESTIONS

1. What are the similarities and differences between the first attempt to implement the simple spreadsheet and the second relational Web-based system? What people, system, and information aspects drove the outcomes?
2. What issues of information sharing for faculty appeared to drive their behaviors and reactions to the system?
3. Is faculty access to student information necessary in order to carry out department-wide planning? How does this impact university-wide goals and objectives?
4. How can information technology leaders address non-technical issues that may interfere with the design and implementation of information systems?

REFERENCES

Davenport, T.H. (1997). *Information Ecology: Mastering the Information and Knowledge Environment*. New York: Oxford University Press.

Green, K. (1999) *The Campus Computing Project, The 1999 National Survey of Information Technology in Higher Education*. Encino: CA. Available online: http://www.campuscomputing.net/summaries/1999.

Lyytinen, K. and Hitschheim, R. (1987). Information system failures—A survey and classification of the empirical literature. *Oxford Surveys in Information Technology*, 257-309.

Morgan, G. (1986). *Images of Organization*. Newbury Park: Sage Publications.

Senge, P. (1990). *The Fifth Discipline*. New York: Currency Doubleday.

Chapter XII

Risks and Rewards: Good Citizenship and Technologically Proficient Faculty

Scott R. Sechrist
Old Dominion University

Dorothy E. Finnegan
College of William and Mary

INTRODUCTION

One of the more often cited objectives found in university and college mission statements is the goal of promoting future good citizenship among students. Indeed, American higher education institutions have been improving society by educating its community leaders since the founding of Harvard in the early seventeenth century. Beyond the direct training of future leaders, college administrators also have recognized the societal need for volunteers to fill gaps that community resources cannot cover. Volunteers enable organizations to thrive beyond their means and their members to receive otherwise unavailable benefits.

This case study describes the role of good citizenship that is performed by two technologically proficient faculty (techno-profs) who are approaching crucial career evaluations at Suburban State University (SSU), a public institution in the mid-eastern area of the United States. It explores the conundrum that faced the SSU Dean of the College of Arts and Letters as she speculated about the outcome of the evaluation of these two faculty members as a result of the existing promotion and tenure criteria. The case also considers the impact of the incorporation of technology into the contemporary role of faculty in a situation in which necessary resources are not provided by those who mandate changes in the existing reward structures in higher education. And, finally, this case study illustrates the existing and potential impact of these mandates on the careers of two techno-profs who act as good citizens for their organizations.

CASE QUESTIONS

- To what degree is good citizenship rewarded in higher education institutions?
- How does acting as a good citizen affect the careers and opportunities of faculty?
- Why do technologically proficient faculty volunteer their efforts to others in their institutions?
- How has the diffusion of technology into academia changed the faculty role?

CASE NARRATIVE

Background

Suburban State University (SSU) is a public university that was established 105 years ago and is located on the outskirts of a moderate-sized city of 130,000 inhabitants. A Doctoral II University, SSU serves approximately 10,000 students, half of whom are residential. Five colleges comprise the University: Education, Sciences, Allied Health, Law, and Arts and Letters. The largest unit, the College of Arts and Letters, is headed by Dean Patricia Rogers. The institution maintained a modest regional reputation throughout its history and has been an attractive choice for local commuting students in addition to those wishing to live on campus.

Employee attrition, program curtailment, and spending reductions eased declining enrollments and diminished resources from the mid 1980s to the early 1990s. In 1995, SSU's President together with the new Provost, established an institutional goal of achieving national stature in the field of technology-delivered education. As part of the strategy to ensure the outcome, Provost Tom Savant directed the university to expand its offerings by reaching out to a new niche—students who were unable to attend classes on campus. In particular, Provost Savant guided a recent redefinition of the university mission statement which now includes several new goals:

> The university is committed to gaining a leadership role in both synchronous and asynchronous technology-delivered education at both the undergraduate and graduate levels. The university also seeks to incorporate technology into the existing curriculum as well as expanding our offerings to include new, innovative degree lines.

Fleshing out these goals during his monthly meeting with the deans of the University, Provost Savant outlined the strategy:

> The incorporation of technology into the existing curriculum provides the groundwork, the backbone upon which the future of this university lies. Technology will make a profound impact upon the mission of the university, the role of the faculty, and ultimately, the extent to which we measure our successes. We must therefore redirect our resources, both monetary and personnel alike, through policy and procedure to the immediate incorporation of technology into the classroom. Our strategic initiatives for the next three years are to: increase class sizes, increase the number and scope of our distance and asynchronous offerings, and increase the presence of technology throughout the curriculum when and where appropriate. With this as our focus, we can achieve the president's vision of a University of the 21st Century.

Each dean was charged to implement the strategy by devising their own tactics that would be applicable to their college's culture, resources, and needs. The Provost's directive to "increase the use of technology" within the College of Arts and Letters, however, was accompanied with only a modicum of resources. The Dean, Patricia Rogers, could only augment the budget enough to upgrade the hardware and software for some of the faculty as money was not available to allocate for personnel.

Defining the Problem

For several years, Dean Rogers had been aware that several faculty in the College, who were considered "technology wizards," were quick to assist when their colleagues experienced computer problems. Until the Provost's recent dictate, however, computer proficiency had not been crucial and faculty had been able to learn to use the technology at their own pace. The "technical wizards" responded to the requests of colleagues on an informal and neighborly basis even though their acts have not been a part of their regular faculty duties. As more faculty have learned to utilize computers for their courses, scholarship, and communication, the Dean assumed that the questions and assistance needed would increase in complexity and would begin to place a strain on the time that these few technologically proficient faculty could offer.

In an effort to evaluate her College's technological assets so that a strategic plan could be developed, Rogers began to gather data. Each department chair was asked to assess the technical capabilities of the faculty as well as their computer equipment. Quickly, she realized from informal updates by the chairs that although the departments maintained moderately adequate hardware and software, troubleshooting technical problems falls on the few faculty who are considered computer experts by their colleagues. Faculty generally did not solicit help from the University's centralized office of technical computer assistance, as they appeared to be more comfortable asking questions of knowledgeable colleagues.

The Dean then asked the department chairs to assist her in identifying the "technical wizards." For each of the College's departments, she conducted a social network analysis. The faculty members in each department were asked to identify the faculty colleague they sought out for assistance with technological problems associated with software, hardware, educational, or Internet issues. She constructed socio-grams for each department, which distinguished the faculty identified as the techno-profs. Rogers then asked several of these technologically proficient faculty to join her for lunch so that she could begin to understand the demands placed on them by their needy colleagues. As a result of the informal discussion at lunch, the Dean recognized that these faculty provide a significant amount of consultation to their colleagues out of the goodness of their hearts. Voluntarily, they assist department colleagues who have a host of technical problems, often taking a considerable amount of time out of their harried schedules. Virtually, they act as good citizens for the College. Yet, the College has no formal method of recognizing or rewarding the good citizenship donated by these faculty.

Wondering about the importance of this issue, Rogers returned to the socio-grams and immediately focused on two particularly energetic faculty members. In the English Department, the techno-prof was Dr. Jennifer Dorn. Dr. Bob Lane was the techno-prof in the Department of History. Thinking about these two "good citizens," the Dean realized that she had to evaluate both faculty members for promotion within the month. Dr. Dorn was under review for tenure and promotion, and Dr. Lane had applied for promotion to full professor. However, the promotion and tenure system had yet to recognize organizational citizenship. Immediately, she asked her assistant to make appointments with these two faculty and to pull their personnel files for her.

The Techno-Profs

The Department of English consists of 25 full-time faculty and 30 adjunct faculty. Most full-time faculty have been teaching at the university for more than 10 years, while most of the adjunct faculty have been hired during Dean Rogers' tenure. Hired as an instructor in the department six years ago, Jennifer Dorn was promoted to a tenure-track assistant professor position when she received her doctorate the following year. As a technical writing specialist, Dorn uses technology extensively to teach writing to students in the sciences and professional fields.

The English Department maintains a 20-station, networked computer laboratory that is connected to the University's main server. Students have access to a variety of general software programs, as well as applications that are specific to writing, composition, and literature. Although generally filled with students from the department of English, the computer lab is also open to general use by faculty and students for access to the World Wide Web, word processing, or e-mail. With only a one-course release per term, Dorn serves as the faculty advisor to the Computer Laboratory for the department and, as part of that role, manages the facility and its two staff members.

Dorn had published one article each year in her field's top journals since completing her doctorate and was currently working on a manuscript concerning the use of the World Wide Web to teach technical writing in the health professions. She had received three grants, two internal grants for $6,000, and one moderately sized, externally funded grant for $165,000 to develop and expand the use of technology in teaching technical writing. Abiding by her contract, she submitted her promotion and tenure portfolio for review this year.

The Department of History consists of 23 full-time and 15 adjunct faculty members. The faculty offices are located in Billingsley Hall. Dr. Robert Lane is a tenured, senior member of the department who began teaching at Suburban State in 1979. He specializes in American History and prides himself on being technologically competent. Computers and technology are an avocation for him, and he enjoys working at home on his personal computer. His scholarly activity (a variety of refereed journal articles, a book, and eight book chapters) was considered to be productive during his first 15 years, but tapered off over the last five years. In the last few years, his use of computers in his classes and his creation of a Web-based historical archival project has invigorated him so that he is again excited about his scholarly activities. He has even been contacted recently by his national professional organization to develop a template for the development of other Web-based archives. Several publishers have approached him to develop and market his innovative Web workspace design. With the conviction that he qualifies for the highest rank, Dr. Lane submitted his portfolio for consideration for promotion to full professor. The bulk of his dossier contains the technological scholarship that he has produced over the past five years.

The Dean's Interview with Dr. Dorn

Dean Rogers, in order to make more informed decisions regarding the promotion and tenure cases under her review, met with both faculty to find out exactly what technology-related contributions they provide to their department colleagues in particular and thus to the College in general. She first met with Dr. Jennifer Dorn. When the Dean asked her what kinds of assistance she provided as the department's techno-prof, Dorn answered the question, while adding an assessment of the state of technological affairs at SSU:

> I feel pretty proficient with technology. I tend to help people mostly with Internet, World Wide Web, and software problems mostly, less so with hardware or network problems. This is a campus with Computer Center problems. Faculty do not want to wait three days for their problems to be fixed. They come to me because they know I can and will help them.

The assistant professor, sensing a sympathetic ear, continued to voice her opinion to the dean:

> There's much political currency to be gained by spending money on new technology, and there's little to be gained by spending money on supporting that technology. I think that is the problem here at SSU.

Rogers directed the young woman by probing her to define her informal contributions. Dorn replied:

> I feel like I am overwhelmed sometimes by the sheer number of people who ask me questions. They tend to come when it is an emergency and expect me to drop whatever I am doing and help them. The problem is I am still junior to most of the ones who come to ask for help. I like helping people but it is affecting my work.

The Dean asked:

> Is it just colleagues who ask for help? Isn't that part of your role as faculty advisor to the English Department Computer Lab?

Dorn replied:

> My chair tends to put me on every committee with the word 'technology' or 'computer' in the title. I feel like the token techno-person in the department. There has got to be someone else who can represent the department with regards to technology. Often I am put in a position of making decisions outside my area of expertise even in technological matters.

When asked why she offered so much assistance, even with the time demands it imposes, Dorn replied:

> I'm a pretty decent person, I like helping others. Plus I think it has gotten my name out there among the senior faculty. They know I have an expertise of value. At least I hope so!

The Dean said:

> Is that it, you do this because you are nice and have a good reputation?

Dorn replied:

> Faculty see my use of technology as practical and useful, and I seem to have a knack for explaining it to people who are not technologically inclined, so they seem to ask me a lot about incorporating it into their courses. People get freaked out because they are on deadlines, so when they have a problem, they come to me because they can't count on the Computer Center or the help desk to respond quickly enough. That pressures me to help. It pulls me from my work. One of the senior faculty members even pulled me out of class once with a printer problem!

When asked who she helps, Dorn laughed and said:

> Who don't I help! Most of the time it is faculty—and I have a lot of repeat customers—several people who seem to come to me more often than others, but I also offer a lot of help to the staff, the secretaries, even people from other departments seem to call me for assistance. And I think part of it is I am pretty good at diagnosing what their real problems are. I always follow up on a problem if I see a faculty member in the hall that I've helped the previous day.

When the Dean asked why Dorn thinks that so many of the faculty are seeking help with computer problems, she commented:

> The pressure from the administration for all departments in the College to "get technological" is putting a lot of pressure on me personally because my colleagues are getting scared they aren't technologically proficient enough.

Shifting the discussion, the dean asked Dorn about the impact of her being the techno-prof for the English department, and for her to speak to the advantages and disadvantages that she incurred because of it. Dorn replied:

> Well, I hope it's been a positive one, I mean, I've tried to tie what I do professionally together with my interest in technology. I get the latest equipment and software, which is nice! I also feel "connected" to the department, since most of the classes I teach are offered at night, it feels good to come in during the day and help people with their technology problems. Another positive aspect is that it has led me to a few grant opportunities regarding teaching with technology. The down side is of course, the amount of time I spend doing this kind of thing....several hours a week helping people when it's not really my job per se. I mean, since the Computer Center is overwhelmed where are my colleagues supposed to go? I am right down the hall so I don't blame them for coming to me. My fear is that I am not taken seriously as a scholar, I have serious content level, and I don't want to be a technological janitor for the department.

Rogers inquired:

> Not being taken seriously as a scholar, Jennifer? What do you mean?

Dorn pondered a second, then replied:

> Being a "technology person" is different from being the "Shakespeare person," or the "Stats" person. It's a content area in its own right, I think. I've got shelves and shelves to attest to that. But it's a different type of position than most academic departments are used to. I approach being the technology person by combining my research, teaching, and service in ways I don't think other people in the English department have ever experienced those three areas. I had just hoped that the promotion and tenure committee would recognize the value of what I do for the faculty, the department, and the College.

The Dean's Interview with Dr. Lane

The next morning, the Dean met with Dr. Bob Lane. Again her goal was to find out what types of voluntary citizenship he exhibits, whom he helps, and what impact it has on his academic career. She asked him about the types of things he does to help other faculty and he answered:

> Well I get a lot of Internet questions now that I'm working on the Web-based archive project. It has really opened doors for me and my research. The Web project has really invigorated my work. Of course the others still come to me for help with the proprietary software questions, as they have for years, but the Internet WWW assistance I provide seems to be increasing dramatically over the last year or so. The number of pedagogical questions has also increased. My colleagues want to know how to incorporate technology into their courses much more now than in the past, probably due to the big push by the administration to get technology into the curriculum.

The Dean nodded and Lane continued:

> The number of "can you fix my monitor" type questions has dropped off during the last couple of years, I think because I just tell people 'no' more often and then they go elsewhere for help with that sort of problem!

The Dean then asked:

Why do you help the faculty?

Lane exclaimed:

Well I really don't know...perhaps because it's exciting! I love a puzzle and every problem is just that, an unknown to me. I'm not as altruistic as I used to be. I find myself picking and choosing whom I will help. I don't actually withhold assistance, but I will refer some people to other sources if I can. I see myself as a broker, as the clearinghouse. I know where to send people when they have a problem I can't handle.

The Dean asked Lane:

Whom do you help?

Lane paused and then replied:

Mainly faculty, some students and staff, but rarely. There is a small group of faculty to whom I seem to have become a "technology" mentor! I have spent an inordinate amount of time with this group, getting their Web-based instructional units up and running. I think they came to me because I have the PhD in History. I can understand the disciplinary portion of what they are doing and help make the leap to the technological presentation of what they are seeking to accomplish.

Rogers asked him:

What impact has being the techno-prof had on your career thus far?

Lane remarked:

The advantages to me have been both tangible and intangible, I think. I certainly have gained a new perspective on my teaching and scholarship. I have been doing this for 30 years and never have I been so excited about a project. The Civil War archives/distance education project I am working on now uses a number of asynchronous discussion groups/chat rooms and interactive media to teach about that conflict. It has made me approach how I teach in a whole new way. The national exposure of this project has led me to serve on several committees in my discipline, especially where technology is involved. I have been approached by two different publishers to develop and market my course. Beyond that even, I am working to make my Web-based course a template for future course creation in a wider range of historical areas.

The Dean asked:

So you have reaped a lot of benefit professionally then?

Lane smirked and added:

Of the more mundane benefits, I am usually the first in line to get any new computers in the department, which is nice. No one complains since they know I will try and get the most out of the latest equipment. One benefit has been a "higher status" in the department I think.

The Dean said:

So your computer work is paying off in a lot of different ways for your career, isn't it?

Lane replied:

All this helping other faculty has been very time consuming. I find myself either working late or doing my regular work at home since my time here is often spent troubleshooting someone else's problems.

Lane leaned forward in his chair and looked directly at the Dean and continued:

May I be frank though? In the long term I think being the techno-prof has been more detrimental than helpful to my career. My interest and use of technology and things technical had absolutely no impact on my achieving tenure many years ago. As far as promotion and tenure go, it was probably a disadvantage in that it wasn't traditional scholarship. I tell all of our new faculty that technology is wonderful, but make sure that they do the traditional things well too or they won't see a seventh year here. Being proficient technologically has no bearing on achieving promotion and tenure. Ultimately I believe my technological work will hinder my quest to achieve full professor status. If I had spent the amount of time I have on technological things and instead had written a "pen and ink" type book, I might be closer to my goal.

Rogers asked Lane if he regretted the time spent assisting other faculty. He replied:

In the long run, I think my helping other faculty for so long with technology problems has been most rewarding in that it has provided me a certain amount of personal satisfaction and the respect from my colleagues.

The Dean concluded her meetings with Lane. She now had the task of writing her recommendations on promotion to the Provost. She had to decide on each case independently of the other, yet both involved similar issues on the work-life of faculty.

ANALYSIS

The Dean's Dilemma

The immediate challenge to the dean was to decide the type of recommendations she must send to the Provost for these two faculty members in her College. However, she immediately realized that she had uncovered a much larger issue. Were the unrecognized helping activities of the techno-profs unique or did types of organizational citizenship behaviors (OCB) exist in the College? How important are OCB to the College and to the University?

Can OCB be recognized within the existing faculty evaluation criteria? And specifically, can and should Dorn and Lane receive acknowledgment and credit for their technology-related OCB activities in the course of their evaluation?

Organizational Citizenship
Behaviors and Technologically Proficient Faculty

In almost all social and organizational groups, some members contribute beyond their role expectations to make the organization a more effective entity (Katz, 1964). These spontaneous, extra role behaviors found:

[...] within every work group in a factory, within any division of government, or within any department of a university are countless acts of cooperation without which the system would breakdown. ...These everyday acts are taken for granted and few of them are included in the formal role prescriptions for any job (Katz and Kahn, 1966, p. 339).

Building on the early identification of Katz, Organ (1988) designated these generalized helping behaviors in the workplace as organizational citizenship behavior (OCB). He defined OCB as those individual behaviors that are discretionary, not directly or explicitly recognized by the formal reward system, and that in the aggregate promote the effective functioning of the organization. Indeed, the sum of actions of individuals across time as well as the sum of the actions of several individuals across the organization in the aggregate benefit the institution, although any one action might be considered modest or trivial.

OCB exists because no organization has the resources to reward every action that is necessary to maintain its proper functioning, nor can it shift as quickly as needed when environmental pressures effect change in its functions. As the use of technology expands in society, the pressure and lure for faculty to adopt and use technology increases. Concurrently, the need for experts to assist faculty in this adaptation grows. If support services do not expand to meet the increased demand for training and assistance, faculty must increasingly find other sources of assistance. Faculty are educated in their specialties, not necessarily in technology. Their primary role rests in their specialties, not technology.

To whom do the faculty go for assistance? Faculty are often reluctant to admit they do not know a particular topic or cannot use a particular piece of equipment or software. Rather than utilize an already understaffed, overstretched technical support structure, they often prefer to go to one of their own colleagues for assistance. In every work group one person generally is recognized as the "technology expert" since she/he understands and uses technology more than anyone else. By default, this "expert" is sought out by other members of the work group for assistance and advice on technological matters (Blumfield, 1997). Referred to as "alpha geeks"[1] (American Dialect Society, 1999), these individuals are called upon, often on short or no notice, to troubleshoot technology problems. Although helping others with technical problems is generally neither their primary function nor part of their job description, they seem to relish the attention and are generally more than willing to help others within the organization with their technological problems. Blumfield also noted:

> While it might be flattering for "alpha geeks" to be appreciated for their skills, having co-workers ask for assistance on a regular basis can undermine their own performance (Blumfield, 1997, p 42).

Organ (1988) originally delineated five elements of OCB: Altruism, Conscientiousness, Courtesy, Sportsmanship, and Civic Virtue. In addition to these forms of behavior, additional research has focused on who benefits from the actions (Williams and Anderson, 1991; Skarlicki and Latham, 1995). OCBO refers to behaviors that benefit the organization, whereas OCBI benefit an individual. The latter category, originally defined by Organ as altruistic behavior, includes discretionary behaviors that assist a specific individual with an organizational task or problem.

In this case study, it is seen that the techno-profs are satisfying—at least on a minimal level—the need that faculty have for technical assistance, and that techno-profs often provide this assistance as part of their pro-social, collegial, or discretionary behaviors. Traditionally, faculty have had broadly defined work roles and have been typically evaluated on their activities in teaching, service and research. Often they are expected to be "effective" teachers or "excellent" researchers, yet few guidelines or criteria are specified to accompany these ratings. Contemporary faculty find themselves working in a world in which technological innovation is diffusing at an ever increasing pace. No longer the purview of just the innovators and early adopters, access to, and the use of, technology has become a standard practice among the mainstream faculty whose work environment now includes the use of e-mail, the Internet, and computers in virtually all aspects of teaching, research, and administration. Although each problem for which techno-profs provide assistance may be minor on the surface, the aggregated assistance serves also an organizational need to ease the often overwhelming frustration that accompanies this new complexity in the workplace.

Computer technology and applications exponentially require more sophisticated competence than the level of understanding often displayed by most faculty. To adapt technology into pedagogy is often beyond the ability of many faculty who cannot seem to employ even the most mundane software and hardware, much less a technology-driven lecture or a Web-based course. The assistance provided by the techno-profs is therefore an invaluable part of the daily operation of the department.

Furthermore, taken in the aggregate, the assistance they provide affects the department and organization on several levels. At the most base, it prevents a slow down of work since the computer support staff need not be called to repair, install or assist faculty through the myriad problems that occur daily in a department. In a greater sense though, they demonstrate to mainstream professors that faculty can use technology effectively in their academic work.

OCBO benefits the organization and was originally identified as conscientious activity on the part of a worker (Organ, 1988). In these instances, organizational members perform behaviors well beyond the minimum required levels of their jobs. Academe presents somewhat of a problem in organizational analysis however, since the responsibilities of faculty members are loosely defined and encompass a wide range of behaviors and roles. Faculty tend to be individualists—independent thinkers working within their specific disciplines—and try to find time to "do their own work." Part of the appeal of academe is the lack of routine mundane work, control over one's calendar, and a flexible workday. Thus, the tendency for most faculty is to work alone. Yet, "the collegium is relational, not autonomous, [and needs] connectivity, not separation" (Bennett, 1998, p. 27).

The discretionary assistance that a co-worker provides to another without reward, or even official recognition, arises within the helper and directly benefits the person in need. In this case study, the two techno-profs assist colleagues with technical problems that would otherwise prevent the smooth operation of the academic process or the incorporation of technology into instruction or scholarship. The assistance is often of short duration and modest in scope and magnitude. However, as Organ notes, altruistic behaviors (or OCBO), if reliably exhibited throughout the organization, obviate the need for the institution to devote what scarce resources exist for purely maintenance functions. In other words, as long as the good citizens take up the slack, the organization need not acknowledge or address an on-going demand.

Ken Green, in his Campus Computing Survey (1997), notes that fully one-third of the 605 responding institutions indicated that "assisting faculty to integrate information technology into instruction" and "providing adequate user support" are the top two information technology challenges confronting their institutions. Clearly, college administrators recognize the needs of their faculty concerning computer technology. Yet, as long as institutions do not provide adequate support, the importance of faculty-to-faculty influence with regards to the adoption of instructional technology cannot be underestimated (Gilbert, 1995). The adoption of new technological innovation appears to be a function of the resources available, the perceived value that faculty ascribed to the innovation, and whether faculty members have communication with other adopters of the innovation (Marcus, 1985). But, adoption at what cost?

Only 12 percent of institutions responding to Green's survey formally reward or recognize faculty use of technology within the promotion and tenure process. "Colleges and universities are sending a clear if somewhat punitive message to faculty: do more with technology, but acquire skills on your own time and do it in addition to your other professorial responsibilities" (Green, 1997). Of further concern is the effect of the altruistic behavior on the careers of the good citizens—the techno-profs. Communication, the social ties, and networking between faculty in the departmental unit form the basis of this case study. Gilbert suggests the use of early adopter faculty as peer mentors as a means to increase the quality and availability of support services (Gilbert, 1996). Ostensibly the techno-profs would receive stipends or release time as a reward for their mentoring. However, Gilbert is honest in his appraisal that "....if these faculty are untenured, the benefits of being a mentor are not so obvious, and the time required can jeopardize career progress" (Gilbert, 1996). As more and more institutions adopt post-tenure review, mid-level and senior faculty who might serve in this capacity would also risk career progress.

The Dean's Solution

The Dean in this case decided to recommend to the Provost that both faculty members should be awarded promotion, and in the case of Jennifer Dorn, tenure. The Dean based her decision on the fact that Dr. Dorn has demonstrated competent and competitive scholarship as well as meritorious service based upon her techno-prof behaviors. In the case of Dr. Lane, she decided his technological work has received national attention and was worthy of inclusion as scholarly activity. To avoid any conflicts in the future, however, the Dean instructed the Promotion and Tenure Committee for the College to create less ambiguous guidelines for teaching, scholarship, and service. She also charged them with including broad definitions of organizational good citizenship so that activities such as technological innovation and mentoring can be rewarded. Using a conceptual model (see Figure 1), the Dean also made a case to the Provost that such guidelines should be incorporated into the University Promotion and Tenure policies. She argued that by recognizing OCB as part of the traditional category of service, both the institution and the individual gain and neither are hurt, and furthermore, if faculty were to cease contributing their altruistic behaviors, the opera-

Figure 1: Conceptual Model for Faculty Organizational Citizenship Behavior

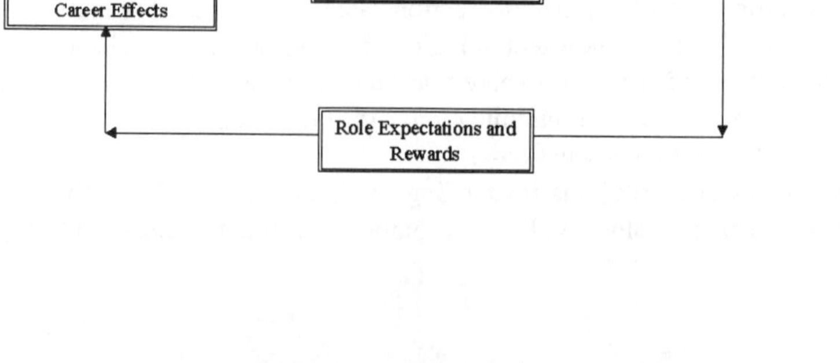

tions of the institution would suffer. As the Dean stated in her comments to the Promotion and Tenure Committee:

> As long as the institution does not recognize the time and effort involved in OCB, the individuals and their careers suffer. And in the long run, the institution and academe loses these valuable people.

CONCLUSIONS

Social network analysis of the two departments in this case suggests that techno-profs do indeed exist. They are faculty members to whom other faculty go with regularity for assistance with a wide range of technological problems. The techno-profs assist their colleagues and others for various reasons, usually based on a genuine desire to be helpful or to enhance their reputation within the organizational unit. The techno-profs are typically not motivated by the promise of monetary or tangible rewards, although these types of rewards often do occur in the form of new equipment, software, or release time.

Techno-profs provide a range of organizational citizenship behaviors (OCBs) generally directed towards individuals (OCBI), but also towards the organization as a whole (OCBO). The aggregate behaviors benefit the organization in that the existing technical support structure need not be burdened further. Other benefits include cost savings for training, increased productivity through reduced down time, and an enhanced diffusion of technology throughout the organization. Intangible benefits include a heightened sense of collegiality within the organization as faculty help other faculty, and heightened departmental status through the use of technology (in an environment which values the use of technology).

The major disadvantage of acting as the departmental techno-prof seems to be the amount of time it takes to help the faculty who ask for assistance. Concomitant with the time drain comes the inability to get one's own work done, often at the expense of performing research and scholarship. This expense in turn can ultimately have negative consequences upon promotion and tenure decisions for the faculty. Techno-profs generally understand that the behaviors they exhibit are not part of their traditional role of teaching, research, and service, although they expect that the OCBs they exhibit will be recognized and rewarded at some level by administration. The junior faculty member in this case study hoped that her behaviors would be considered during her promotion and tenure process. She also hoped that her technological expertise would be understood and recognized by the members of the review committee. The senior faculty member, having survived the traditional promotion and tenure process, had his academic career reinvigorated by the use of technology. He also was hopeful that the promotion committee reviewing his latest work would recognize his work as the equivalent to that of more traditional scholarship.

This case study demonstrated the dilemmas present in many higher education institutions as they establish goals to incorporate more technology into their instructional operations. While it is often promoted vigorously by university administration, adequate resources are not dedicated to training and system maintenance. Thus, the organization must rely on the good citizenship of those faculty who are early technology adopters. Furthermore, the academic reward system has not been adjusted in most cases to incorporate the activities of the faculty necessary to effect the adaptation. In the end, neither the techno-profs nor the mainstream faculty receive organizational credit for complying with institutional goals. Faculty therefore are often left to their own devises to learn about, adopt, and employ computer technology into their courses and academic pursuits. Until the organizational mandates are backed with the resources necessary to support them, some faculty may virtually pay for institutional success with their careers.

Techno-profs do exist in higher education. They are the faculty who have adopted technology, are using it, and are helping the rest of the academy with their problems.[2] The contributions the techno-profs make may be small, even insignificant when viewed as single helping events. Taken as a whole, however, the impact they have on the organization can be great and the institution should recognize the contributions these individuals make and reward them accordingly.

DISCUSSION QUESTIONS

1. Should technologically proficient faculty be recognized for their organizational citizenship behaviors? If yes, what forms should this recognition take?
2. Should the contributions of techno-profs be recognized in the promotion and tenure process as scholarly work? As the performance of service?
3. Do you agree with the Dean's recommendation that Dr. Lane be rewarded with promotion and Dr. Dorn be rewarded with promotion and tenure?

EPILOGUE

This case study is derived from seven interviews that included deans and information technology administrators as well as techno-profs. Analysis of these interviews revealed a hopeful anticipation from more junior faculty that the organizational citizenship behaviors they exhibit will somehow count towards their eventual promotion and tenure decision. They equate the immediate gratification of new equipment and the latest software with recognition and hope that this recognition will carry over when the time comes for a tenure decision.

Techno-profs appeared to possess certain common characteristics: an early exposure and sustained use of computers at home and at work, a desire to help people, a love for technology and the application of technology to daily and disciplinary problems, and an interesting ability to teach themselves without having to attend classes or reading manuals when confronted with new technology.

While the deans who were interviewed by and large knew about the techno-profs in their college, they admitted that many good faculty slip below the "dean's radar." In this case, they must rely on their chairs to recognize which faculty are excelling in certain areas. Each dean also stated that traditional scholarly activities carried the greatest weight during promotion and tenure decisions, but that technologically oriented organizational behaviors were not "unnoticed." However, older faculty recognized the reality of the current reward system. They understood that unless excellent teaching and traditional scholarship are performed, no amount of service will help during the promotion and tenure process. Each dean said that technologically based instruction, coursework, and scholarship needs to be included and addressed in promotion and tenure guidelines and that these new guidelines and expectations must be communicated unambiguously to all faculty entering a tenure track position.

REFERENCES

American Dialect Society. Words of the Year—1996 From: http://www.americandialect.org/woty.shtml. (19 August 1999).

Bennett, J. (1998). *Collegial Professionalism: The Academy, Individualism, and the Common Good*. Phoenix, AZ: Oryx Press.

Blumfield, M. (1997) The accidental trainer, *Training, 34*(9), 42.

Gilbert, S. (1995). Teaching, learning & technology—The need for campus-wide planning and faculty support services. *Change, 27*(2), 47-52.

Gilbert, S. (1996). Making the most of a slow revolution, *Change, 28*(2), 10-23.

Green, K.C. (1997). *Campus Computing 1997*. Encino, CA.

Green, K.C. (1999). *Campus Computing 1999*. Encino, CA.

Katz, D. (1964). The motivational basis of organizational behavior. *Behavioral Science, 9*(2), 131-146.

Katz, D., & Kahn, R. (1966). *The Social Psychology of Organizations*. New York: Wiley.

Marcus, J. (1985). Diffusion of innovations and social learning theory: Adoption of the context text-processing system at Stanford University (Doctoral Dissertation, Stanford university, 1985). *Dissertation Abstracts International, 46*, 3553.

Organ, D.W. (1988). *Organizational Citizenship Behavior: The Good Soldier Syndrome*. Lexington, MA: Lexington Books.

Pflueger, K.E. (1995). Collaborating for more effective integration and use of technology. *Proceedings of the 1995 CAUSE Annual Conference*, 4-4-1 to 10.

Skarlicki, D. & Latham, G. (1995). Organizational citizenship behavior and performance in a university setting. *Canadian Journal of Administrative Sciences, 12*(3), 175-181.

Williams, L., & Anderson, S. (1991). Job satisfaction and organizational commitment as predictors of organizational citizenship and in role behaviors. *Journal of Management, 17*(3), 601-617.

Young, J.R. (1999). University of Washington tries a soft sell to woo professors to technology. *The Chronicle of Higher Education*, May 28, A23.

ADDITIONAL RESOURCES

Barnes, J. A. (1972). *Social Networks*. Reading, Massachusetts: Addison-Wesley.

Batson, T., & Bass, R. (1996). Teaching and learning in the computer age. *Change, 28*(2), 42-47.

Dill, D.D., & Friedman, C.P. (1979). An analysis of frameworks for research on innovation and change in higher education. *Review of Educational Research, 49*(3), 411-435.

Dolence, M.G., & Norris, D. M. (1995). *Transforming Higher Education: A Vision for Learning in the 21ˢᵗ Century*. Society for College and University Planning: Ann Arbor, MI.

Edwards, G. (1997). Concerns of faculty members in higher education about using computers (Doctoral Dissertation, University of Illinois at Urbana-Champaign, 1997). *Dissertation Abstracts International, 58*, 3897.

Evans, R.I. (1968). *Resistance to Innovation in Higher Education*. San Francisco: Jossey Bass Inc.

Geoghegan, W.H. (1994). What ever happened to instructional technology? Paper presented at the 22nd Annual Conference of the International Business Schools Computing Association. Baltimore, MD, July 12-20, 1994. http://ike.engr.washington.edu/news/whitep/whg/wpi.htm.

Geoghegan, W.H. (1996). In response—four viewpoints, *Change*. 28(2), 30.

Geoghegan, W.H. (1997). Instructional technology and the mainstream: the risks of success. Maytum distinguished lecture series, SUNY College at Fredonia, from the CMC Users Group Home Page, http://www.rodwell.com/Gap.htm.

Gilbert, S. (1995). An "online" experience—Discussion group debates why faculty use or resist technology. *Change,* 27(2), 28-45.

Gilbert, S. (1996). Double visions—Paradigms in balance or collision? *Change,* 28(2), 8-9.

Gilbert, S. (1997). Four swinging pendulums. 11/11/97 AAHESGIT Listserv posting.

Granovetter, M. (1973). The strength of weak ties. *American Journal of Sociology*, 78.

Green, K.C. (1996). The coming ubiquity of information technology. *Change,* 28(2), 24-31.

Knoke, D. & Kuklinski, J. (1982). *Network Analysis.* Beverly Hills, California: Sage Publications

Marsden, P., & Lin, N. (1982). *Social Structure and Network Analysis.* Beverly Hills: Sage Publications.

Morehouse, D. L., & Stockdill, S. (1991). Understanding the influence of a change age organization on technology use by university faculty and staff. *Educational Technology,* 31(6), 61-62.

Rodwell, G. (1997) . Bridging the Gap—CMC Users Group—online discussion. http://www.rodwell.com/Gap.htm. (March 19, 1997).

Rogers, E. (1983). *Diffusion of Innovations* (3rd ed.), New York: The Free Press.

Rogers, E. (1995). *Diffusion of Innovations* (4th ed.), New York: The Free Press.

Scott, L.J. (1986). A study of the factors which influence computer adoption by community college faculty in Virginia (Doctoral Dissertation, College of William and Mary). *Dissertation Abstracts International,* 47-08A, 2915.

Schuster, J. (1990). The need for fresh approaches to faculty renewal. *Enhancing Faculty Careers*, San Francisco: Jossey-Bass

Smith, K.L. (1997). Preparing faculty for instructional technology: From education to development to creative independence. *Cause/Effect,* 20(3), 36-44,48.

Spotts, T.H., &Bowman, M.A. (1995). Faculty use of instructional technologies in higher education. *Educational Technology,* 35(2), 56-64.

Young, J. R. (1997). Rethinking the role of the professor in an age of high-tech tools. *The Chronicle of Higher Education.* October 3, A26.

ENDNOTES

1. Since the term "geek" is rather pejorative, *technologically profi*cient *prof*essors—*"techno-profs"*—is proposed as a better term.

2. At California Lutheran University, a program has been adopted whereby technologically proficient faculty, acting as experts or faculty mentors, assist the mainstream faculty to adopt technology. The directors of this program indicate that non-technical faculty were more likely to respond to assistance from a colleague and prefer a one-on-one mentor format, and that faculty preferred learning in their own offices (Pflueger, 1995).

Section III

Teaching
and
Learning

Chapter XIII

Higher Education Culture and the Diffusion of Technology in Classroom Instruction

Kandis M. Smith
University of Missouri

INTRODUCTION

The diffusion of an innovation takes, on an average, 25 years in an educational setting. Many factors contribute to this slow acceptance rate. Rogers' (1995) theory on the diffusion of innovation and the influence of culture on such diffusion is used to shed light on the causes for this slow diffusion. While not a full explanation of this slow rate of change, this case study shows that the academic culture, within which faculty function, has a strong influence on the diffusion of the use of technology in classroom instruction. This case study provides a point of reference for further study of diffusion of technology in classroom instruction.

This case focuses on a Research I institution in the Midwest that has made a number of commitments to the integration of technology into the curriculum and has channeled many resources into this campaign. While the institution has invested large sums of money in the development of the infrastructure, the rate at which faculty have adopted the use of technology in their teaching has remained low. In order to determine the perceptions of faculty and develop some framework for understanding why the infusion of technology into classroom instruction was so low, faculty members on the campus were interviewed, focus groups were conducted, and meetings between faculty and administrators concerning technology issues were observed. Because additional issues exist with distance education, the scope of this case study research was limited to on-campus classroom instruction and support.

CASE QUESTIONS
- Do the values and beliefs of academic culture promote or discourage a pro-innovation social climate?
- What aspects of academic culture hinder or promote the diffusion of innovation, specifically, the process for adoption of the use of technology in higher education?
- How do disciplinary differences affect the adoption of technology?
- What roles do faculty play in the diffusion of technology in the classroom?
- What tools and support structures drive successful technology integration into the classroom?

CASE NARRATIVE
History of Technological Innovations in Higher Education

As an innovation, technology has been diffusing throughout institutions of higher education since 1946 (Heterick, 1993). Some of the earliest research in higher education resulted in the development of ENIAC at the University of Pennsylvania in 1946. By 1965, Thomas Merrill, Lawrence Roberts and Leonard Kleinrock had developed and implemented the first wide-area computer network, operating between Massachusetts and California (Leiner et al., 1998). By 1969, ARPANET was operational at the University of California-Los Angeles, Stanford Research Institute and the University of California-Santa Barbara, and was connected to the University College of London in England and the Royal Radar Establishment in Norway by 1973. In the 1980s, BITNET was connected between City University of New York and Yale University and the National Science Foundation established five super-computing centers, enabling connections for many universities.

During the 1950s and 1960s, funding from agencies such as the Ford Foundation, the Carnegie Foundation, and the Kettering Foundation enabled institutions of higher education, usually research institutions, to acquire large computers (Saettler, 1990). Many of these were used for administrative purposes and were not available to the general faculty or to students. With the passage of the National Defense Education Act and the Elementary and Secondary Education Act, the federal government became a primary source of funds for institutions of higher education desiring to integrate technology into education (Saettler, 1990). By the late 1960s, spurred by these federal research grants, more faculty were investing in technology (Knapper, 1988). Katz (1993) stated that by the 1970s most of the research institutions were using mainframe computers extensively for three major activities: "... numerically intensive research, ... instruction in computer science, and ...administration" (p. 15).

By the 1980s, desktop computers were available to individual faculty and students (Mason, 1996). Cartwright (1993) indicated that the first uses of technology in the classroom were demonstrations of how a computer could analyze data. However, faculty also began to develop interactive processes of using technology in teaching. One example was Patrick Suppes and Richard Atkinson's program of computer-assisted instruction in mathematics and reading, which was designed for "...individualized, instructional strategies that allowed the learner to correct his [the student's] responses through rapid feedback..." thereby allowing active participation by the student (Molnar, 1997, p. 3). By 1992 the World Wide Web made access to information around the world possible from desktop computers. Today in some classrooms, faculty are using multimedia, integration of text, video, audio, animation, or graphics, which are often interactive in design. They are also using technology for simulations, acquiring information, communicating with others in the classroom and outside the classroom, and transmitting assignments electronically. According to Ringle (1996), technology is now a part of the curriculum. Usage by faculty and students is found across a wide spectrum and includes:

> [...] access to literary and historic databases, simulations in the social sciences, digital imagery in art, theater and architecture, virtual laboratories in chemistry, biology, and physics, and many other things (p. 6).

Higher education institutions are undergoing some major changes as they incorporate technology into the curriculum. Gilbert (1995) stated that although the changes occurring in education are not the result of technological changes, the character of the changes may be guided "...by our own thoughtfulness of the role of technology in education" (p.1). Based upon this premise, Gilbert (1995) listed several indicators of changes that are already happening. First, faculty report that their best teaching efforts do not appear to be working with today's students. Second, one-third of college students do not purchase required textbooks for classes. Third, in 1994-95, over 50 percent of all freshmen had used technology in their academic endeavors, and approximately one-fourth of all students owned personal computers. Fourth, approximately five percent to 15 percent of faculty reported that by using technology in instruction, significant improvements in the quality and effectiveness of their teaching were achieved. Fifth, students on many campuses have voted to increase student fees by up to $150 per student in order to subsidize computer-related purchases and services. Sixth, more and more faculty are developing customized course packs, often in CD-ROM or Internet/Web format, in conjunction with traditional textbook publishers.

Another development, which is having an effect on American higher education, is the national technology plan. The plan, *Getting America's Students Ready for the 21st Century*, is aimed at elementary and secondary education, but has some far-reaching implications for higher education. The thrust to have all teachers trained to help students learn through the use of computers with adequate support and resources implies that institutions of higher education must train the elementary and secondary education teachers to use technology, and that the students entering institutions of higher education will expect to use technology in their college classes (Clinton, 1996). According to Plotnick (1996), society is insisting that teachers become "technologically literate" and educational technology is one of the top policy issues in education. Green (1996) said that students in institutions of higher education expect technology to be incorporated into their learning experiences.

Alvarez (1996) stated that the use of technology is changing expectations to the extent that institutions that do not incorporate technology into classroom education will not be able to attract good faculty and good students. Additionally, a 1996 Campus Computing survey showed that the most important technology issue for institutions of higher education was helping faculty to integrate technology into educational instruction (Green, 1997).

Lever-Duffy (1991) noted that most institutions of higher education have made significant resource commitments toward supporting technology, that unit costs of technology have declined, and that technology has become increasingly easy to use. With these changes, faculty in higher education are adopting technology, but at a slower rate than would be expected, especially given the popularization of technology through the media and the expectations of society, parents, and students.

As indicated by increased budget allocations for implementation of technology projects, expectations of students, parents, legislators and business executives concerning the importance of technology in education are increasing. However, Lee (1996) stated technology integration in higher education is failing and one of the main reasons for the failure is that the perspectives of faculty are ignored. According to Neal (1998) this lack of integration of faculty perspective was one of the main reasons for the failure of Instructional Television in the 1960s and 1970s. Whitaker and Ekman (1998), in discussing the potential for the application of technology to instruction, stated that such efforts must be faculty driven in order to be successful; they cannot be imperatives from the top. Ely et al. further stated that "...the individual teacher or professor is the single most important factor leading to appropriate implementation of media and technology for learning" (Ely et al., 1992, p. 7). In her introduction to *Rethinking University Teaching*, Diana Laurillard (1993) stated that the impetus for changes in higher education should be from within the system. She argued that academic values, which promote the advancement of learning, continued research and freedom, must be the driving force behind changes in higher education. The implication of such an assertion is that faculty must be the impetus behind change in order to protect and promote those academic values which make higher education unique as an institution. Although the culture of the institution frames the perspectives of the faculty who are the primary impetus for changes that occur within the institution (Ely et al., 1992; Laurillard, 1993), prior research on diffusion of innovation has not concentrated on aspects unique to a given culture (Walsh, 1993).

Diffusion of an Innovation

Rogers (1995) defined diffusion as a process which incorporates four specific elements: (1) the innovation, (2) communication channels, (3) time, and (4) a social system. Each of these components interacts with and reacts to the other three components. Therefore, no single element may be fully considered outside the context of the other elements.

An innovation, idea, process or object is defined as something new to an individual, department, or institution. An innovation need not be a new or recent discovery as measured by time, but is considered new based on the perceptions of the individual or other organizational unit. In this study the innovation was defined as a computer-mediated tool for communication. This included multimedia, electronic mail, commercial courseware, CD-ROM materials, computer simulations, World Wide Web-based resources, and Internet-based resources.

As Rogers (1995) indicated, two types of communication channels have been studied: (1) mass media and (2) interpersonal. At different stages of diffusion, the different channels have varying impacts upon decision making. In the early stages of beginning knowledge, mass media may provide the initial information to spark interest in the innovation. As an individual moves through the decision-making process, channels of communication with peers usually have a greater effect on the process.

The time element begins with the period of initial awareness of the innovation and progresses until the individual either implements or rejects the innovation and confirms the decision. In diffusion research in the field of education, innovations such as kindergartens and team teaching have been the subjects of study. Although the rate of diffusion in education appears to be accelerating, Miles (1964) cited several studies that indicated a relatively slow rate of diffusion of innovations in education. Research on innovations in higher education by Getz, Siegfried and Anderson (1994), in which they examined 30 innovations in academic and administrative areas at 238 institutions, showed that the average time for adoption of an innovation within institutions of higher education was 25 years. The time needed for adoption differed according to discipline, with innovations in computer and library science diffusing faster than other fields. The rate of diffusion of innovations in higher education in computer and library science was similar to the rate of innovation diffusion in industry.

No aspect of the process occurs in a vacuum. The social system of the individual or institution exerts influence upon the entire process. Within organizations, such as higher education institutions, the diffusion of innovation is related to the internal and external characteristics of the institutional structure and the characteristics of the individuals within the institution (Getz, Siegfried & Anderson, 1994). The social structure of the system—within which the individual perceives the innovation and the communication channels developed within the system—greatly influences the number of individuals who adopt an innovation and the length of time it takes for the individual to adopt or reject the innovation (Rogers, 1995).

Institutional Background

The University, established in 1839, became a land-grant institution in 1870 under the Morrill Act of 1862. Although the University was predominantly a residential campus composed of 18 schools and colleges, and more than 20,000 students, there was also a strong emphasis on continuing education and outreach.

In 1980, the campus technology services were mainly mainframe computers allowing administrative access to information. By 1990, as a result of increased demand and technological changes, the system included connectivity to remote sites and network segmentation. As the technology grew, services to support the technology were maintained at the departmental level. Due to differences in commitment and funding, departments provided differing levels of support for technology. Some departments provided little support while other departments built their own separate networks.

Over the past five years, the institution has made both fiscal and written commitments to the integration of technology into the curriculum. The official institutional technology plan listed as a major goal the integration of instructional technology programs throughout the university curriculum, and over $25,000,000 was budgeted for this purpose. Projects developed to achieve the goal included upgrading of the library technology system, participation in innovative technology development, and increased infrastructure. This strength of administrative commitment at this institution appeared to contradict much literature, which indicated a lack of commitment and administrative support as one major barrier to incorporation of technology in classroom instruction (Albright, 1996; Bryon, 1995; Geoghegan, 1994; Knapper, 1988).

During this time period, several changes occurred on the campus relative to the use of technology. For students the changes included automatic e-mail accounts upon enrollment, the requirement of several hours of classroom instruction in courses that were considered technology enhanced, and the increased accessibility of on-line support services. For the faculty, an instructional technology teaching and support group was formed to provide new avenues of access to learning about how to use technology in the classroom. In some cases, grants were provided to faculty for development of technology-enhanced instruction. Also, for the students, faculty, and staff, a desktop replacement program was initiated and computer labs were upgraded. Administratively, the leadership in the information and computing services division changed and a new committee structure was initiated to increase participation in planning.

The University had several specialized centers for the support of faculty who desired to use technology in their classroom instruction. One center provided support to faculty and students through such services as the help desk, specific training programs, and hardware support and repair. Another center for faculty support provided services such as equipment rental, media materials preparation, and audiovisual supplies (such as audio and video equipment). A third source for faculty support was a center composed of faculty, staff, and students. This center was one of the primary sources of faculty support for the integration of technology into classroom instruction. Programs included faculty training institutes, workshops, and a faculty-mentoring program.

Faculty Perspectives on the Use of Technology

According to Clark (1987) and Austin (1990), university faculty operate within four overlapping, yet distinct, cultures: 1) the academic profession in general, 2) the individual disciplines, 3) the specific institution as an organization, and 4) institutional type. These four cultures provide the framework for a discussion of the findings of this case study on the diffusion of technology for classroom instruction at this institution.

The Academic Profession

Faculty who were using technology agreed that the use of technology in the classroom provided some benefits that encouraged them to continue to explore the use of technology in their classroom teaching. They stated that the use of technology in their classrooms enhanced student learning, and faculty and student interactions, leading to increased empowerment of students. Additionally, faculty felt that the use of technology had increased their awareness of teaching principles and forced an examination of the way they teach. Another benefit, according to the faculty that were using technology in their classroom instruction, was that the development of materials and the determination of what to use had led them to consider the pedagogy of their classroom instruction. One faculty member said:

> [It is] rethinking the way we teach anything. Because...a typical college professor, they went to school, they did well under the system. So they get their PhD, they come and they use the system that they learned under. And so, lectures, three lectures a week, a laboratory room, write a paper, turn it in. Technology doesn't lend itself to that.

Another faculty member explained reasons to incorporate technology as such:

> I chose this profession not just to become a researcher. I chose the profession also because I wanted to teach. ... I wanted to learn about the psychology of teaching. I wanted to learn about teaching methodology. ... I just wanted to improve the teaching process. ... So I was thinking, well, how would you put some of these things [technology being used] ...integrate them into education.

One issue that participants perceived as very important was the return to learning for the faculty member. Faculty who reported using technology in teaching viewed themselves as able to learn from their students in a new and different way. They indicated that the empowerment of the students had changed the student-faculty relationship and now, although the faculty member was still the expert, the students and faculty members have become participants in a collaborative learning community.

The following was one professor's description of how electronic mail, listserves, and the World Wide Web had changed the communication in the classroom and thereby the faculty role and the role of these students:

My role has changed. Everybody is talking. It has moved from me doing all the talking, to working with the student on something that they want to do, which I love. It allows me to take a class of 15 or 20 students and essentially collaborate with every one of them. And then they talk to each other about what they are doing. So the learning moves from me telling you, to me working with you, and then us telling everybody...everybody in the class. And that has set a very high standard.

All of the interviewed faculty, whether they used technology in classroom instruction or not, were concerned with teaching and the effect of technology on the profession and on student learning. Every individual considered him or herself a good teacher and researcher and committed to academe and the traditional institutional mission of a Research I institution. This commitment indicated strong support for Austin's (1990) academic cultural value of the "...notion that the purpose of higher education is to pursue, discover, produce and disseminate knowledge, truth, and understanding" (p. 62).

Faculty who were using technology in their instruction still felt that the professional autonomy of others who did not use technology must be respected and maintained. The continual pursuit of knowledge and dissemination of knowledge within the autonomy and freedom of the academic institution were values of all of the faculty. Their support of the conservative diffusion of technology in education and their assertion that faculty should not be pushed to use technology, unless it is essential to the content of the course, indicated that they value this aspect of the culture of the profession.

The Individual Disciplines

Clark (1980) stated that the power of the disciplines is the strongest for faculty. It is easier to change institutions than to change disciplines. The individual faculty member has spent years being socialized into the particular discipline as a student and faculty member. Special organizations in each discipline increase the sense of belonging to the discipline on a national or international basis and thereby enhance the individual self-identity as a member of the discipline.

In the use of technology in instruction, several differences were evident among the various disciplines. Disciplines, such as journalism and veterinary medicine—in which the use of technology was a specific component of the curriculum—were more heavily involved in using technology such as multimedia and Web-based interactions in classroom instruction than were disciplines for which the use of technology was not a component of the curriculum, such as English or social work. Faculty from disciplines considered a "hard paradigm," such as chemistry, indicated greater acceptance of using technology, such as specialized software programs, in instruction than did participants who were from disciplines considered a "soft paradigm," such as history. In addition, disciplines, like chemistry, in which students would be required to use technology in their careers, were more supportive of the incorporation of technology, such as Web-based instruction, into classroom instruction than disciplines, like languages, in which students might not have to use technology in their careers.

Another disciplinary difference was evident when faculty discussed support for technology in general. Faculty in disciplines that were well funded indicated they received higher levels of fiscal support from their departments whereas faculty in disciplines that were less well funded found it difficult to obtain departmental support. As one faculty member said:

> I have never had to want for expendables, hardware, and software. Now, that is an important point because I am probably the exception. Probably a lot of teachers really don't have the resources that they need.

Several other faculty members in other disciplines who stated that they could not obtain the equipment they needed supported this view. One faculty member actually stated that many of the hardware and software items that were used for classroom instruction were purchased with personal funds because the department did not have the necessary funding. Another faculty member gave the departmental rationale for refusing the request for portable equipment. This faculty member was told that getting a laptop would be supporting personal work and that "...the computer might be used for consulting or something..." and therefore the department could not purchase such an item.

The Specific Institution

Despite the institutional technology plan and the fiscal commitment by administration, faculty described a number of major problems related to the institution and the use of technology in the classroom. Among the issues was a perceived lack of coordinated effort at the institutional level to support faculty use of technology. A faculty member who did not use technology in classroom instruction saw the lack of technology standards across campus as a major issue. Although a number of auditoriums and classrooms across campus were capable of supporting the use of various forms of technology, such as multimedia presentations, what worked in one room might not work in another. This faculty member indicated that since the professor was responsible for using the equipment in the classroom, each individual would have to learn several operating systems and be prepared to provide several types of equipment, such as a variety of connector cables.

A connected issue was the lack of assurance that a classroom would have the necessary capability for using a certain form of technology in instruction. One professor who was incorporating multimedia technology into instruction described the process of using this form of technology in a non-multimedia configured classroom in a building on campus that belonged to another discipline.

> I had to pick up a portable computer, video projector ... and haul it all over there all the way from .... I used my luggage cart because they won't deliver the video projector unless somebody over there will sign for it. And since we are not a part of [that department] ... . There is a lab right next door [to the classroom], a dedicated undergraduate computer lab, and of course we could not use it.

Another professor who was not using technology in teaching said that this issue was a major reason for not using technology in general:

> My attitude is, if the university wants me to use technology, they better guarantee me that its going to be there for me. And I don't think I can get that.

Another faculty member who was using multimedia technology was frustrated because, although the classroom equipment and connections were available, there was no one available to teach one how to use it. This faculty member stated that no one in the department had the skills to use the equipment and no training was available, so everyone was on their own to learn. Additionally, if something suddenly did not work, faculty had no idea who or where to call for help. The process had become very frustrating for faculty and students. This faculty member further stated that as a result of this frustration, only two faculty members in the entire department were using technology in their classroom instruction.

This problem was echoed in another area that also, according to the faculty member, had only two faculty in the entire department using technology in the classroom. One of these two faculty members described it thus:

> It isn't routine and standard yet and people don't understand. So, if you want to teach with technology, you have to become an expert, I find, in connections, wiring, and you have to spend time teaching yourself because not many people can help you.

One faculty member who had used Web-based technology in classroom instruction for a couple of years stated:

> [When I began] we didn't have anybody to answer the basic questions of where do you start, what do you do first, what do you do second. There was no one. ... I think now the support team is fragmented. I still can't seem to find out where, if I have a question, where I need to go with it.

Rogers' (1995) theory of innovation diffusion stated that the communication channels that promote the diffusion become individual channels as awareness increases. As stated in the literature on the current status of the use of technology in education (Ely et al., 1992; Green, 1996; McCollum, 1998; Olien, 1998), faculty were aware of the use of technology in education. However, the participants in this study indicated that the personal communication channels were not well developed. Individual faculty, although generally aware of the use of technology in education, did not have access to the communication channels that, as Rogers (1995) stated, are essential to the diffusion of an innovation.

The Institutional Type
Another major issue for faculty at this institution was the lack of incentives and rewards for incorporation of technology into classroom instruction. One of the faculty members who began using technology, such as computer simulations and listserves, before receiving tenure stated:

> [...] A person who is on the tenure track needs to be focusing on research and creative activity. I wouldn't encourage them, if they didn't already have the skills to learn enough about it, to get into technology and instruction. I just wouldn't do it.

Most of the participants indicated that while including the use of some form of technology in evaluation criteria was an issue that was discussed, opposition to including criteria related to the use of various forms of instructional technology in the evaluation process was strong. One of the faculty members who was untenured stated that using technology in classroom instruction was perilous at this career point:

> [But] even though it doesn't count for tenure decisions, if I use the information here and don't make tenure, there are a number of schools that will want me.

One explanation given by a number of the faculty members for the lack of incentives and rewards was that teaching itself was not highly valued institutionally. They indicated that as this institution was a Research I institution, the highest value was on research and it was research that was rewarded.

ANALYSIS

The participants in this case study indicated that core values within academe might affect their use of technology in classroom instruction. The beliefs and values of the academic profession culture emphasize learning, dissemination of knowledge, and autonomy in teaching. The continual pursuit of knowledge and dissemination of knowledge within the autonomy and freedom of the academic institution were values of all of the participants. It was evident from the data collected that these beliefs and values were supported by the incorporation of technology into classroom instruction for those faculty who are using technology. Those faculty who were not using technology in classroom instruction also shared these beliefs and values but were asking for proof that the use of technology did provide support for these cultural values. Their support of the conservative diffusion of technology in education and their assertion that faculty should not be pushed to use technology, unless it is essential to the content of the course, also indicated that they value this aspect of the culture of the institution.

Additionally, the findings supported the cultural differences among disciplines. The participants in this study acknowledged that there are major differences in funding and support for technology among schools and departments, and that these differences affect their ability and desire to use technology in teaching. Since the wealth of the department determines whether or not the equipment is even available, it was obvious that this aspect of the individual disciplines had a strong effect on the diffusion of technology into classroom instruction. Additionally, disciplines in which the use of technology was part of the culture of the discipline showed greater involvement in using technology in classroom instruction.

Interviewees indicated that general attitudes and the climate toward the use of some form of technology for instruction were different depending on discipline. Further, despite the potential described in the literature for doing so, the participants in this study have not crossed disciplinary boundaries through the use of technology, either in research or teaching, but have remained well within their institutional, national, and international disciplinary boundaries. It is perhaps this continued disciplinary perspective that has supported the faculty viewpoint of isolation and lack of support for their efforts.

The official workload for tenure evaluation of faculty at a Research I institution is roughly 40 percent teaching, 40 percent research, and 20 percent service. Faculty, at this particular institution, felt that the lack of incentives and rewards for using technology was the result of the lack of emphasis on teaching and higher emphasis on research. The general perception was that to achieve tenure, it would be wiser for a faculty member to concentrate on research and not on using technology in teaching.

CONCLUSIONS

Despite the campus technology plan and the strong fiscal support from the administration, faculty saw several institutional issues that slowed the diffusion of technology in classroom instruction. One was the lack of campus-wide technology standards, which forced faculty to learn different operating systems and equipment. Another was the lack of coordination of effort to provide support for faculty who wished to learn how to use technology. It was perceived as especially difficult for faculty members to learn to use the technology, since, although the equipment might be available, they did not know where to seek help and few in a given department could help.

This case study has not only provided support for the literature, but also provided findings on the diffusion of technology into the classroom instruction that may increase understanding of diffusion of this innovation in higher education. These findings included: 1) the development of a more collaborative learning environment through the use of technology provided a potential for increased learning for faculty as well as students; 2) personal communication, essential to the diffusion of technology, was fragmented across disciplines and across the institution; 3) the faculty perception of lack of support contrary to administrative perceptions of commitment leads to difficulties in the institutional communication process; and 4) the value of teaching relative to research was low.

Results of this study indicated that faculty and students experienced enhanced classroom learning when technology was incorporated, which supported the values of the academic profession in general. The results of this case study indicated that at this particular institution, incongruities in the values and beliefs reflected by the administration and the perceptions of the faculty were barriers to the increased use of technology in instruction. Finally, as a Research I institution, faculty indicated that the emphasis that was reinforced by the current promotion and tenure system was on research rather than teaching. This emphasis further hindered the diffusion of technology in classroom instruction.

DISCUSSION QUESTIONS

1. What could the institution/faculty do to promote the diffusion of technology into classroom instruction?
2. What might be the effect of culture on the diffusion of technology at other types of higher education institutions, such as community colleges?
3. What other aspects of higher education might explain the slowness of diffusion of technology?

REFERENCES

Albright, M.J. (1996, February). Instructional technology and higher education: Rewards, rights, and responsibilities. Keynote address, Southern Regional Faculty and Instructional Development Consortium. (ERIC Reproduction Service No. ED 392 412).

Alvarez, L.R. (1996, May/June). Why technology? Technology, electricity and running water. *Educom Review* [Online], 31, 3. Available: Http://www.educom.edu/web/pubs/review/review/Articles/31324.html.

Austin, A. (1990). Faculty cultures, faculty values. In Tierney, W.G. (Ed.), *Assessing Academic Climates and Cultures*. (pp. 61 - 74). San Francisco, CA: Jossey-Bass Inc.

Byron, S. (1995, December). Computing and other instructional technologies: Faculty perceptions of current practices and views of future challenges. (ERIC Reproduction Service No. ED 390 338).

Cartwright, G.P. (1993). Part one: Teaching with academic technologies. *Change*, 6 (November/December), 67.

Clark, B.R. (1980). *Academic Culture* (Report No. YHERG-42). Higher Education Research Group, Institution for Social and Policy Studies, Yale University. (ERIC Document Reproduction No. ED 187 186).

Clark, B.R. (1987). *The Academic Life: Small Worlds, Different Worlds*. Princeton, NJ: Carnegie Foundation for the Advancement of Teaching.

Clinton, W.J. (1996, November). Introduction: Achieving the goals — Goal 5 - First in the world in math and science technology resources [Online]. Available: http://www.ed.gov/pubs/AchGoal5/intro.html.

Ely, D.P., Foley, A., Freeman, W., & Scheel, N. (1992, June). Trends in educational technology. ERIC Clearinghouse on Information Resources, Syracuse University. Syracuse, NY.

Geoghegan, W.H. (1994, July). What ever happened to instructional technology? Paper presented at the 22nd Annual Conference of the International Business Schools Computing Association, Baltimore, MD. [Online]. Available: http://w3.scale.uiuc.edu/scale/library/geoghegan/wpi.html.

Getz, M., Siegfried, J.J., & Anderson, K.H. (1994). Adoption of innovations in higher education. Vanderbilt University. Nashville, TN.

Gilbert, S.W. (1995, September/October). Technology & the changing academy: Symptoms, questions, and suggestions. *Change* [Online]. Available: http://contract.kent.edu/change/articles/sepoct95.html.

Green, C. (1997). Past, promise and potential: Tracking change via the campus computing project. 1997 TLTR Summer Institute presentation. [Online]. Available: http://www.wilpaterson.edu/aahe/si97/cg/sld.htm.

Green, K.C. (1996, November). The 1996 national survey of information technology in higher education: Instructional integration and user support present continuing technology challenges. *The Campus Computing Project*. [Online]. Available: http://ericir.syr.edu/Projects/campus_computing/1996/index.html.

Green, K.C. (1996, January). The 1995 national survey of information technology in higher education: Technology use jumps on college campuses. *The Campus Computing Project* [Online]. Available: Http://ericir.syr.edu/Projects/campus_computing/1995/index.html.

Heterick, R.C., Jr. (1993). Introduction: Reengineering teaching and learning. *CAUSE Professional Paper Series #10* [Online]. Heterick, R.C., Jr. (Ed.). Available: http://cause-www.colorado.edu/information-resources/ir-library/text/pub3010.txt.

Katz, R.N. (1993). Silicon in the grove: Computing, teaching, and learning in the American research university. *CAUSE Professional Paper Series #10* [Online], Heterick, R.C., Jr. (Ed.). Available: http://cause-www.colorado.edu/information-resources/ir-library/text/pub3010.txt.

Knapper, C.K. (1988). Technology and college teaching. Young, R. E., (Ed.). *College*

Teaching and Learning: Preparing for New Commitments. New Directions for Teaching and Learning, 33, 31-47.

Laurillard, D. (1993). *Rethinking University Teaching: A Framework for the Effective Use of Educational Technology.* New York, NY: Routledge.

Lee, J. (1996). Information technology at the gate: Faculty perceptions and attitudes about technology-mediated instruction innovation in higher education. (Doctoral dissertation, University of California, Berkeley). Available: http://wwwlib.umi.com/dissertations/fullcit?170476.

Leiner, B.M., Cerf, B.G., Clark, D.D., Khan, R.E., Kleinrock, L., Lynch, D.C., Postel, J., Roberts, L.G., & Wolf, S. (1998). A brief history of the Internet. Available: http://www.isoc.org/internet-history/brief.html.

Lever-Duffy, J.C. (1991, November). Strategies for empowering educators with technology: A presentation for the League of Innovation. (ERIC Document Reproduction Service No. ED 387 168).

Mason, J. (1996). Building an overview: Fitting information technology (IT) into the educational setting [Online]. Available: http://sunsite.unc.edu/horizon/mono/CD/Change_Innovation/Mason.html.

McCollum, K. (1998, March 20). Information technology: 'Ramping up' to support 42,000 student computers on a single campus. *The Chronicle of Higher Education,* A-27-29.

Miles, M.B. (1964). Innovation in education: Some generalizations. *Innovation in education* (pp. 631-662). New York: NY, Bureau of Publications, Teachers College, Columbia University.

Molnar, A.R. (1997). Computers in education: A brief history. *T.H.E. Journal* [Online]. Available: http://www.thejournal.com/SPECIAL/25thani/0697feat01.html.

Neal, E. (1998, April). AAHESGIT73: Faculty skepticism & judgement vs. laziness. [Online] Discussion list aahesgit@list.cren.net.

Olien, D. (1998, February). New technologies bring challenge in dealing with governors and state legislatures. *NASULGC Newsline,* 7, 2.

Plotnick, E. (1996). Trends in educational technology. *1995 ERIC Digest. ERIC Clearinghouse on Information and Technology.* (ERIC Document Reproduction Service No. ED 398 861).

Ringle, M. (1996, May/June). Why technology? The well-rounded institution. *Educom Review [Online].* 31, 3. Available: http://www.educom.edu/web/pubs/review/review articles/31324.html.

Rogers, E.M. (1995). *Diffusion of Innovations* (4th ed.). New York, NY: The Free Press.

Saettler, P. (1990). *The Evolution of American Educational Technology.* Englewood, CO: Libraries Unlimited, Inc.

Timeline: 50 years of computing. (1997). *T.H.E. Journal* [Online]. Available: http://www.thejournal.com/SPECIAL/25thani/0697feat01.html.

Walsh, S.M. (1993). Attitudes and perceptions of university faculty toward technology-based distance education. (Doctoral dissertation, University of Oklahoma, 1993).

Whitaker, G.R., & Ekman, R. (1998, February). Initiative on the cost-effective uses of technology in teaching: The Andrew W. Mellon Foundation [Online] Available: http://ww.mellon.org.cutt.html.

Chapter XIV

The Impact of Information Technology on Roles and Role Processes in Small Groups

Robert Heckman
Syracuse University

Dave Maswick
Bard College

Jamie Rodgers, Kevin Ruthen and Gary Wee
Syracuse University

INTRODUCTION

In both corporate and academic organizations, collaborative work is frequently accomplished and managed in small work groups. These can take either the form of formal work groups or ad hoc task groups. The formal work group has relatively permanent membership, ongoing tasks, and routinized reporting relationships within the organization. Over time, skills and information of group members become more group-specific and norms more implicit. There is less communication on how to work together and more on the work itself (Finholt, Sproull, and Kiesler, 1990). Some types of work are, however, best performed in ad hoc or quickly formed task groups. According to Finholt, Sproull, and Kiesler (1990), such groups are convened for a particular purpose, consist of members who otherwise would not work together, and disband after completing their assigned task. These task groups permit an organization to respond rapidly to changes in the environment and to non-routine problems by calling on expertise regardless of where it resides in the organization.

In higher education, a particular form of ad hoc task group is familiar to many instructors—the student project team. Such teams are commonly formed to allow students to tackle projects that are too big to handle individually, to allow students to teach and learn from one another, and to create opportunities for practicing the intricate dynamics of collaborative work. Given the benefits claimed for ad hoc task groups, it is presumed to be a good thing for students to gain hands-on experience in their function.

Advances in information and communication technology today help many corporate task groups confront problems such as physically dispersed members, lack of information-sharing routines, and short-term deadlines. After almost two decades, the use of computer-mediated collaboration technologies has become common. These technologies range from basic email systems to sophisticated computer and telecommunication systems capable of providing various functions, allowing groups to communicate, collaborate, and coordinate beyond the limitation of time and space.

At a somewhat slower pace, higher education has similarly embraced these technologies, and is now using them to create and promote a wide variety of distance education offerings. It is arguably more important than ever to continue the tradition of assigning students to collaborative project teams. However, little is known about how technology can best be used to promote successful collaborative learning. The ability to use collaboration technology effectively is an important issue when students are all on the same campus and have the opportunity to meet their instructors and each other in the classroom. It becomes critical in distance education. In order to gain any of the benefits of collaborative learning in distance education, the conditions that lead to successful use of collaboration technology must be understood.

This case study reports the experience of a single group of four geographically distributed graduate students who collaborated with great success on a number of projects over a period of two years. During the period reported, they were enrolled in the Master's of Science in Information Management program at The School of Information Studies, Syracuse University. They participated in this program under the Independent Study Distance Program (ISDP), which at the time of this writing has been offered for three years. Their story is worthy of study because, in technology-mediated collaborative learning, they represent the far positive end of the outcome continuum. Unknown to each other before enrollment, they quickly learned and embraced a broad array of communication technologies and became adroit in using different technologies to accomplish different objectives. They formed a strong group identity, and went out of their way to work together on every group project possible, including their final degree exit requirement. They received a grade of "A" on every project they worked on together. They had fun. They became friends. Because they had infrequent opportunities to meet face-to-face, they accomplished these things predominantly through the use of a technology-mediated communication environment.

By choosing to work together on several projects, this group began to take on some of the characteristics of a formal work group. Skills became understood, norms became implicit, and the group was able to spend its communication energy on the work itself rather than on how to work together. However, since the group was re-formed at the beginning of each semester and disbanded after its end, had no ongoing formal standing, and disbanded for good after its final project together, it lacks the defining features of a formal work group. In many ways, this group is a better exemplar of a "hot group," a label coined by Leavitt and Lipman-Blumen (1995). A hot group is defined by a distinctive philosophy, attitude, and pattern of behavior. It is intense, sharply focused, and task obsessed. It has high standards for both thinking and doing. Like an ad hoc task group, it generally disbands when its task is complete. Hot groups are capable of achieving unexpectedly high levels of performance. The goal in studying this group is to learn something about the conditions that cause, or at least allow, such high performance learning teams to form in technology-mediated educational environments.

In this two-year longitudinal case study, group members' written reflections provide the primary data for the narrative and analysis reported below. The analysis focuses on the impact of information technology on the roles and role processes that characterized this group. Finally, the chapter concludes with a discussion of what this story tells about the prerequisite conditions necessary for success in technology-mediated learning teams.

CASE QUESTIONS

- How does information technology (IT) affect the process of role assignment in technology-mediated learning teams?
- How does IT affect the exercise of leadership in such teams?
- How does IT affect the role structure in such teams?
- What are the necessary conditions for high performance in technology-mediated learning teams?

CASE NARRATIVE

Background

The Master's of Science program in Information Management at the School of Information Studies, Syracuse University is offered in both a traditional on-campus mode and as an independent study distance program (ISDP). The ISDP program relies heavily on the use of information technology for the delivery of course content. Students participate while situated in different locations and time zones around the world.

Professors and students use a suite of Internet-based technologies to deliver lectures, carry on discussions, and complete assignments. Included in this suite are email, asynchronous bulletin boards, and synchronous discussion environments. The program's professors rely quite heavily on small class groups to deliver a variety of collaborative course assignments using this technology.

The Syracuse model of distance education also includes short,three-four day, on-campus residencies at the beginning of each semester. These residencies consist of all-day class sessions, and are used for a variety of purposes such as technology instruction, case study discussions, role-play assignments, simulations, and other group exercises. Perhaps their most important function, however, is to allow students a brief opportunity to meet and get to know one another before returning to their homes, where they participate in the majority of their course activities. About half the courses in the ISDP program have a residency period. The others are conducted entirely online.

The technology suite used in the Syracuse model of distance education is based on an open, relatively simple, publicly available technology environment. For their collaborative assignments, students are generally allowed free choice of the technology support they wish to use. Students may use all of the technology resources provided by the university in their collaborative work, or they may choose to use none of it, relying instead on telephone, FAX, traditional mail, and/or courier. Thus, use of any particular configuration of technology support for collaborative work is discretionary.

Specifically, the Syracuse suite of technology consists of the following:

- *Email*: Available through Internet browsers, as well as the University's UNIX system.
- *Internet-based asynchronous discussion software*: Such as those available in Internet newsgroups as well as some proprietary Java discussion packages.
- *The Palace synchronous discussion software*: The Palace is an avatar-based synchronous chat system in which groups can meet and interact in real time. It employs small picture icons to represent a participant in a synchronous discussion, and records all comments made. The software features tools for facilitating discussion such as a blackboard, sounds, and visual cues for members to use when they want to speak. Text-based synchronous chat is also available.
- *World Wide Web sites*: For posting documents for review by other members of the group.

The collaboration support provided by the technology suite includes the following characteristics:

- *Communicators are identified*: Each submission by a member of the group is tagged with the member's name, email address, and the date and time of the submission. This is true of the synchronous and asynchronous communications channels.
- *Synchronous and asynchronous communication are supported*: The Palace software and the text-based chat rooms deliver synchronous communications capabilities, and the bulletin board software offers the asynchronous capabilities.
- *All keyed input is recorded*: Both synchronous and asynchronous discussion submissions are available for retrieval and reference.
- *Immediate feedback is provided*: For both the synchronous and asynchronous software, the user is provided with immediate confirmation that his or her message was received.
- *Unstructured agenda*: All discussion that occurs within the technology suite is unstructured, free-flowing conversation.

The Group

The group members described in this case—Dave, Jamie, Kevin, and Gary—were four men with full-time professional jobs, of different ages (between 25 and 40), with different job responsibilities, and in different stages of their careers. They lived in different areas (one in New York City, one in upstate New York, and two in widely separated suburbs of Toronto). One member of the group was a member of an ethnic minority. Each was seeking a Master's degree in Information Management through the Syracuse University ISDP program during the time period described in this chapter.

They met for the first time during their initial residency at the Syracuse campus in August 1996. They worked together for the first time as a team in the following semester, which began in January 1997, during their first required group project in the program. Thus, their history as a group began in their second semester in the program.

The course IST775, The Information Industry, began with an intensive four-day on-campus residency, and after that was conducted entirely online. Each of the team members had the opportunity to interact with the others face-to-face during this residency, and they also spent time together socially during the evenings after the all-day classes ended. Once the online team project was assigned, they expressed a mutual desire to work together for the assignment. The assignment (creation of a Web site on a segment of the Information Industry) was relatively unstructured, allowing the group wide latitude in their choice of operating procedures and in the format of the final deliverable. In their subsequent reflections, each team member recalled an initial uncertainty as to how they would interact and function as a group, especially in an online environment that was new and unfamiliar. But it soon became clear that they would be able to work very effectively using the available communication technology.

One incident occurred during the residency that foreshadowed the group's subsequent experiences. After teams had been formed, a training session for the Palace synchronous chat system was held in a large computer lab. Team members were separated throughout the room, and instructed to communicate with each other using only the Palace software, without speaking. While several of the teams had difficulty with the technology, Dave, Jamie, Kevin, and Gary took to it immediately. The silence in the large room was punctuated by their laughter as they exchanged virtual jokes across the interface.

Back at their homes, the group was free to choose among different technologies for communication, but they relied most heavily on the Palace synchronous chat environment.

It did not take long before mutual patterns and social cues were established, leading to orderly and effective communication:

> The event that most influenced our interactions was the introduction of the Palace software to the group. At our first exposure to it, it became quite clear that the Palace was the medium of choice for our real-time distance communication needs. We quickly became facile with the interface and also developed an altered social order that would compensate for the lack of physical cues and sound in proximate group discussions (Dave).

The graphical interface and the simple aids to synchronous discussion provided by the Palace created a virtual environment that was comfortable for this group:

> The avatars definitely served as an effective mutual symbolic representation of ourselves. We also learned and got used to the way certain members abbreviated words and their style of communicating in the Palace. As time went on we learned certain member patterns and established the use of virtual hand raising for less interruptions and cutoffs of member communication. It was common for us to recognize when someone was finished expressing a thought and then who would likely be the first to respond next or to move onto another subject (Kevin).

The group generally held Palace meetings weekly throughout the semester to discuss the project. They primarily used email to set up and confirm Palace meetings, distribute project documents and meeting logs, and to ask or to clarify any questions prior to a meeting. Thus they adopted a flexible technology use pattern that depended on multiple technologies. They also established a fluid pattern of role assignment, and the Palace technology seemed especially suited to this adaptive approach to roles:

> The role(s) of each person in the group quickly developed and matured with our continued use of the Palace. Each member of the group functioned at various times as leader, facilitator, communicator, and as a passive observer depending sometimes on overt nomination ("Kevin...you moderate.") or by virtue of information that needed to be communicated to the group (Dave).

An online, interactive Web site on the subject of information technology procurement negotiations was created as the deliverable for this project, and it received a grade of A. Successful use of the technology, members' general comfort level with each other, and effective ability to work together online created a desire to work together in the future as a team. As Kevin described in his reflection:

> We all have very unique personality traits and very different background experiences, which for some groups may cause conflicts and barriers to be erected, but it has been quite the opposite for our team. We relied upon flexibility and open mindedness along with our desire to learn from each other to build, mesh, and strengthen our relationships as a team, which has also led to friendship (Kevin).

In the following semester (Fall 1997), all four members of the group registered for two common courses (IST642, Electronic Commerce; and IST653, Telecommunications). There were no on-campus residencies for these classes. They were conducted entirely online.

IST642 required a collaborative group research project, and the professor specified that each group was to consist of six members. Dave, Gary, Kevin, and Jamie quickly agreed to work together, and expanded their group size to six by selecting two other members through online correspondence. As they worked on the project, conflict arose in the expanded group. The newcomers did not share the original group's facility with the full range of available technologies (especially the Palace). The original group members had developed certain behavior patterns and patterns of role assignment in the Palace environment that were not equally shared by the new participants. The expanded group did not work as smoothly as the original four. Dave recalled:

> I perceived it as the infiltration of our group by interlopers, and that their presence was counter-productive or at least a hindrance to the speedy completion of the project.

Ultimately, the contribution of the two new members was apparently judged acceptable, however, and an online report regarding WebTV technology was submitted and received a grade of A.

In their second course together during that semester (IST653, Telecommunications), the four-member group was once again able to work as an intact team. In this course, a number of brief online research reports were posted and discussed in an asynchronous discussion forum (bulletin board). The professor required that weekly postings, each representing a group's consolidated opinion on a particular report, be shared with the class. This generated much email back and forth between members due to the short time frames, number of reports, and consolidated submission demands. Since this class was taken simultaneously with IST642, Palace meetings were often used for discussions on both class projects.

Thus, once again, the team was able to move smoothly back and forth between technologies, using email, asynchronous bulletin boards, and synchronous chat technologies as appropriate. By this time, the group had developed effective technology-mediated work and role assignment processes. As Jamie noted:

> We almost always unanimously agreed on the approaches we took on projects, and we all exhibited approximately the same level of commitment to get things done. The different roles that needed to be played to make a team successful were shared effectively among our members.

During this semester the four original group members strengthened their social identity as a team. They adopted a name, the *Virtual War* (reserved for the four original members). A *Virtual War* Web site was created, with humorous pictorials and fictitious biographies. It also served as a central posting and submission area for documents to be viewed by "outsiders." In the Palace, they discussed obtaining team paraphernalia such as jackets and caps. They discussed the possibility of a recreational trip together. By this point they had also developed a high performance standard for collaborative course work based on an aggressive, competitive team identity. The four team members also sensed a shared ease and familiarity with technology, and a balance of skills and abilities which became a key component of their desire to maintain the team.

As they progressed through their degree programs, members of the *Virtual War* continued to seek opportunities to work together as a team. For the Social Research course (IST501) in Spring 1998, the *Virtual War* team worked together to conduct literature review research regarding the use of introspection for social research. Research findings and write-ups were passed back and forth via email and discussed at length during Palace meetings.

In Fall 1998, the members of the *Virtual War* sought and received permission to work collaboratively on their final degree program exit requirement. The idea to work as team on a large research project was first proposed Spring Semester 1998. This led to a number of emails and Palace meeting discussions to refine the idea, the purpose, general outline, and timeframe. A final outline and schedule was agreed upon in the Summer of 1998. Fall Semester 1998 and part of Spring 1999 were spent conducting a literature review, collection of data, analysis, and writing the final report. Drafts of individual submissions were shared via email attachments and through postings to the *Virtual War* Web site. Palace meetings were used to discuss issues, submissions, tasks, and timeframe milestones. The project was completed in Spring, 1999, and, as with their other collaborative efforts, received a grade of A.

All members of the *Virtual War* met the requirements for completing their degrees. Even though they had relatively few opportunities to meet face to face over the two-year life of the *Virtual War*, they felt that they have developed a strong relationship. Kevin commented:

> We believe the technology we utilized, and the projects we worked on together helped us to overcome distance barriers, allowing us to develop a strong bond and relationship both inside and outside of school that might not have existed had we only met occasionally on-campus.

ANALYSIS

The case suggests that technology can facilitate a dynamic process of role assignment. Bormann (1990) defined a role within a group as a dynamic set of recurring behaviors, both expected and enacted, within a particular group context. A member of a group, therefore, does not assume a role until common expectations about what that member will say and do have been established. In Biddle's (1979) approach, roles are the result of group member interaction within a certain context that occurs uniquely at a moment in space and time. Leavitt and Lipman-Blumen (1995) supported this dynamic aspect of the process of role development in their work on hot groups. They argued that roles and responsibilities change quickly as the task or objectives change. Context can change the perceived task, and thus change the roles required to respond to that task. Roles must be able to change and develop over time according to the context defined by group objectives, environment, and external forces. Thus, the process of role assignment and management must also be both dynamic and fluid if the group is to be successful.

In the experiences of the *Virtual War*, one can see evidence that a dynamic process of role assignment and development existed. Roles rotated freely and dynamically from project to project, within a current project, and sometimes within the course of a single online meeting. As tasks became more clearly focused and defined, the roles required to undertake the task changed accordingly. Further, it is clear that the technology suite supported this process. That is, the technology facilitated rather than hindered the ability of the group to function dynamically, and to quickly assume roles and shed them as necessary. Probably the most significant impact of technology resulted from the group's use of the Palace software, as the following comment illustrates:

> The Palace allowed us to quickly try and change the type of role we would assume during a meeting. The Palace environment also allowed roles to quickly emerge

and change. I think it is much more difficult to clearly take on the role of a facilitator or leader when conversing asynchronously (Kevin).

But it is also apparent that the availability of a wider array of communication technologies was important to the development of the group's role assignment process. Because all members were comfortable using the Palace (synchronous), email (private asynchronous), bulletin board (public asynchronous), and Web site (public and private archive), the group had the capacity for dynamic role assignment:

> The technologies allowed each member of the group to act in one of many roles depending on the situation. That is to say that any member of the group could act in any role at anytime (Dave).

In summary, events suggest that the dynamic role management processes employed by the *Virtual War* were enhanced by the array of information technologies available to them. The *Virtual War* group performed successfully and at a high level because the IT supported a dynamic process of role management that allowed different members to take the lead when appropriate and to perform whatever task was needed at particular points in time. The IT also supported the concept that tasks themselves could be adjusted over time as familiarity with the subject matter and with the other members of the group matured. As familiarity with the technology improved, it became essentially transparent to the team and allowed the group to fill roles that have been proven essential in traditional face-to-face groups.

The team's experience indicates that available technology can facilitate dynamic leadership in technology-supported groups. Lipnack and Stamps (1997) noted that small groups typically have at least two kinds of leaders—social leaders and task leaders. On a broader scale, Bales and Slater (1955) also noted that social systems need two types of leadership roles, a task leader and a social-emotional leader.

The task leadership role deals with problems of defining the task, suggesting solutions, and moving the group towards achievement of goal production. Task leadership is usually oriented to expertise, activities, and decisions required to accomplish results. It is expertise that most often defines one's role in task-oriented virtual teams. The measure of this type of leadership is productivity, and because of the task-centric nature of most virtual teams (or hot groups), the critical importance of task leadership cannot be overstated.

The socio-emotional leader occupies a less visible type of role and, when the task leader dominates group discussion by suggesting solutions or criticizing contributions, acts as a buffer and helps to maintain group cohesion. Social leadership arises from the interactions that generate feelings of group identity, status, desirability, and personal satisfaction. Group cohesion is the measure of social leadership. In a traditional hierarchy, social leadership is sometimes a function of position or rank in the authority structure, as opposed to task leadership, which is usually a function of individual expertise.

The members of *Virtual War* did not describe any issues related to rank. All group members appeared to share equal hierarchical status:

> No one member dominated the group and this is what I feel made my experience the favorable one it was (Jamie).

Indeed, the role of rank in small groups is both unclear and difficult to resolve. Although rank can sometimes be a positive factor in the success of small, task-oriented groups, the experience of the *Virtual War* would seem to suggest that it is possible to operate effectively in absence of it.

Biddle (1979) classified the roles played by participants in small groups into two categories: task roles and group-building (socio-emotional) roles. Task-related roles include Proceduralist (procedure person, moderator, agenda-keeper); Recorder (record-keeper); Evaluator (devil's advocate, critic); Explainer (elaborator, coordinator, orienter, summarizer, amplifier); Information/Opinion Seeker (questioner); Information/Opinion Giver; and Idea Generator. Group-building roles include Follower (listener, information receiver); Motivator (energizer, encourager); Gatekeeper (participation monitor/expediter); Mediator (harmonizer, compromiser, conflict handler); and Tension-Releaser (jokester).

Using Biddle's role classifications as a guide, group members seemed to assume one of two leadership roles dynamically depending on either the appropriateness of that person's expertise to the current situation or the location of the group in the task-completion continuum. The first type of leadership role dynamically assigned between group members was that of task leader. Functions of task leadership include task coordination, explainer, and evaluator. The second, socio-emotional leadership, included group-building roles (follower, motivator, mediator, and tension-releaser). While virtual teams may sometimes have single leaders, shared leadership may be the norm rather than the exception. What has been observed in this group was a dynamic division of leadership roles between those of task and socio-emotional task leadership.

The case suggests that technology can simplify group role structure by assuming certain roles. The observations above suggest that, in high performing technology-mediated groups, roles are transferred dynamically between members at different times. The experience of the *Virtual War* also seems to suggest that the number of roles available to group members can be reduced by reliance on technology as the primary means of interaction. Again, using Biddle's small group role classifications, it can be argued that technology assumes the roles of proceduralist, communicator, recorder, and gatekeeper, as described below:

- *Proceduralist*—The constraints imposed by any technology demand that certain procedures be rigorously adhered to. The Palace software in particular imposes certain demands on the communication styles of members. Thus, the constraints imposed by communication technology narrow the range of possible operating styles, and serve as a kind of "Roberts Rules" for the group.
- *Communicator*—By easily handling broadcast distribution, one-to-one distribution, or rich combinations of the two, ideas and information can be disseminated in ways that previously required human intervention.
- *Recorder*—The logs and journals automatically generated by most communication software fulfill the role of recorder.
- *Gatekeeper*—The combination of password security and technological skill requirements serve to limit access to those who are invited and those who are knowledgeable.

Zigurs and Kozar (1994) also found that technology in a technology-mediated environment could assume some of the roles that people were previously expected to fill. Their survey respondents reported that the top five roles performed by technology were recorder, proceduralist, gatekeeper, motivator, and mediator. It is interesting to note that the gatekeeper, motivator, and mediator are considered group-building roles. This suggests that technology does not just assume task roles, but may also perform socio-emotional roles as well. For example, the *Virtual War* reflections suggest that lack of skill in using the technology can present a very real barrier to inclusion in the group.

It has often been noted that the use of technology for group communicating reduces social context cues such as eye contact and body language. However, the use of richer graphic interfaces such as that used by the Palace software may allow group members to find other ways to express these social context cues. This may entail, for example, the use of symbolic text characters or the use of 3-D objects to express social context cues. For example, a rich set of fictitious identities and inside jokes was developed by the *Virtual War* in their use of the Palace. These cues in some ways partially assumed the tension-releasing role of the Joker.

By eliminating some roles entirely, and partially assuming or enriching others, technology can simplify the role structure, thus releasing group energy for other tasks and roles. For groups that are technologically skillful, this may permit a more concentrated focus on task, a central attribute of hot groups.

CONCLUSIONS

The two-year experience of the *Virtual War* permits the following observations about hot groups in technology-mediated educational environments:

- The process of role development, assignment, and management is dynamic and fluid, and is shared among team members. Any information technology that does not positively facilitate this concept will negatively affect group performance.
- Leadership roles are likely to be fluid, dynamic, and not formally specified. Both task-oriented and socially oriented leadership roles may be assumed by different group members at different times.
- The number of roles available to group members is reduced when technology is the primary means of interaction. When technology assumes the traditional roles of proceduralist, communicator, recorder, and gatekeeper, the simplified structure of remaining roles can permit greater task concentration, a key characteristic of hot groups.

If technology can facilitate these important attributes of high performing teams, it remains to be asked why such groups do not form more frequently whenever technology is present. Most teachers would probably agree that such groups are unfortunately the exception rather than the rule. Several conditions, believed to be prerequisites for the formation of such teams, are:

- *Discretionary use of suitable technology:* There must be a broad array of available communication media, and groups must have freedom of choice in their use of technology. Without both availability and discretion, groups will find it difficult to align technology with task and the personal styles of members. The *Virtual War* would have performed very differently if they had not had access to both synchronous and asynchronous communication technologies. They were especially adroit at dynamically choosing the technology that met their needs at any given moment.
- *Capacity to use:* Group members must share a level of technological readiness to employ the technologies that are available in the array. The *Virtual War* members embraced the graphical interface of the Palace software almost immediately, while many of their

classmates never reached the level of comfort required to use it effectively.

- *Shared standards of thinking and doing:* The members of this group quickly found that they held similar standards of thinking about task performance. This commonality prerequisite is especially problematic for all fast-forming, fast-dissolving task groups, and student project teams are no exception. To create more student groups like the *Virtual War,* ways to create this shared bond must be found.
- *Opportunities for social bonding:* The intensive, on-campus residency component of the Syracuse ISDP program provided an effective way for these four people to meet, and to discover that they shared the two previous prerequisite conditions. They also had a chance to begin the development of an open and trusting relationship. Such bonding is difficult when no face-to-face encounters are possible, although this case shows that a high level of social integration is achievable through interactions that are predominantly technology mediated.

Each of these four items may represent a necessary condition for the formation of a high-performing, technology-mediated work group. Perhaps all must be present in some form. It remains for future research to test this hypothesis. Meanwhile, it remains the task of practicing educators to find innovative ways, through trial and error, to do the best job possible of creating the necessary conditions for high performance in technology-mediated learning teams.

DISCUSSION QUESTIONS

1. In addition to the traditional roles assumed in this case—proceduralist, communicator, recorder, and gatekeeper—are there other roles that technology might replace or simplify?
2. Are there ways in which the applications of information technology described in the case could inhibit role development in groups?
3. Would greater in-person contact positively or negatively affect the advantages of technology-mediated work groups found in this case?
4. How does the addition of new group members affect the relationship and interactions of an established small group?

REFERENCES

Bales & Slater. (1955). Role differentiation and small decision-making groups. Parsons & Bales (Eds.), *Family, Socialization and Interaction Process*, 259-306. MacMillian.

Biddle, B.J. (Ed). (1979). *Role Theory Concepts & Research*, Krieger Publishing Company.

Bormann, J.E. (1990). *Communicating in Small Groups: Theory and Practice* (5ᵗʰ ed). Harper and Row.

Finholt, T., Sproull, L. and Kiesler, S. (1990). Communication and performance in ad hoc task groups. Galegher, J., Krant, R. and Egido, C. (Eds.). *Intellectual Teamwork Social and Technological Foundations of Cooperative Work*. Hillsdale, NJ: Lawrence Erlbaum, 291-325.

Leavitt & Lipman-Blumen. (1995). Hot groups. *Harvard Business Review*, July, 109.

Lipnack, J., & Stamps, J. (1997). *Virtual Teams. Reaching Across Space, Time, and Organizations with Technology*. John Wiley and Sons.

Zigurs, I. & Kozar, K. (1994). An exploratory study of roles in computer supported groups. *MIS Quarterly*, 18(3), 277-294.

Chapter XV

The International Negotiation Modules Project: Using Computer-Assisted Simulation to Enhance Teaching and Learning Strategies in the Community College

Rosalind Latiner Raby
California State University, Northridge

Joyce P. Kaufman
Whittier College

INTRODUCTION

This chapter presents a case study of the International Negotiation Modules Project (INMP). The INMP utilized computer-assisted simulation is a tool to enhance teaching and learning strategies about international negotiations. Simulation in this context was more than merely playing a game or participating in a predefined exercise. Rather, it encompassed the entire class structure and affected all learning modalities. International topics that depicted real-life negotiation issues were incorporated into a simulation that was infused into a wide range of selected community college classes, including English, French Language, Math, and Psychology. The non-conventional pairing of disciplines, the non-traditional use of integrated technology, and the often diverse student bodies enhanced the overall quality of the simulation and the direct learning experience.

Moreover, the INMP demonstrated a direct relevance for the use of information technology in community colleges. In total, a cross-section of 30 community college classes participated in the three-year pilot project. They represented both rural and urban areas across California, Hawaii, Maryland, New York, and Texas. This case addresses critical issues such as methods involved in implementing alternative instruction and information technology, effects of its implementation on the faculty and students, and problems associated with Internet technology access.

CASE QUESTIONS
- How can the integration of technology across the curriculum be used as a tool for research and communication?

- Should students be expected to acquire computer literacy skills in a class that is not explicitly technology related?
- In what ways can computer-assisted communication be used to develop global perspectives?

CASE NARRATIVE

Background

The International Negotiation Modules Project (INMP) grew from a collaboration between the University of Maryland ICONS Project, Whittier College, Immaculate Heart College Center, and the consortium, California Colleges for International Education (CCIE), whose membership currently includes more than 68 California community colleges. A $221,000 FIPSE Comprehensive Program Grant supported funding for the three-year pilot INMP project.

The International Negotiation Modules Project (INMP) adapted the International Communication and Negotiation Simulations (ICONS), a networked computer-assisted simulation of international negotiations, to the community college environment. ICONS was designed for application in political science and international relations classes at the University of Maryland. Over the past 20 years, it has expanded into high school social studies classes across the United States and in several countries around the world. ICONS is a proven pedagogical method that teaches students about international issues and the negotiation process, with computer technology as a tool to support the substantive issues.

ICONS software was developed at the University of Maryland and resides in an on-site host computer. This software was originally designed in the late 1970s as a text-based/DOS system, and was called POLNET (Political Network). In 1995, POLNET was radically updated to become a Wet-based Windows application usable on any computer. One factor that highlights the educational uniqueness of the ICONS software is that it allows the simulation coordinator to review all messages sent by all teams for content, accuracy, and language. This control center is called SIMCOM (from Simulation Control). During the course of a simulation, SIMCOM reviews and keeps a running record of all Internet interactions, and has the ability to communicate directly to each team. Even messages that are designated "private" in the context of the simulation can be viewed for educational purposes by SIMCOM.

ICONS's growth parallels the escalating use of technology and computer-assisted communication within post-secondary education. Its popularity also correlates with an increased recognition in education of the idea that the individual student constructs his or her own knowledge (Wilkenfeld and Kaufman, 1993; Torney-Purta, 1996; Vosniadou, 1996). An important aspect of the method of knowledge construction is that a student often enters a class with preconceived knowledge. It is only through active processing of new cognitive structures that this knowledge takes new meaning and becomes ingrained as part of the student's consciousness (Torney-Purta and Pavlov, 1998).

The connection of INMP to the community college environment was made because of the significant impact community colleges have on contemporary U.S. society. Within the United States, community colleges provide a wider range of educational choices and serve a greater proportion of youth than in any other nation (Raby and Tarrow, 1996). Indeed, in 1998, more than six million U.S. students enrolled in credit courses and four million in noncredit continuing education courses in more than 1,200 community colleges. This accounts for 45 percent of all higher education students and 52 percent of all noncredit adult and continuing education students. Of students attending four-year universities, 51 percent of all domestic and 25 percent of all international students were community college transfers. In 1998, in California alone, 1.8 million students attended 107 California community colleges, and 50 percent of California State University and 20 percent of University of California bachelor degree recipients were community college transfers (Raby, 1999). Most significant, however, is that for the majority of students community college remains their sole venue for higher education, as they provide educational opportunities for students whose academic background is lacking, who cannot afford university tuition, and who do not fit a traditional profile.

In the new century, the United States faces an undisputed need for community colleges to cultivate adults who are competent in dealing with the complexities of the world. With more than half of all U.S. college students currently enrolled in community colleges, these institutions find themselves on the post-secondary front lines. They face a challenging dual mission: to prepare students for continuing their education in a four-year setting and to provide critical training for direct applications in the work place. For both venues, all students must be able to meet the demands of an international, multicultural, and technologically advanced work force. It is now recognized that international issues are an integral part of every community college discipline and the task of internationalizing the curriculum not only can, but should, be internationalized in all areas of the college environment (Raby, 1999).

Adaptation of INMP to community colleges has at its root the introduction of innovative teaching methods to a non-traditional and often diverse student body. Community college students bring to the classroom backgrounds and skills that enrich the simulation experience in ways not seen with traditional undergraduate populations. Furthermore, a synergy exists between current community college computer literacy requirements and international education projects and the INMP, which inherently internationalizes any course in which it is implemented, and integrates computer technology into the learning experience. Therefore, the information technology that is learned as a result of the INMP experience assists community college students in both their education and for direct application in the current job market.

SELECTION AND DESIGN

In spring 1994, a small team of community college faculty and administrators from the nine-college Los Angeles Community College District were brought together to give input about what would be most important to them in the application of information technology in the classroom via INMP. Previous ICONS experiences indicated that the more faculty/participant ownership of the program that existed from the beginning, the greater the chances of success.

The uniqueness of the community college itself prompted three specific changes from the original ICONS model. First, INMP needed to be multi-disciplinary in its approach and applicable to academic, occupational, and vocational disciplines. This was a significant departure from ICONS which was utilized solely in political science and international relations classes. Secondly, each class represented either a nation-state or a non-state actor, whereas ICONS utilized only nation-state players. The combination of both voices reflected the way in which international discourse currently exists and reinforced knowledge that was pertinent to community college students—that negotiations occur at many levels. A primary objective of the INMP was not to train students to be professional negotiators (as it is often used in ICONS settings), but rather to provide a solid grounding that would enable students to understand and assess better the process of international relationships, communication, and most importantly, information technology. The skills gained were ones that would assist community college students in all future endeavors. The final objective was to fully incorporate information technology as an intricate component of the community college learning experience.

The first year of the pilot project included only faculty from California community colleges. California was chosen as the initial site because community colleges play a significant role in the higher education mix in the state. Thirty applications were received and nine faculty members were chosen to participate in Year One.[1] In the second year, INMP became a national program with the addition of colleges from Hawaii, Texas, and New York.[2] By the third, and final, year, more colleges were added to the mix from Maryland and across California.[3] Disciplines represented in the simulation over the three-year pilot program included "traditional" classes such as those that are included at the university level, as well as "non-traditional" classes such as English, French, Math, and Texas Government.[4] In addition, some faculty took the opportunity to team-teach the class with colleagues within, or even outside, their departments. What made INMP especially impressive, however, was not simply the number of colleges which participated, but rather the range of courses in which the simulation was integrated.

In total, more than 300 students participated in the program during the three-year period. The mean age was 25, with the youngest at 18 and the oldest at 49 with considerable variation in average age across locations. The ethnic backgrounds of students varied with college location, with many classes consisting predominantly of minority students. In all colleges, there was an almost even distribution of male and female students. Ninety percent of all students held a job for at least five hours a week during the semester in question. The consequence of such a mixture of students was that the skills required in information technology were ones that could be readily ascertained by all students.

Implicit in INMP was the infusion of international perspectives and technological skills into any course through innovative and creative means. The use of networked computers employed both active and collaborative forms of learning. Throughout the INMP, students were cast in the role of decision-makers for specific countries or non-state actors, and their task was to work together to solve common problems. The simulation engaged students by enabling them to understand better how different countries and cultures perceive contemporary thematic and policy issues, along with building skills towards the international negotiations and communication process. Although problems exist with the use of simulations, the benefits in the case of the INMP far outweighed the drawbacks, as the simulation remained an effective teaching tool because it engaged students and made them active participants in the learning process (Kaufman, 1998a).

Faculty participants received a small monetary stipend for participation in the program. They were selected based on four criteria: 1) demonstration of accessible technology at the college for faculty and students; 2) administration support; 3) faculty interest in making their teaching style more effective; and 4) faculty and college interest to help broaden students' perspectives about the world, regardless of the discipline, by internationalizing their curriculum. Final consideration of candidates was also contingent upon assuring a geographical balance between urban/rural, majority/minority, and west coast/east coast community colleges. In addition, a balance in terms of the substance of the courses taught was also sought. "Non-Traditional" courses were emphasized as this breadth contributed to the use of INMP to internationalize across a range of disciplines. All faculty members were required to attend a two-day training orientation in the Fall semester and participate in an online debriefing session in the Spring.

During the Fall, there was a faculty orientation workshop. Faculty members were instrumental in choosing their "country," deciding whether their class would act as a state or non-state actor, and providing the issues that were to be represented in the negotiation scenario. Country selection was dependent upon personal interest, course content, and student composition. For example, Hartnell College, which is located in Salinas, California, represented the Philippines, because of the large Filipino population that resides in the city and attends the college. The match of "country" to the student population at each participating community college also allowed incorporating both international student and immigrant student populations as a project resource. Selected issues corresponded to existing curriculum guidelines for each class, so that required course content would not be neglected during the semester in question. Therefore, integration of INMP into a class required significant work and preparation on the part of each faculty member, and the method of choosing issues that were woven into the scenario also reflected the need to be broad enough to be relevant to a range of courses.

In Year One, two topics were chosen that reflected the curricular needs of all participating faculty: international trade and global ethics. International trade had been a standard issue in all ICONS simulations because of the role it plays in the international system. Global Ethics, however, introduced a new topic pertaining to the rights and responsibilities countries have toward one another. By couching the issue in broad and general terms, the teams addressed human rights, the environment, and natural disasters as part of this discussion area. The two broad topics satisfied the needs of all faculty in the project from World History to English, Geography, Sociology, and Psychology. In the second year, the increased number of faculty allowed for five issues to be selected: 1) international trade/development—highlighting free trade zones, global inequalities, and ways to foster trade across trade blocs; 2) drug trafficking—including narco-terrorism; 3) nuclear proliferation—focusing on the spread of nuclear technology; 4) human rights—aimed at whether countries can arrive at an acceptable definition of human rights based on the Universal Declaration of Human Rights; and 5) immigration/migration—concentrating on the movement of peoples within and across borders.

All faculty agreed that the issues in the scenarios were strong enough for all students to be able to make vital links between the real world, the simulation, and the course materials. In the final year, five issues again were chosen: 1) international trade—emphasizing the World Trade Organization; 2) environment—specifically addressing ways in which countries could implement the December 1997 Kyoto agreement; 3) health—with an emphasis on what countries can do to stop the spread of AIDS and other STDS; 4) drugs—including drug trafficking and crop substitution; and 5) human rights—with an emphasis on issues surrounding immigration, migration, and refugees. This particular mix of issues was applicable across all courses in which INMP was implemented.

Prior to the Spring semester, the INMP scenario was written by the simulation director in such a way that it reflected the issues and countries discussed in the orientation workshop.

Each year, the scenario reflected the needs, interests, and curricular constraints of the particular mix of participating faculty. The curriculum director later guided participants in various techniques for infusing this scenario within their total course structure. Within the first two weeks of the Spring semester, all faculty members shared with their students the particularities of project participation, the technology requirements, and the internationalized curriculum.

The first task was for each faculty to guide their students in researching their role as a specific country, that country's perspective on the selected issues, and the perspectives of the other countries represented in the simulation. Introduction to Internet research, e-mail exchanges with other classes in selected countries, and reading online international English-language newspapers facilitated this process. For many students, this exercise constituted their first introduction to information technology. At the conclusion of the research component, each class produced a position paper outlining their views and strategies for the negotiation simulation.

The second component of the INMP was the simulation itself. During a four-week period, student teams engaged in direct communication with other teams via e-mail. Students were not given any personal information about INMP participants outside their own classroom, such as what colleges they represented, where they lived, their gender, ethnicity, age, etc. In fact, extreme care was taken to preserve this secrecy, even if multiple classes from each campus participated. On the first day of the simulation, each team sent an opening message by e-mail to begin the negotiation process. They also received messages from other country teams. This process of sending and receiving comments, strategies, and basic information facilitated the learning process.

During the four-week period, SIMCOM analyzed all messages sent and provided direct feedback to each team. At the conclusion of the four-week period, a series of "summits"—90-minute real-time chats—were offered, to which all teams were invited. There was one "summit" scheduled for each theme. During the "summits," teams could engage in both public (where all teams received all messages), and private (where one team sent a private message to another team) negotiations. SIMCOM moderated all exchanges for their educational content. One challenge was to establish real-time "summits" in which all community colleges, from New York to Hawaii, could participate. It attests to the success of the program that students would participate in these sessions, even when they occurred in the early morning or late evening hours.

At the conclusion of the four-week simulation, there was an online briefing and wrap-up. It was decided not to do a face-to-face meeting because that would demystify the players and minimize the total learning experience. For the remainder of the semester, the INMP faculty continued to refer to the simulation in support of their course curriculum.

PLANNING AND IMPLEMENTATION

In both the planning and implementation stages, four external factors emerged as being potential problems to be addressed. The first concerned accessibility to and quality of technology. INMP depended on student and faculty access to technology when and as often as needed. In many cases, unfortunately, this was not available. Even in cases where an institution promised support, it was not always forthcoming. Many participating faculty lacked access to computer facilities and technological support due, in part, to unwillingness on the part of the institution to commit computer resources to the program. In Years Two and Three, this problem was addressed by requiring a letter of commitment from each participating college's Director of Instructional Technology, Computing Services, or the equivalent to ensure technological support. While helpful, it did not alleviate all the problems. In general, colleges that had the most successful experience were those with the easiest access to the technology, and conversely, the most difficult were those where access to the technology was blocked or limited. Since the success of a technology-based program depends on access to that technology, it is essential to ensure that there is real commitment, support, and access for all faculty and student participants.

The second problem related to the administrative structure of community colleges in which administrative personnel frequently change positions and even colleges. Knowing this was a possibility from the onset, a letter of support and commitment from the Academic Vice President or Dean of Instruction was required in order to insure institutional commitment to the faculty member. Unfortunately, obtaining a letter did not necessarily mean that the administrator was fully aware of the program, nor that he or she was willing to commit resources to implement or support the program, nor even that all promises could be kept. During the duration of the pilot, several Deans who signed the required letter pledging support left mid-year, leaving the faculty member working virtually alone or with a new Dean who knew nothing of the project. Although this was not true in all cases, a lack of administrative support, coupled with unfulfilled promises, contributed to frustration of the faculty. One conclusion that can be drawn from the pilot is that campus-wide support is a critical part of each college's contribution to the project.

One of the more surprising problems was an element of jealousy between traditional technology disciplines at the college and the incorporation of a non-traditional discipline with information technology. Several faculty members had to compete with colleagues outside their department for computer time/access and sometimes needed to confront jealous colleagues within their own department who also wanted to access these labs. Clearly, this type of jealousy or even hostility is not unique to community colleges. However, what made the problem especially difficult was that the resources for many community colleges are severely limited. Hence, this was defined by some to be a "zero-sum" situation—i.e., if one faculty member was promised additional resources or the use of a computer lab, then another (perhaps equally as deserving) faculty member would not have it.

Finally, in retrospect, it remains unclear whether the INMP would ever have been created without FIPSE funding. The FIPSE grant provided the start-up costs that included recruiting, training, development of materials, on-site school visits, face-to-face debriefing sessions, and evaluations. These costs were far too high to be accomplished successfully without external funds. The FIPSE grant also covered each individual college's participation fees. Since the INMP was created specially for the community college structure and had to be tailored to reflect the individual diversity of each college, the start-up costs were significant. After the first year, on-going costs included supporting and upgrading technology, annual connection to ICONS at the University of Maryland, production and dissemination of an instructor's manual, annual training sessions, and biannual evaluations. During the project's duration, the cost for on-site visits to the local colleges was not an issue, but the costs to colleges outside the Los Angeles area were included in the overall budget.

Faculty Participation

A consistent theme throughout the INMP was that of faculty participation. Faculty chose which countries and actors their class would represent, helped choose the themes of the simulation, and were active participants in altering both their curriculum and teaching methods. They also were engaged in evaluation of the program itself. At the end of each Spring semester, an online debriefing session was conducted in which faculty evaluated the program from their individual perspectives.

The primary requirement for successful implementation was a willingness to look at a class from a new and often different perspective and to be open to new ways in which to teach that class. For example, in the class entitled "Anger and Conflict Management," the professor previously focused on micro-levels of conflict (between individuals). For the INMP, the class was modified to illustrate macro-level and micro-level conflict (as it exists among individuals at the international level, and how negotiation can be an important conflict resolution tool at each of those levels). Another professor, who implemented INMP in a required English class, initially met with opposition from students who could not understand how representing China and participating in the simulation could help improve their writing and grammar skills. However, over time, students agreed with the professor that the primary basis of the INMP is writing and that they were doing more research, writing, and analysis than they would have been expected to do otherwise in a more traditional introductory English class.

Finally, teaching methodologies were positively affected by the INMP as faculty assumed the role of facilitators while students became directly involved in and responsible for their own learning. The use of collaborative groups facilitated this process, as students needed to work together in groups to do research and to draw and act upon conclusions. As members of a team, students needed to research their groups' position on a range of predefined issues, and in the process students were encouraged to create and test negotiating strategies, collect and analyze information from different perspectives, and make decisions based on prior research over the course of the simulation. Effective communication skills (among those in their own group, between other groups, and between other classes), critical thinking of content, and ability to use the Internet for research and communication were vital ingredients of the INMP process.

Challenges

Significant alteration to the way in which faculty teach as well as what they teach was an inherent part of the INMP. Faculty had to make an extra effort while in the classroom, as they modified their course to allow the INMP to support the subject content and to encourage students to participate in a different way. Two examples are the use of group learning dynamics and the transition of the INMP from teacher to facilitator. Special techniques involved in internationalizing the curriculum and in utilizing information technology were provided at orientation workshops and through consultations with an international curriculum specialist. For some faculty, these revisions were consistent with what they had been doing and required relatively minor modifications beyond simply incorporating the scenario. For others, however, INMP was a radical departure that required major rethinking of their classes. As a result, careful training and preparation of faculty was essential.

Another challenge was to keep students involved and prevent a large attrition that was likely because the course had become so different from what students normally expected.

While some faculty felt that a larger than normal number of students did drop the INMP class, all agreed that those who stayed were more committed and excited about what they were learning. In fact, one faculty member noted a higher retention rate in the required 20th Century World History Class than would otherwise exist, because of the program itself. A final challenge concerned the assessment of student performances, which because of the type of participation could not be appraised using traditional means. Hence, faculty had to make a concerted effort to determine how best to evaluate student learning in this non-traditional setting.

Bringing the faculty together, face-to-face, at the annual Fall orientation workshop helped to ease certain problems, while raising discussion on others. Experts were invited to lead discussions on topics that INMP faculty raised during the INMP experience. Other concerns emerged as a result of group discussion. One such issue involved use of the ICONS "POLNET" software, that during Year One caused extreme frustration as it was text driven and cumbersome. Faculty complaints resulted in a replacement, in the second year, to a Windows-based program that was noticeably more "user friendly." Another issue involved a lack of required communication structure during the period after the Fall workshop and up to the start of the simulation. During Year one, a communication structure was adhered to and there was much more cohesiveness among all faculty. During Years Two and Three, the communication structure was more lax, and this made a notable impact on the mood of the faculty and their inclination to work together as a team.

EVALUATION

One of the most important facets of the INMP was integration of technology across the curriculum as a tool for research and communication. Because communication is based on the written word, students' reading, writing, and critical thinking should improve as a result of this experience. In particular, careful evaluation of the program showed that nine goals were met (Kaufman, 1998b).

Goal 1. To acquire factual knowledge

Acquisition of factual knowledge about particular countries and the international system occurred throughout the program. Initially, students had to learn about the country that they represented and that country's position on particular international issues and negotiating strategies. Later, students had to learn about the same issues from other countries' perspectives so that they could negotiate in a realistic fashion. It is clear from reading student-written evaluations that this objective was met (Kaufman, 1998b):

> I've enjoyed spending hours in different book stores reading about Malaysia and other Pacific Rim countries. I now own a world encyclopedia and have read quite a bit about other countries.

> I've come to realize that the Business section of the *LA Times* is not so boring after all and is actually very interesting. I have been able to carry intelligent conversations with my own opinions when talking about the pros and cons of open trade, NAFTA and GATT.

> On an academic level I have enjoyed the experience of learning how to begin a research project, document my sources of information, and write an essay

objectively. Another benefit I gained from this project was definitely a deeper understanding of and greater interest in world affairs at large .... In closing, I would just like to reiterate how very much this experience has opened my eyes to many issues the world faces today.

The internal evaluator's final report further substantiated significant student growth in factual knowledge (Torney-Purta and Pavlov, 1998).

Goal 2. To illustrate interconnections among issues

On the cognitive level, the nature of the representation of knowledge was enhanced as students assessed connections between concepts. Pre-testing indicated that the concept maps of novices were relatively sparse, consisting of a few poorly understood concepts with few links to other concepts. As the student acquired new knowledge and experiences, those linkages became more numerous and significantly stronger. Realization that decisions cannot be made in one country without affecting other countries became manifest not only in the way in which students' perception of the world changed, but also in the different manners in which they looked at international and immigrant students on their own campus as a result of this experience. By the end of the simulation, students drew the obvious conclusion that the world is becoming smaller and more interconnected (Kaufman, 1998b).

Goal 3. To secure decision-making skills and to understand the role of negotiation in the context of the world

During the semester, students became familiar with policy decisions, how those decisions were generated, and how they could support their own decisions. This type of learning occurred on different levels throughout the simulation. Initial negotiations began as students within the same class were divided into teams. Students learned first to negotiate within their own group and then within their own class team in order to arrive at a single position that they all could agree upon. They then had to negotiate with teams from other classes/countries in order to see if they could reach agreement on the issues within the confines of the INMP scenario. Those negotiation and communication skills that they learned are invaluable when applied in the work place, as part of further schooling, or at home.

Goal 4. To enhance critical thinking skills

From preparation to the simulation itself, students learned to address problems and formulate negotiating strategies that enable them to achieve solutions. Students were put in a position of not only responding to input from other country teams, but, simultaneously, reevaluating and adjusting their own positions and ideas. At the conclusion of the INMP, during the debriefing stage, the students analyzed and assessed the experience, tying their "hands-on" experience to the theories that they had studied in class. All forms of evaluation indicated that such critical analysis did occur in the classroom.

Goal 5. To foster communication skills

Group efforts helped foster an understanding and appreciation of collaboration, which ceases to exist without effective communication. On the individual level, students needed to communicate their own ideas to other students. Writing about these ideas was important, but a vital contribution to learning also occurred as students voiced those ideas to other students and sharpened them through discussion with classmates. Situations in which students moved back and forth between written and oral expressions are of special value in the process of knowledge construction. INMP encouraged both modes—written messages sent during the simulation and face-to-face group discussion within their own teams. Two students summarized what was learned:

> I learned how to work together as a group to set our goals and to deal with [those goals] with other trading partners.

> The most valuable part of this experiment is allowing me to express my opinions on different issues and to hear the viewpoints from other students. Many students had different viewpoints that help us think and challenge us. Education involves communication. Without communication, being educated is useless.

Goal 6. To acquire skills that can be used in the workplace

The INMP was structured so that students were required to work together in groups to solve real-world problems, master technology in a number of forms, learn negotiation techniques, and apply in practice ideas that they learned in theory. During the simulation, they also developed a familiarity and comfort level with global economic issues and a context within which they could address such issues in the workplace. The comments of the students themselves identified the level of success in achieving this objective:

> [...] with thorough preparation things go much smoother. I guess I can say that from this project, I learned a little about life. That is, the value of being prepared.

> I have learned some economic concepts and business details. It really helped me to develop my knowledge, especially [since] my major is business.

> This activity also opened my eyes to a new 'economic' perspective that I had never paid attention to before. I was also introduced to the Asian way of thinking that is valuable knowledge if one is to live in a truly global community.

Goal 7. To develop a global perspective and enhance one's association of cultural differences

One outcome was to increase students' abilities to look at the world from a different, and wider, angle of vision. Through the experience, not only did students view the world differently, but they also started to see one another differently as well. The relatively large number of immigrant and international students in the community college population became an asset, as students gained new appreciation for their classmates that in many cases fostered self-esteem skills. Even when students were not officially enrolled in the class, many students became "advisors," helping the members of the class understand more fully the country, culture, and context that they were representing. Again, evidence of the students' changing perspectives can be found in their comments:

I learned to appreciate the differences between cultures.

I learned that each country had its own way of making themselves powerful and using that source to negotiate with other countries. What was interesting was the smaller countries still had a lot to offer, and in some cases the smaller countries were more powerful than the larger countries.

Goal 8. To enhance use and understanding of computer technology

In that, the INMP was designed to utilize computer technology to support class content and, through it, the learning experience. One of the most important programmatic objectives was to enhance computer literacy in a way that was not intrusive but rather supportive of the larger educational goals. A secondary goal was to have the student be able to take charge of technology in the learning process, rather than allow technology to control the student. Realization that computer literacy is an important skill for both college-bound and work-oriented students strengthens technology as an integral aspect of the curriculum and learning experience. The INMP focused faculty on finding ways to encourage students to use the Internet even more as a tool for their work, but, most importantly, it validated that technological innovations introduced into the classroom must have a context. Introducing the use of technology is not sufficient unless it can be tied into and used to support the substance of the course. While the computer software gave students the tools for research and negotiation, it was the learning that took place within the context of substance that showed pre/post-test change.

Goal 9. To make a significant impact in the way participating faculty teach

Emphasis on active and cooperative learning, both of which remain central to the INMP, facilitated student learning. An Austin Community College professor, who teaches Texas State and Local Government, wrote of the experience:

I teach Texas State and Local Government and had to work very hard to demonstrate to students links between global issues and our state. The experience turned out to be a great learning challenge for me and them...I now teach the course very differently in order to stress to the students the importance of understanding that there is often a direct impact of national and international policies on the state of Texas, a linkage that students had not been making previously. Because of the simulation, the students could see the direct impact of NAFTA on the economy of Texas, or what a change in the immigration laws means to their state directly.

Another faculty member from Hawaii stressed that students loved the idea of working in a setting where they had to take responsibility for their education, a point which was echoed by some of the students in their written evaluations.

ANALYSIS

Throughout the course of the pilot, it became apparent that the INMP is not for all faculty members. A number of faculty joined the program with great enthusiasm but found that it was far more difficult to implement than they had expected. As the simulation is student-centered, it meant giving up "control" of the classroom, something that not all faculty were comfortable doing. Furthermore, it entailed teaching a familiar subject quite differently. The use of technology was very frustrating to some, either because they could not get access to it or were simply not comfortable with it themselves. INMP further required that faculty utilize different types of procedures to evaluate student learning. However, those faculty who did stay with the program became very committed to it and maintained that it significantly altered the way in which they teach not only the INMP course, but other courses as well. They appreciated the differences that they witnessed in their students, and the individual growth that occurred from participating in a program such as this one (Kaufman, 1998b; Torney-Purta and Pavlov, 1998).

From the outset, it was speculated that there would be a demonstrable increase in student learning. To determine this, a multi-faceted evaluation model was designed to answer questions about student learning. In addition, such evaluation would provide feedback from which modifications could be made to strengthen the program.

On the micro level, pre- and post-tests on issues and concepts that were addressed in the course of the simulation helped to evaluate individual student learning. Developed by the second evaluator, these tests measured cognitive learning (what students learned about politics, economics, culture, and other specific forms of knowledge) and procedural knowledge (what students learned to do in actual negotiations). The evaluation indicated that INMP students:

1. Learned more and retained more than students who were in "traditional" classes
2. Substantially increased their knowledge of the issues and saw more relationships between both abstract and concrete concepts which were central to discussions (not just concepts in one area such as economics or human rights)
3. Felt highly involved in the decision-making process and believed that they have contributed cognitively to it
4. Developed critical thinking skills
5. Became involved in the group process which surrounded the project
6. Excelled when involved with the computer aspects of the program, even though some had been most reluctant to participate in class discussions

In general, the experience using the INMP had a particular effect on the construction of knowledge, which reinforces the notion that when students are directly engaged in their learning, they internalize a new vision of knowledge. The INMP, by making group work and discussion a central part of the program, is extremely effective for constructing knowledge among community college students.

It is significant to note that many students indicated that they learned from the reading and writing assignments, while others noted that they learned and benefited more from on-going discussions that were very much a part of the simulation. Evaluations concurred that the INMP was especially appropriate in meeting the needs of many of the older non-traditional community college students, who "reported participating more fully in both the cognitive aspects of the simulation experience and in helping their group's functioning" (Torney-Purta and Pavlov, 1998, p. 11).

Torney-Purta compared the results of the community college INMP to a simultaneous ICONS simulation with University of Maryland students participating. She found both groups had high involvement, were engaged, and this was positively correlated to student learning. Community college students started the semester with less cognitive knowledge, but by the end of the semester had the same level of knowledge as those in the university setting—i.e., the learning curve was steeper for community college students (Torney-Purta and Pavlov, 1998). In short, evaluations confirmed the hypothesis that community college students who participated in the INMP learned and benefited from it directly.

Annual orientation and evaluation workshops, conducted by INMP staff for participating faculty, were designed to reflect upon what transpired during the previous year and to plan for subsequent years, incorporating changes as necessary. For example, limited access to technology, class expectations that were unclear to students, and non-traditional class structure were concerns echoed in the first year which were dealt with in the second workshops and were not noted as problems subsequently (Kaufman, 1998b).

Many faculty shared anecdotal evaluations that provided important feedback about what occurred in each classroom. This allowed each faculty member to assess issues that were unique to institution/class, and to highlight particular achievements. A Leeward Community College (Hawaii) faculty noted a significant benefit of INMP was the ongoing communication with students from the "Mainland." A professor from Austin Community College (Texas), an urban, largely minority college, found that the program brought out leadership skills in her students. She also was able to create a situation in which the diversity of her classroom was a benefit. A professor from Los Angeles Valley Community College (California) noted that one of the Chinese students "blossomed" as the class represented China. In addition, an e-pal exchange with a group of graduate students in China who were learning English added an international dimension that further helped to improve students' learning. Finally, a faculty member from rural Butte Community College (northern California) started integrating technology into the teaching of all classes, because of the acquired firsthand knowledge of technology uses.

The evaluation process also raised pedagogical concerns. The Los Angeles Valley College faculty, whose students played China, noted that:

> I am both pleased and perturbed. I am pleased that this class reached so many students, all of whom describe themselves as non-verbal learners, those not inclined to enjoy the lecture format. They loved the set-up-and-move environment of group work, although the chaotic nature of the curriculum combined with the sheer volume of work often threatened to overwhelm them. I am perturbed because I worry that the simulation and its research requirements might have interfered with the success of those students who are likely to fail the course. I keep thinking of all those lessons on reading and writing that they might have missed had we not been involved with this project. But bored students don't do well either; they were not bored. I am on the whole encouraged by what the students themselves had to say about Kung Fu English.

All faculty observed that students seemed to be better prepared for the future because they learned to think critically, and they saw self-esteem increase as a result of the responsibility inherent in the program that, in turn, contributed to the students' setting higher expectations for themselves.

CONCLUSIONS

Both anecdotal information, formal evaluations, and the experience itself confirm that incorporation of INMP into community college classes helped to increase students' understanding of international issues and perspectives, and learning the joys of diversity within their school community. Furthermore, international and immigrant students found a special role in the INMP process. In addition, computer literacy, writing, and critical thinking skills were all significantly enhanced during the simulation. Hence, INMP became an innovative approach to community college teaching and learning.

One of the more surprising outcomes of the INMP was the unintended consequence of securing information technology competency for both students and participating faculty. All of the participating faculty noted that upon completion of the program, they intended to incorporate technology into the remainder of their classes either through Web pages, bulletin boards, and/or e-mail assignments.

Replication of this model requires that potential problems that are unique to community colleges be addressed. Some examples are frequently revolving administrators, inequitable use of technology on campus, and students who may question non-traditional teaching methods. This does not suggest that problems were consistent across all colleges nor does it mean that all projects involving community colleges will have these problems. Quite the contrary; in some cases, colleges were extremely cooperative and supportive from the administrators through faculty. Indeed, the many successful faculty had support from their administrators from the beginning. Requiring administrators to attend the Fall workshop would have ensured administrative enthusiasm and sustained institutional support. Finally, in an age where every institution of higher learning talks about the importance of computer literacy, the project staff were stymied simply by the lack of access to the technology on some campuses. This was not anticipated when the program was planned.

This program was envisioned as a way to significantly alter community college curriculum by adding an international dimension across a range of disciplines, reforming teaching methodologies and curriculum design, and enhancing computer literacy. As implemented in the community colleges, INMP took advantage of the non-traditional nature of the students and their special skills and interests. It incorporated significant advances to a proven simulation program by developing negotiation scenarios appropriate to applied areas of international discourse. It expanded the ways in which technology is used across the curriculum and altered significantly the ways in which faculty members teach. Both students and faculty members who participated in the INMP benefited from the experience academically and personally. Finally, in that the INMP blends together an emphasis on raising technology and international literacy skills, it fulfills an important need for community colleges for the new century.

DISCUSSION QUESTIONS

1. How can technology be used to promote curricular reform? What type of effort is required?

2. How did the simulation project assist students in developing a global perspective and enhancing their understanding of cultural differences?
3. How did the simulation assist students in developing decision making and critical analysis skills? What else might the simulation have been used for?

EPILOGUE

From the outset, the goal was to create a program that would be institutionalized by the conclusion of the three-year FIPSE grant. Even though start-up costs would no longer be a concern, it remained apparent that the INMP is expensive to run. At the final Fall workshop held during the grant period, all faculty were reminded that participation in the post-grant period simulation would be contingent upon either securing additional grant funds or payment of participation fees. Faculty were reminded that, since grant funds are far from assured, they needed to begin dialogue with their own institutions to raise the required funds.

The costs required to duplicate this program have remained relatively low because the prototype has already been established. The duplication costs depend on the particularities of the program, such as how many colleges are participating, the distance between the colleges, the number of classes in each college, the number of total faculty participants, etc. These costs can typically range from $700-$1,200.

The FIPSE-funded portion of the INMP concluded in June 1998. During the 1998-1999 academic year, a smaller, yet equally successful implementation of INMP occurred among six community colleges (one from New York, another from Texas, another from Hawaii, and three from California). Four of the colleges from the pilot program continued and an additional two others were added. A larger program was implemented during the 1999-2000 academic year with 12 participating colleges from across the United States.

REFERENCES

Kaufman, J.P. (1998a). Using simulation as a tool to teach about international negotiation. *International Negotiation,* 3, 59-75.

Kaufman, J.P. (1998b). The International negotiation modules project: Integrating international simulation into the community College. *FIPSE Grant Final Report.* Unpublished document.

Raby, R.L., and Tarrow, N., (Eds.). (1996). Dimensions of the community college: international and inter/multicultural perspectives. *Garland Studies in Higher Education,* 6(1075). New York: Garland Pub., Inc.

Raby, R.L. (1999). *Looking to the Future: Report on International and Global Education in California Community Colleges.* Sacramento: State Chancellor, California Community Colleges.

Starkey, B., and Wilkenfeld, J. (1996). Project INCONS: Computer-assisted negotiations for the IT classroom. *International Studies Notes,* 21(1), 25-29.

Torney-Purta, J. (1996). Conceptual changes among adolescents using computer-networks in group-mediated international role playing. S. Vosniadou et al. (Eds.), *International Perspectives on the Design of Technology Supported Learning Environments.* Hillsdale, N.J.: Erlbaum.

Torney-Purta, J., and Pavlov, V. (1998). Evaluation Report: International Negotiations Modules Project—Integrating International Simulation in the Community College. *FIPSE Grant Final Report.* Unpublished document.

Vosniadou, S. et al. (Eds.). (1996). *International Perspectives on the Design of Technology Supported Learning Environments*. Hillsdale, NJ: Erlbaum.

Wilkenfeld, J., and Kaufman, J. (1993). Political science: Network simulation in international politics. *Social Science Computer Review,* 11(4).

ADDITIONAL RESOURCES

ICONS Home Page <http://www.icons.umd.edu/about/index.html>

ENDNOTES

1. In the first year of the grant, participants included faculty from the following California community colleges: Butte Community College, Canada Community College, Hartnell Community College, Los Angeles Valley Community College (two faculty members), Mt. San Antonio Community College, Pasadena Community College, Rio Hondo Community College, and San Jose Community College.

2. Second-year participants included faculty from the following colleges: CALIFORNIA COLLEGES: Butte Community College; Canada Community College; East Los Angeles Community College; Hartnell Community College; Los Angeles Valley Community College; Los Angeles Harbor Community College; Mt. San Antonio Community College; Rio Hondo Community College; San Jose City Community College; HAWAII COLLEGES: Kapiolani Community College; Leeward Community College; NEW YORK COLLEGE: Jamestown Community College; TEXAS COLLEGES: Austin Community College; Tomball Community College; Tyler Junior College.

3. Final-year participants included faculty from the following colleges: CALIFORNIA COLLEGES: Butte Community College; Canada Community College; Long Beach Community College; Los Angeles Harbor Community College; Marin Community College. The following colleges had two faculty participants: East Los Angeles Community College; Los Angeles Valley Community College; Los Angeles Mission Community College; San Diego Mesa Community College. EAST COAST COLLEGES: Jamestown Community College (New York); Prince George Community College (Washington, DC); HAWAII COLLEGES: Kapiolani Community College (two faculty); Leeward Community College; TEXAS COLLEGES: Austin Community College; Tomball Community College; and Tyler Junior College.

4. Examples of INMP "traditional" classes are: International Relations, Political Science, World Civilizations and World History. Examples of INMP "non-traditional" classes are: American Government; American Studies; Business (International and Introductory); Economic (Introductory); English (Composition, Grammar, and 20th Century Literature); French Language; Geography (Cultural, Physical and Economic); Government; History; Latin American Studies; Management; Math; Political Science; Psychology (Anger and Conflict Management); Religion; Social Science; Sociology (Culture and Migration); and Texas Government.

Chapter XVI

The Harvey Project: Open Course Development and Rich Content

Robert S. Stephenson
Wayne State University

INTRODUCTION

The rise of the Internet has started a knowledge revolution whose extent can only be guessed at. The last revolution of this magnitude, brought on by the printing press, led to the proliferation of books and the rise of the modern university system. If universities are to survive the latest knowledge revolution, they must adapt with unaccustomed speed and learn how to use the Internet for more effective teaching.

Most universities adopt a limited approach to building on-line courses. However, many studies have found that merely transplanting materials to the Web does not significantly improve learning (Russell, 1999). In fact, handouts, slides, and viewgraphs that have been "repurposed" for the Web are sometimes derisively referred to as "shovelware" (Fraser, 1999). So while moving existing materials to the Web may increase their accessibility, it will not necessarily improve their effectiveness.

The Internet's real value as a medium and teaching platform is that it makes possible rich, interactive content such as simulations, animations, and 3-D models. These learning objects, or rich content, can significantly enhance learning, especially in the sciences, and can be just as useful inside the classroom as outside. The difficulty is how to create this enhanced content, since the task demands a broad range of technical skills and enormous effort. Besides faculty domain experts and experienced teachers, rich content development typically requires illustrators, Web designers, programmers, instructional designers, testers, and Webmasters. The only way faculty and institutions can meet this challenge is to embrace collaboration more broadly and seriously than they have in the past. One approach is the multi-institutional consortium. Another solution is a collaboration of faculty to build rich content in their discipline. This chapter chronicles an example of the latter sort: a bottom-up, cross-institutional project.

For such a grass roots collaboration to succeed, it must recruit many faculty pioneering the use of the Internet in their teaching, as well as artists and technical professionals. It must offer collaborators an incentive to participate, and it must attract not only volunteers, but also institutional and agency funding as well. Finally, as a pioneering project, it must create standards and develop paradigms as it goes. This case study describes a work-in-progress to solve these issues.

CASE QUESTIONS

- What is the best example you have seen of pedagogically effective rich content? What makes it effective? Could it be improved??
- What tools were used to create it? How much effort do you think its production required?
- Can you think of faculty who are pioneering the development of rich content in their discipline today?
- What incentives might motivate teachers and researchers to collaborate within their discipline and build rich content?

CASE NARRATIVE

Background

For the last three years, the author has taught an on-line human physiology course (http://www.science.wayne.edu/~bio340). The course has both lecture and Internet-only sections, and it is based on 600 static Web pages (converted from PowerPoint) as well as RealVideo asynchronous broadcast of the videotaped lectures and an electronic discussion board.

Although students in this course seem to grasp the superficial details easily, many have great difficulty understanding and manipulating the physiological principles that underlie the material. Physiology, like many sciences, deals with complex chains of causality and laws of chemistry and physics that are generally remote from students' everyday experience. To convey these notions more effectively they need to be brought to life for the students. This requires simulations so students can experience for themselves the consequences of these laws, animations so they can grasp complicated dynamic processes, and 3-D models so they can see how different molecular or anatomical structures are related.

An innovative approach was needed to build the rich content necessary to take the course to the next level. On the one hand, the University was neither willing nor able to help with this enterprise (at that point there was only one other on-line class in the entire university). On the other hand, it was clear that the instructor could not attempt the task on his own. Because of the amount of time and skills required, the most that could be hoped for would be an incomplete and imperfect job that could be eclipsed at any time when another, better equipped and better funded effort came along.

The solution adopted was that physiology teachers and researchers should collaborate across institutions to develop world-class rich content for physiology, and make these materials freely available to other faculty and institutions. Surprisingly, there was no precedent for such a collaboration in other disciplines of higher education, although there were a few distant parallels.[1]

This collaborative venture, which started in the summer of 1998, was named the Harvey Project after Sir William Harvey, a 17th Century English physician and teacher. A pioneer of physiology, Harvey was renowned for discovering the circulation of the blood and for the clarity of his exposition.

The Open Source Movement

Although the Harvey Project had no parallel in higher education, an excellent precedent exists in software development. One of the most successful models of software development has been the free or open source software movement. Individuals around the world who are interested in solving the same problem interact via the Internet, donating their time to contribute a small part of the overall project, making design and implementation decisions democratically, and producing a product that is entirely public and nonpropri-etary. Two of the foremost products of such cooperation have been GNU/Linux, a free version of the Unix operating system, and the Apache Web server.

The Linux operating system is running e-mail and other Internet services at large corporations and universities around the world. In fact, 31 percent of Internet servers are running Linux, more than any other operating system (*Wall Street Journal*, 1999). The Apache Web server is regarded by many as superior to its counterparts from Netscape and Microsoft, and is currently running on 60 percent of the world's servers (Inktomi, 2000). Even Microsoft is concerned about competition from the open source, free software model, according to internal documents.[2] The open source model has also been embraced on a limited basis by some large corporations such as Netscape, AOL, IBM, and Apple Computer.

The Harvey Project and Rich Content

The Harvey Project aims to create rich content and tools that will empower individual faculty to create their own world-class physiology courses. The project is not about creating an on-line course or textbook, nor is it about competing with existing institutions. It is a collaboration in support of physiology faculty everywhere.

The cornerstones of the Harvey Project are collaboration, peer review, standards, and openness. Together they define what could be called the "open course" development model.

Collaboration

Collaboration and widespread participation are essential to making the work move quickly. Without the participation of a broad community of educators and technical experts, the project would not be able to meet its ambitious objectives. A corollary of this collaborative philosophy is that the responsibility for teaching physiology becomes shared by the entire discipline. If examples in the field of software design are any guide, collaboration can lead to a more accurate and effective course because the material incorporates many different points of view. To paraphrase a motto of the open source movement, all errors become obvious when seen by enough eyes.

Peer Review

Materials developed under this paradigm must be peer reviewed to ensure that they are scientifically accurate, pedagogically effective, and technically sound before being released to the public. This triple review process is essential to ensure the quality and integrity of the content. It will bring the project a reputation for accuracy, usefulness, and trustworthiness. In addition to initial peer review, project materials will be subjected to careful use-testing at participating universities and further revised accordingly.

The reviewers are project members with a specialty and/or interest in the area concerned, and the e-mail reviews are rapid, constructive, and signed (i.e., not anonymous). When necessary, reviewers are recruited from outside the project. A number of project collaborators are active researchers, and they play an important role in ensuring the accuracy of proposed materials. Review for effectiveness proceeds in the same way, except that the principal reviewers are instructors and instructional designers.

Every set of materials has a "credits" link that lists those who participated in its creation and improvement, citing their specific roles. Reviewers are also credited. Besides ensuring the quality of the project, peer review is necessary so that contributors receive scholarly credit and recognition for their work. As much intellectual effort and scholarship are required to build a module of rich course materials as to write a chapter in a textbook or publish most research papers, and these need to be rewarded. Because the Harvey Project is peer reviewed, those who help build it can claim credit towards promotion, tenure, or raises. The more widely the Harvey materials are adopted, the greater the value of this credit.

Standards

Conformance to recognized standards is an essential part of the project. Technical standards ensure that different materials work together, and that they work well for most users. Design and interface standards ensure that project content is clear, effective, and easy to use. Other standards ensure that the materials are useful to the broadest group of students, and that they will interoperate with other teaching materials and educational systems.

All the Harvey Project materials are designed to be accessible from any platform with a Web browser such as Netscape Communicator, without additional plug-ins, and with only a modem connection to the Internet. Wherever possible, they are based on open standards. The technologies used include HTML, ECMAScript (a.k.a. Javascript), Java, PHP, and Macromedia Flash.

Project materials will incorporate the evolving IMS standard (IMS, 2000) for metadata to identify and describe individual blocks. The IMS also sets technical standards for exams and student tracking. The Project will support the ADA Web accessibility standards (Waddell, 1998). Although being developed initially in English only, they are designed with multiple language support in mind. Wherever possible, the Harvey Project will adopt standards for multiple language support and internationalization of embedded text. It is following the standard curricula developed by the American Physiological Society for medical schools (Carroll, 2000) and by the Human Anatomy and Physiology Society for undergraduates (HAPS, 1994). The project is developing its own standards for design of the Web pages and the user interface presented to the student. Adherence to all these standards is essential to ensure that the learning objects fit together seamlessly and that they be useful in a variety of different contexts.

Openness

Finally, openness means that educational institutions can use, copy, and modify the materials without charge so long as they give the original authors credit. Making the materials open encourages their widespread adoption and improvement. It also fosters a spirit of cooperation, non-competitiveness, and humanitarianism that helps attract others to the enterprise.

The Harvey Project holds copyright for project materials. The project license, similar to the copyleft of the Gnu project,[3] states that the materials are free for any nonprofit institution to use, distribute, or modify, but a) the original attribution must be maintained and b) any improvements must be re-released under the same license (and also resubmitted for peer review, if they are to remain part of the Harvey Project).

The project aims to create rich content for teaching all aspects of human physiology. When complete, these materials will cover physiology not only in its breadth but also in depth, since the range of materials is intended to satisfy students from advanced high school, through undergraduate and nursing schools, to medical and other professional schools. Specifically, the rich content includes animations, simulations, 3-D models, interactive problem solving, and on-line quizzes. It incorporates the best teaching materials and methods that are publicly available and is designed to help students master underlying principles. The learning objects are as interactive and stimulating as possible, so as to draw students into the material and foster interest and understanding.

The basic unit of the Harvey Project is a building block consisting of one or a few Web pages with embedded rich content that explains a basic concept, such as how myelin speeds propagation of the action potential, for example. Most blocks are designed to be useful in lectures and are therefore more graphical than textual.

So far, the project has completed half a dozen animations and simulations, with many more in the development pipeline.

Harvey Project Tools

From the beginning, Harvey Project members realized that many faculty found it difficult to incorporate rich content into their courses. This technical problem threatened to limit the Project's usefulness for more technically naive faculty. Another problem was how to make learning objects that could be both text-poor (for use in a lecture) and text-rich (for self-study). To address these issues the project is developing a suite of open source Java-based tools to build lecture presentations or on-line course modules easily out of individual Web pages.

The first of these, called Beads&String, is a system of navigation that allows a professor to choose which Web pages to cover in which order, like stringing beads for a necklace. The instructor then delivers this "string" to her or his students for them to follow. Beads&String means that faculty do not need to edit the HTML of each block to link them together. A "content browser" will allow them to specify which Web pages they want in which order, and it will create the "string" file for them. Beads&String allows one instructor to assign students learning objects A, B, D, and F, in that order, while another class may be using the same materials at the same time in the order F, E, B, A, and C.

Another tool, still under development, will allow an instructor to embed an optional audio explanation (possibly extracted from the class lecture) into a block for students to review on their own. In this way, the blocks resemble the display cases in museums that offer recorded descriptions at the push of a button.

A third tool will create on-line quizzes. Learning objectives and corresponding questions are associated with each building block. Questions from a number of blocks can be gathered into review quizzes at the end of each module. Students' performance on these will be tracked in a database and reported to the instructor. These data will also provide feedback to the Harvey Project on student mastery of the content and, therefore, on the effectiveness of project materials. In this way, project materials will be continually use-tested by participating universities and revised accordingly.

Although it provides rich content and quizzes, the Harvey Project will not include lectures or exams. To provide them would usurp the role of the individual faculty member, and a one-size-fits-all approach to these would surely be unsatisfactory. The project will also not host materials directly for student use. Instead, individual institutions will need to mirror the materials to their own Web servers and handle authentication and tracking of their own students. The project will, however, provide them with software, instructions, and, if necessary, technical support to accomplish this.

The Harvey Community

From its inception in July of 1998 until February 2000, the project has grown to 85 participants in eight countries. Members include physiology teachers, researchers, students, department heads, physicians, programmers, Web designers, and instructional designers. For the Harvey Project to succeed, however, physiologists around the world need to know about it.

To reach them, the project has been building relationships with professional societies such as the American Physiological Society, the Physiological Society (London) and the Human Anatomy and Physiology Society. Harvey Project members make presentations at national physiology meetings to make participants aware of the project and its materials, and to demonstrate how to use them. In addition, the Project has a Web site (http://harveyproject.org) which is both the focus of this on-line community, as well as a "portal" and "reputation manager"[4] for physiology.

The Web site includes a searchable database of physiological sites elsewhere on the Web. Each site is described and classified according to topic and whether it includes rich content. The list of sites is interactive, so anyone can add a new site to the list or make a comment on an existing one. The database currently includes about 600 Web pages.

Besides being a useful resource for physiologists, the database is also a good way to identify potential contributors. The most effective way to recruit participants to the Project has been to contact those who had started to build similar materials on their own. These developers have much-needed technical skills, are quick to understand the benefits of a collaboration such as the Harvey Project, and may have already built materials that can be incorporated directly into the Project.

Besides the database of physiology sites and a compendium of course materials developed by the Project, the Web site includes profiles of members, a calendar of events, and a list of ongoing projects. A version-tracking repository keeps records of who is working on which project, as well as saving the latest and all previous versions. Other collaborative tools include a list server, an on-line bulletin board, and conferences by both Internet chat and telephone. Plans include organizing an annual conference as a satellite to a national scientific meeting.

As a collaboration, the Harvey Project supports its members in many ways. It brings together participants with the various skills needed to build rich and effective content. It educates its members in the use of digital technology and effective methods of teaching. Through its members, it will provide technical support for institutions wishing to use its materials. This will provide a source of income both for the Project and for its members. The Project will offer more general expertise and consulting for institutions or companies wishing to develop rich content, and to other open course projects. It provides a means for members to receive publication credit for their contributions. Finally, it could provide a placement service for members whose skills are in demand.

ANALYSIS

In the past, faculty have often been reluctant passengers on the train to on-line course development. This is likely to change, however as universities come under increasing pressure to improve their teaching and develop on-line courses. Faculty may soon face a choice between losing their traditional teaching autonomy or participating actively in rich content development.

The Harvey Project includes technical experts who provide skills that faculty may lack. Many former faculty and students have quit their discipline to work in more lucrative computer-related fields and may be willing to contribute to a worthy program in their spare time. The lure of renown is a great motivator, and many of them may see helping to build the physiology courses of tomorrow as a valuable opportunity.

One of the benefits of the open course model is to open up the development process and reduce the barrier to participation. Every scientist has a stake in how his or her discipline is taught. Until now, the only way researchers could shape the teaching of their discipline was to author a major textbook, something few can find the time to do. The collaborative development model allows researchers, teachers, professionals, scientific societies, and even graduate students to contribute to what is taught and how it is taught, and therein lies its great power.

Richard Dawkins (1990) coined the term "meme" to describe the unit of cultural inheritance that reproduces itself non-genetically in human society. Among other things, knowledge in a discipline consists of memes. It is in the interest of every researcher to ensure that the memes of her or his specialty get transmitted accurately to future generations. Without that, research in the field would stagnate due to a lack of trained graduate students, and society would be less likely to fund a field that it does not understand. That is a strong motivation for researcher participation in open course development. Researchers are also used to working in science collaboratively, based on openness, standards and peer review. Conversely, researcher participation is the best guarantee that course materials will be complete and accurate. The lesson from the open source movement is that as more developers contribute to a product, it becomes more rigorous, effective, and useful.

Even the venerable doctoral dissertation can be an engine for developing Internet-based teaching materials. Most theses contain a chapter that reviews the literature in their specialized area. With encouragement and direction from his faculty advisor, a graduate student in the Harvey Project has chosen to develop Chapter I as a series of interactive animations that will become part of the Project. In this way, the dissertation is transformed from a rather sterile, academic exercise into a contribution that will help shape how physiology is taught. It will also help ensure that Project materials are kept abreast of the latest research. Finally, it gives the student an opportunity to receive publication credit for the rich content and exposure for his thesis.

Although volunteerism remains the principal engine of the Harvey Project, it is obviously not enough by itself. Financial support will come from a variety of sources. The Project is currently supported by grants from the National Science Foundation and from some of its members' host institutions, as well as by donations of equipment and software from commercial companies. Grants will probably continue to provide the largest part of its support, as they do now. Since open course initiatives like the Harvey Project can make a critical contribution to the future good health of universities, host institutions and funding agencies should see such projects as both worthy and cost effective. Many of the costs of rich content development are eliminated because faculty volunteer their collaboration. Medical groups and international agencies will see the Harvey Project as a way to further medical education, especially overseas. High quality medical teaching materials are desperately needed in the Third World.

Other sources of funding might be technical support contracts with universities using Harvey Project materials and consulting with businesses and institutions wishing to develop rich content, as mentioned above. In addition, the Project may decide to charge royalties for the use of its materials by for-profit companies and could charge commissions for developing specific materials on a priority basis.

There is need for an Open Course Initiative to foster the development of similar projects in other disciplines. Such an umbrella organization could facilitate the development of shared tools, standards, and expertise. It could also coordinate efforts to attract funding for member projects.

CONCLUSIONS

The Internet is bringing global competition to an industry that has organized itself along largely regional lines. Those universities and colleges that have long benefited from a captive clientele are finding their ecological niches threatened by Internet-based distance learning programs from faraway competitors. So far this threat has been blunted by the often mediocre quality of the distance courses and by questions of accreditation and equivalency. What will happen, however, when the Internet-based competition, offering rich content, is indisputably superior to local offerings? What will happen when students begin to drop classes because they offer "only PowerPoint slides?"

Building rich content and on-line courses that exploit the richness of the digital medium requires a spectrum of talents that most universities lack and is extremely expensive. Commercial Web-based training, for example, typically costs upwards of $25,000 per hour of instruction to develop (Hall, 1997, p. 113). At that rate, a one-semester, three-credit college course would cost a million dollars. Some elite universities have the resources today to develop rich content for their curriculum, and a few are already doing so. Most institutions, however, are not ready to make such an investment in their curriculum. On the other hand, they cannot afford to be unprepared for competitors that are.

In the absence of the sort of open course collaborations described above, colleges and universities will be forced to license many of their courses from other institutions—educational and/or commercial—so as to compete for students and remain in business. Economies of scale, however, favor the content producer rather than the content distributor. Universities that outsource their curriculum face a future where they will compete less on the basis of brand ("Big Blue") or quality and more on the basis of cost. The winners in such a market are likely to be the content producers and probably some community colleges, which have a lower cost structure and are often more "wired" than other higher learning institutions. The losers are likely to be content-distributing universities and four-year colleges, and with them their scholarship, research, tenured faculty, and academic freedom.

This is the dilemma that faces higher education today and is the IT issue which dwarfs all others. Although development of a world-class on-line curriculum is a challenge to many components of the university and is much broader than just an IT issue, no other IT initiative will have as much direct impact on the very survival of the institution. Higher education institutions must devise innovative approaches to building rich content and developing a "wired" curriculum (such as the open course collaboration described here) or face an uncertain future.

The goal of the Harvey Project is to develop rich content to support an entire human physiology course by the end of 2002, and to see this material used in most physiology courses around the world. The Harvey Project is very young, and it is too early to tell whether it will live up to its promise. Whether or not the Harvey Project achieves this ambitious objective, it offers an attractive solution to a critical challenge: building rich content and moving university teaching into the wired future.

Collaborations such as the Harvey Project that make rich content freely available can avoid a crippling "arms race" among institutions to develop the best on-line courses. Higher education institutions should therefore support such open projects. It is in the interest of university administrators to encourage this activity of their faculty with awards, incentives, and release time. It should be the mission of every university IT department to facilitate such collaborative development. It is in the interest of faculty and professional societies to consider creating similar open courses in their disciplines. And finally, granting agencies with an interest in educational quality and the health of our university system should be prepared to fund such open course initiatives. The benefit to students will be great if they succeed. And the consequences for many higher educational institutions could be serious if they do not.

DISCUSSION QUESTIONS

- What factors might influence the long-term success of the open course model embodied by the Harvey Project?
- Do you agree with the statement that higher education institutions which do not develop a wired curriculum face an uncertain future?
- Could a similar, open course project be established in your discipline? Is there a professional society or group that might sponsor it?

REFERENCES

Bloomfield, V. (Ed.). (1999). *Biophysical Society Textbook Online*, http://biosci.umn.edu/biophys/OLTB/Textbook.html.

Carroll, R.G. (2000). Medical Physiology Objectives Project, Jan. 20, 2000, http://www.physiol.med.ecu.edu/objectiv/index.htm.

Dawkins, R. (1990). *The Selfish Gene*. Oxford: Oxford University Press.

Fraser, A. (1999). Colleges should tap the pedagogical potential of the World Wide Web. *Chronicle of Higher Education*, Aug. 6, B8.

Hall, B. (1997). *Web-Based Training Cookbook*. New York: John Wiley & Sons.

HAPS—Human Anatomy and Physiology Society. (1994). Course Guidelines for Undergraduate Instruction of Human Anatomy and Physiology, http://www.hapsweb.org/corecurr.htm.

IMS Global Learning Consortium, Inc. (2000). IMS Meta-Data Specification. Feb. 20, 2000, http://www.imsproject.org/metadata/index.html.

Inktomi, Inc. (2000). Inktomi Webmap, Jan. 18, http://www.inktomi.com/webmap/.

Russell, T.J. (1999). *The No Significant Difference Phenomenon*. Office of Instructional Telecommunications, North Carolina State University (to order, see http://www2.ncsu.edu/oit/nsxflyer.jpg). Also available on the Web at http://nt.media.hku.hk/no_sig_diff/phenom1.html.

Valenzeno, D., Gasparro, F., Smith, K., Brennan, T., Lambert, C., & O'Shea, K. (1999). *The Digital Photobiology Compendium*. Abstract presented at the 27th annual meeting of the American Society for Photobiology.

Waddell, C. D. (1998). Applying the ADA to the Internet: A Web Accessibility Standard, June 17, 1998, http://www.rit.edu/~easi/law/weblaw1.htm.

Wall Street Journal. (1999). Beyond Linux, Free Systems Help Build the Web. Sept. 10, B1.

ADDITIONAL RESOURCES

More information about the Harvey Project is available on its Web site at http://harveyproject.org/.

END NOTES

1. No other open project aims to fill the critical need for discipline-specific rich content. There are, however, several open projects to build Web-based, modular textbooks. The Biophysical Society Textbook Online (Bloomfield, 1999) and the Digital Photobiology Compendium (Valenzeno et al., 1999) are examples of these. There are also, of course, proprietary educational resources on the Web. Many of these allow public access without charge, but forbid reproduction or modification in any form. Some include banner advertisements.
2. The so-called "Halloween documents": http://www.opensource.org/halloween.
3. Copyleft, invented by Richard Stallman, is the foundation of the free or open source software movement.See http://www.gnu.org/copyleft/copyleft.html.
4. The term, invented by Jakob Nielsen, refers to an independent service that rates Web sites or anything else for quality. See http://www.useit.com/alertbox/990905.html.

ACKNOWLEDGMENTS

I would like to thank Drs. Saadia Sabah and Tina Ziemba, Krim and Tleytmas Stephenson, and Marija Franetovic for their thoughtful comments and suggestions. I am indebted to Richard Stallman of the Free Software Foundation for ideas and discussions about the open course license. This work was supported by grants from the National Science Foundation (DUE-9951384) and from the Vice President for Information Technology, Wayne State University.

Chapter XVII

The Role of Computers and Technology in Health Care Education

Jan K. Hart
University of Arkansas for Medical Sciences

INTRODUCTION

The goal of health care education at the University of Arkansas for Medical Sciences (UAMS) is a good nurse, doctor, pharmacist, or allied health professional—a well-prepared health care professional who is knowledgeable, knows how to get information as needed, and knows how to use information in a clinical practice setting. The health care professional is trained and practices in a computer- and network-intensive environment where distributed access to electronic information—the medical literature, medical records, and laboratory data—is needed and is increasingly expected. It is during their education that professionals learn to use and value the electronic tools at their disposal. Institutions like UAMS search for ways to support teaching faculty, clinical educators, and students in making the most of useful computer-based practice tools, information resources, and educational technologies. Computer literacy, faculty development, facilities planning and support, access issues, and incorporation of increasingly sophisticated educational modalities are key elements in successful education at UAMS. The use of technology in health care and health care education is unavoidable and growing more so daily.

The convergence of the Internet and Internet 2 and other federal and state initiatives for faster and more extensive networks, combined with continually falling prices for increasingly powerful computers, has created a climate full of promise as well as unmitigated hype. It is often assumed that everyone is being swept along by the tide of computer technology and that the impetus of the tide will prepare faculty and students for this new age in medical education. It is wrong to assume that all faculty and students are prepared to use and manage sophisticated medical informatics tools. UAMS is looking beyond the myths of computer literacy to make a realistic appraisal of the computer readiness of their faculty and students, so that appropriate help and support is available.

This case study illustrates the ways that information technology is used in health care education at the University of Arkansas for Medical Sciences and other health care education institutions. It addresses the problems that must be overcome and the advantages and opportunities that information technology tools provide for health care education. It examines this in light of the changing face of health care and, consequently, health care education.

```
┌─────────────────────────────────────────────────────────────────┐
```
CASE QUESTIONS

- How can faculty use information technology to best serve students in their health care education?
- In what ways are the information technology needs of health care practitioners similar or different from other disciplines in higher education?
- How can institutions and their academic affairs units support the use of technology in the educational experiences in health care education?

CASE NARRATIVE

Background

The University of Arkansas for Medical Sciences (UAMS) is a mid-sized academic health sciences center with Colleges of Health Related Professions, Medicine, Nursing, and Pharmacy, a Graduate School, and a 320-bed University Hospital. Total enrollment for 1999/2000 is 1,852 students with 835 teaching faculty. The University Hospital and the educational campus are located in Little Rock, with six associated Area Health Education Centers (AHECs) and a Delta Health Education Center located around the state. The Department of Pediatrics is located at Arkansas Children's Hospital two miles from the central campus, and many UAMS faculty members have joint appointments with the Central Arkansas Veteran's Health Care System that is located next to the main campus. UAMS supports the only medical and pharmacy schools in the state and is the central hub for health sciences education and research in Arkansas.

UAMS has been adversely affected by managed care and changes in the funding of health care and health care education, as have many other health sciences academic centers whose fortunes have been reported in the news media over the past year. However, research funding awarded to UAMS has grown at a healthy rate, and "centers of excellence" programs have drawn funds from local and national philanthropists and from state and federal programs. Several clinical programs at UAMS draw patients from around the country and the world. UAMS is currently in the middle of an extensive building program. Income-generating activities, grant-funded research, and clinical care are recognized as vitally important to the well being of the entire institution. In short, UAMS suffers the growing pains and faces the challenges common to many academic health sciences centers juggling educational, research, and clinical missions in very stringent financial straits.

In health care education and health care, generally, four major trends are affecting the incorporation of computers, networks, and telecommunications into the industry. They are: a) reliance on distributed access to electronic information in clinical practice at academic health sciences centers; b) managed care and health care competition; c) demands for access to electronic information and educational programs for distance education students and for students in clinical rotations away from the central campus; and d) accreditation and certification examinations conducted via computers.

Distributed Access to Electronic Information

Computers are found in virtually every aspect of health care—in the hospital ward stations, diagnostic laboratories, clinics, business offices, and physician, resident, and student on-call rooms. Access to electronic medical records, laboratory data, medical decision support tools, online bibliographic databases, and full-text journals and books from these locations requires pervasive data communication networks and health care professionals who can practice in a computer- and network-dependent environment. Although the primary impetus for the robust information resources and networking is clinical care and research, health care education can reap tremendous benefits from access to these extensive networks.

Managed Care and Health Care Competition

Managed care and changes in funding for teaching hospitals have undercut the financial base of academic health sciences centers. Teaching hospitals with the heavy financial burden of a teaching facility must compete directly with non-teaching hospitals and clinics. Academic health sciences centers are responding by assuming corporate characteristics, often at the real and perceived detriment of the educational mission. Increasing emphasis on outpatient treatment and abbreviated hospital stays limits the variety and depth of cases seen by students. Physicians responding to increased time and cost restraints have neither the time for intensive teaching nor the time to investigate new technologies such as the sophisticated clinical simulations and "virtual" clinic experiences that are being developed.

Clinical Rotations and Distance Education

Most health care disciplines require students to participate in clinical rotations or practicums in a hospital or clinic setting. Also, distance education courses and full degree programs, especially degree completion programs for practicing health care professionals, are increasingly being served via compressed interactive video and the Internet. Both rotations and distance education require some mechanism for providing electronic information resources and computer-based educational programs to students away from the central campus and its concentration of electronic resources.

Board and Certification Examinations via Computers and Accreditation

The importance of board and certification examinations and accreditation cannot be underestimated for either the individual student or for the institution in health care education. Nearly all health care disciplines now require board or certification examinations via computer at the completion of the program. Most academic health sciences centers like UAMS familiarize students with computer-based examinations by testing via computers throughout their course of study. These examinations and the facilities and resources to support them are a critical component in the educational experience of students. Also, accreditation teams look very seriously at the electronic resources, student computer facilities, and access to computer-based educational tools as well as traditional print resources during the accreditation review process.

Technology and Health Care Education at University of Arkansas for Medical Sciences

UAMS is poised to use its significant computer and network resources to support the clinical education of health care professionals. The successful integration of computer-based instructional programs into the curricula of the pre-clinical sciences at UAMS has been due to the straightforward nature of the materials to be learned, the many excellent commercially available programs, and the well-defined, relatively rigid structure of the curricula of the colleges. In contrast, clinical education is more often case-based, and it demands analysis and synthesis of information in a clinical setting where several different clinicians with varying computer and medical informatics skills teach clinical skills to students in clinics and hospitals far away from a traditional education setting and central resources. Despite changes in the health care environment that increase the importance of computer-based cases and simulations as demonstrated at other academic health sciences institutions, UAMS faculty and students have been slow to move to a more computer-based clinical education. Faculty development, support, and faculty and student computer literacy are key to success.

UAMS has a pervasive campus-wide area network that is connected to the Internet and to Internet 2. A multi-year project to implement a clinical information system providing comprehensive electronic medical records has been undertaken. The UAMS Library is increasing its number of electronic full-text journals as quickly as possible, providing access to several electronic databases and an online catalog, and it is working closely with the AHEC libraries to provide important resources to students on rotations and in distance education classes.

Traditionally, the UAMS colleges have introduced students to electronic resources through classes, presentations, and orientations covering some or all of the following: the UAMS email system, the Library and library resources, computing facilities at UAMS, and medical literature searching. Many of these activities are successfully coordinated and taught by non-teaching faculty in the UAMS Academic Affairs Division—specifically the Library, the Office of Educational Development, and the Office of Academic Computing. These activities have provided the groundwork for students to use computers as educational tools.

Preclinical Computer-Based Education

Since 1988, the Library Learning Resource Center (LRC) has been centrally funded to support computer-based instruction as a resource for all of the UAMS colleges. The LRC has grown from a handful of stand-alone interactive videodisc and computer workstations to a large multi-functional, multi-location computer laboratory that supports individual study, small group learning, testing, faculty and student instruction sessions, and electronic communications. The LRC has the primary responsibility for assisting faculty in identifying and procuring appropriate computer-based instructional programs and supporting students in the use of software and hardware on campus and remotely.

UAMS has a long and successful history of integrating computer-based instruction programs into the preclinical curriculum of all of the colleges. Students use a wealth of commercially available programs on anatomy, pathology, recognition of heart sounds, muscular physiology, and similar didactic subjects that are primarily based on identification of images and understanding of processes. The LRC, together with the faculty of the colleges, has identified and purchased over 400 programs in support of the curricula. Faculty members will send students to use the program or will take the program to the students in classrooms, lecture halls, or laboratories. Some preclinical faculty have also found that with training and assistance they can learn to develop educational programs with easy-to-use authoring tools. Most UAMS developers have worked through the UAMS Self-Directed Learning Program discussed below.

Almost without exception, students in health care disciplines proceed through their early classes in lock-step through a predefined and fairly rigid curriculum, e.g., sophomore medical students all take exactly the same courses and use the same materials at the same time. This is perhaps one of the most significant reasons why so many computer-based instructional programs are available for health sciences education. Key factors in supporting such a well-defined need are identifying and acquiring the right programs, providing sufficient trained staff to ensure things run smoothly, and planning the logistics to support students from all of the colleges at the same time. It is a challenge to successfully support programs for students in the pre-clinical years. This includes such tasks as determining how to support 150 medical students using a particular histology program over a specific period of time, 85 nursing students coming in small groups to practice using an auscultation of breath sounds program during a similar period, and 30 pharmacy students needing to take a pharmacy law exam sometime during that same timeframe. While challenging, however, it is a relatively straightforward juggling act of students, programs, and computer stations and can be handled.

Probably no academic health sciences centers have computer facilities to seat all students simultaneously; nor do they need to. UAMS instead has maximized its resources by providing access to programs on the LRC servers from other locations on campus, through checkout of software programs on CD-ROMs, via a remote access server, and, increasingly, through Web access to faculty-developed Web pages with educational materials.

Clinical Education Complexities

The comparative ease with which preclinical curricular materials are procured and supported does not necessarily provide adequate preparation for the difficulties encountered in supporting clinical education. Four factors generally differentiate preclinical and clinical education: a) preclinical faculty are a few course directors—clinical faculty are a large number of practicing clinicians with varying skills and interests; b) preclinical education centers on identification, comparisons, categorizing, and processes—clinical education centers on analysis, synthesis, and hypotheses, and requires medical informatics, computerized medical practice tools, and case-based materials; c) preclinical faculty present information to learn—clinical educators show how they work and what tools they use; and d) preclinical students are usually on campus—clinical rotations take students all around the state.

The model used so successfully with pre-clinical students does not hold true for the clinical rotations when students are no longer part of a cohesive group with direct assignments and one course director per subject. Students move into the clinic arena and must look to the clinical educators for direction and for modeling their practice and information-seeking skills. These clinical educators, whose primary job is clinical work, teach in hospitals and outpatient clinics largely by allowing students and residents to accompany them from room to room and patient to patient. Students learn how to behave as physicians, nurses, or pharmacists during these clinical experiences.

The clinical educators are often an overlooked factor in preparing students to use the extraordinary computer-based tools that are available to them. The pressure on clinicians from managed care and financial concerns is a severe constraint on the opportunities of clinical educators to become even familiar with all of the tools at their disposal. Their time and effort is compressed and their opportunities to participate in faculty development programs are very limited. Unfortunately, computer literacy is hit-or-miss among the clinical educators and there is very little clinical education that can be done by anyone outside the professional ranks of physicians, nurses, or pharmacists to assist in this modeling process. Without the day-to-day modeling of the appropriate use of information and educational technology by the clinical educators, most attempts to integrate significant new information technology tools into clinical education are dismissed by the students or just disappear due to lack of use. The loss of a clinical educator who is modeling use of online medical literature or computer-based medical decision-making tools can eliminate an entire area of experience by students.

The current health care environment, as previously mentioned, tends to inhibit the opportunities for broad spectrum, in-depth clinical education of medical students. Clinical educators are under pressure to proceed as quickly as possible and to limit contact time with patients. There is little time or means to provide a focused learning experience to meet specific objectives so that patient encounters, and therefore teaching opportunities, are based on what patients come to the clinic during a student's clinical rotation. Patient encounters may be sporadic, brief, and out-of-the-context of the patient's life.

Computer-based case simulations help overcome the constraints of a clinical setting in which students cannot follow a patient and there is a lack of student engagement with an individual patient's case. A few leaders in technology-based medical education have begun the development of "virtual practicums" based on focused learning experiences under the guidance of a "virtual consultant" who provides feedback. These computer programs present clinical education not as small bits of discrete information but as an experiential, reflective activity requiring engagement on the part of the student and integration of information (Henderson, 1998).

Access Issues

The Web is a rich and far-reaching information resource. While Web access to the Library catalog, electronic journals and books, and online databases is important to students wherever they are located, it is critical for the off-campus students during clinical rotations at AHECs and rural health clinics. Currently, however, for students using home computers connected to the Web via modems, access to the rich image, video, and audio content that is fundamental to health sciences materials continues to be slow. Additionally, thin-client technology allows access via the Internet to Windows-based instructional software on a Citrix Winframe remote access server. Because it is not indexed by any of the search engines, most educational software vendors have allowed site-licensed materials to be distributed to UAMS faculty and students via the LRC's remote access server.

The large student computer labs, including 65 computers in the LRC, 55 computers in Academic Computing laboratories, and 45 computers in the classroom/laboratory, are centrally funded resources. This year, for the first time, the UAMS budget has a plan to support the periodic upgrade of educational equipment. The units have jointly developed a plan that staggers the equipment upgrades so that there is always at least one facility on campus that has state-of-the-art equipment. Each unit knows when its next upgrade is scheduled and what is available in the other labs. This cooperation has enabled the support units to stop competing for resources and adequately serve the colleges with shared computer resources, thereby avoiding the development of large college-based computer labs that would siphon off support for the campus-wide computer facilities.

Small computer labs supporting specific areas, such as Anatomy and Health Information Management, have, however, been established around the campus. Connecting these specialized labs, as well as student computers in departmental libraries and conference rooms, to the centralized resources via the network provides convenient access for students to the LRC's educational programs at locations across the campus while allowing for centralized purchase, installation, and maintenance of educational software.

UAMS is content to purchase some of the excellent commercial educational programs for student use when there is faculty commitment to incorporating the programs into the curriculum. Learning how, when, and where to take advantage of these multimedia educational programs by using them as lecture support, in the laboratory, and in small group discussion settings, and then to evaluate their effectiveness in the curriculum is an important aspect of faculty development. To incorporate computer-based instructional programs into the curriculum, faculty should: a) know the software program; b) correlate the program to the objectives of the course, including testing of those objectives; c) correlate the program to coursework and syllabus; d) demonstrate the program for class and tell students how they are expected to use the program; e) work with the LRC to ensure successful implementation; and f) evaluate the success of the program with students and evaluators in the office of Educational Development when appropriate. No one can provide the same impact as the clinical educator or instructor in demonstrating the use and value of information resources and educational software.

Most faculty at an academic health sciences campus find that computer-based instruction development efforts must be attended to after research and clinical responsibilities. Time is always their most precious commodity. Many are resigned to the notion that promotion, tenure, and monetary rewards for educational activities are minimal. Others forge ahead in the belief that the time is right to gain acceptance of "teaching portfolios," and recognition that development of computer-based instructional resources should be considered seriously in promotion and tenure review.

Nonetheless, easy-to-use authoring and development tools, and computers and data projectors in the classrooms have lured some faculty into developing their own courseware. Many start with presenting PowerPoint lectures and having a presence on departmental Web sites. Some faculty use Authorware, WebCT, or other authoring tools to provide their own more detailed content to students. Generally these materials focus on presenting text, images, self-assessment quizzes, and rudimentary case presentations. But they are extremely valuable to students because they represent what their instructor has selected as important for students to know.

Faculty-Development Mechanisms

UAMS has several faculty-development mechanisms in place, including several campus-wide groups or activities. These include a self-directed learning program, online testing support, campus-wide presentations, teaching scholars program, and a variety of classes and workshops.

The UAMS Self-Directed Learning Program Committee, formed nearly a decade ago, provides assistance, training, hardware, and software to aid faculty in the development of computer-based educational programs. All of the colleges and the academic affairs units have representatives on the committee. The committee does not produce programs but advises faculty and helps them prepare their staff to develop programs. LRC staff provide training and assistance with the flatbed, slide, and transparency scanners; videocapture and videoediting equipment and software; digital camera, imaging, authoring and testing software; and other development tools that are housed in the Faculty Development Room in the Library.

UAMS began giving examinations via computer in 1993. This early adoption of computer-based examinations was motivated by trends toward computerized certification examinations and also by the unique ability of computers to present the high-resolution color images needed in health care education. All colleges now use computer-based examinations to some degree. There have been many successful examinations, several problems, and a few outright disasters. The successes have far outnumbered the difficulties, but a failed examination can be a catastrophic event and a great demoralizer. The support units that have trained and assisted faculty and their assistants have noticed some problematic trends as more instructors move to computer-based examinations.

The instructors who developed computer-based examinations in the early years were "early adopters" who felt comfortable with computers, were committed to setting aside the time to build computer-based examinations, and were interested in development themselves. As faculty members without these interests and skills have begun to develop and use computer examinations, a more intensive level of assistance from support staff has been required. Faculty and their assistants prepare the content, but the actual implementation of the exam should be accomplished with oversight by an assigned liaison from the UAMS Online Testing Team to increase the likelihood of a successful examination. The support groups have learned that it is much better to devote more resources to assure that the examination goes well than to have to spend agonizing time afterward trying to troubleshoot failures.

The LRC sponsors weekly presentations on education technology. The programs are diverse and include presentations by faculty demonstrating how they use educational technology to improve their teaching and student learning, by staff from the academic affairs units showing new technology, software, or new ways to use development tools, and by invited vendors and outside guests.

Each year 24 UAMS faculty participate in a year-long program developed by the Office of Educational Development and the College of Medicine Faculty Development Committee to help faculty improve their teaching methods. Many become involved in projects related to educational uses of technology. They are provided with numerous opportunities to learn about educational technology in theory and practice. Additionally, classes on PowerPoint, WebCT, Authorware, Question Mark, scanning, Adobe Photoshop, and other development tools are given frequently at no charge to UAMS faculty, students, and staff.

Challenges to Implementing New Technologies

UAMS students vary in computer literacy skills—some have virtually no experience while others have advanced skills. Students' off-campus access to computers varies as well. Ensuring that students are not penalized during their early work at UAMS due to a lack of computer skills while making sure that all graduating students have at least moderate computer skills requires a difficult balancing act. Careful attention must be given to how educational technology is applied and whether the opportunities for students to learn and become comfortable with it are available.

Each year more students want access to education and information resources from home, other health care sites, and other educational locations. Making resources available to students away from the central campus involves difficult technology, licensing, and support issues. It is, however, not acceptable to ignore this need.

Most educators in health care programs are also clinicians to varying degrees. This is especially true in the College of Medicine where very few faculty members focus on education as their primary responsibility. For most faculty teaching preclinical courses, the primary professional responsibility is research. For those involved in clinical education, the primary responsibility is clinical care. Most of the clinical skills education of the third- and fourth-year students takes place in the hospital or in the clinics alongside residents and attending physicians where students can closely observe the use of electronic information resources and practice tools. If these resources are not valued by the attending physicians, it is unlikely that students will value them either. Unfortunately, many good possibilities for modeling the use of medical informatics resources are lost as the clinicians simply become increasingly pressed for time by research and clinical duties. As the health care environment becomes more intense and focused on managed care, the educational component is in danger of slipping further out of sight.

Whether to require students to purchase computers has been a recurring issue at the College of Medicine. Several other medical schools require students to have computers or, even more specifically, laptop computers. This issue has been debated nationally in journal articles and electronic discussion lists for several years. Medical students at UAMS are encouraged but not required to purchase computers, and a financial aid program is available for those who wish to do so. The 1999 annual survey of incoming UAMS freshman medical students indicates that 82 percent of the students have a computer and another 12 percent have access to a computer off-campus. In the survey 96 percent of the freshmen stated they were interested in using educational programs from home and 91 percent responded that they have access to the Internet from home.

Several medical schools, including UAMS, are involved in pilot programs to determine the usefulness of palmtops in the clinical years. UAMS is currently conducting a small informal study in response to a group of third- and fourth-year students who have become palmtop advocates. Most likely, the question of the importance of handheld computers in health care and health care education is "when," not "whether."

Many see requiring computers as a step toward greater computer literacy while others do not believe that student computer literacy is the key element in what keeps UAMS from taking full advantage of educational technology and medical informatics. Even among the student population, there is disagreement about requiring students to purchase computers.

Some faculty believe, despite evidence to the contrary, that all students should and will come to UAMS already computer literate. They feel no responsibility for the computer literacy of students. They believe the half-truths and myths about computer literacy: a) all students have powerful computers and know how to use them; b) if students are required to purchase computers, it will ensure that UAMS is a computer-literate campus; c) anyone under 25 is computer literate; d) the faculty is fully aware and ready to use computer technology; e) students intuitively know what to do with computer-based educational materials; and f) others are responsible for computer literacy, and they are doing something about it.

Others believe that it is necessary for UAMS to address computer literacy deficiencies as they are identified, because time after time, the same students repeatedly fail to do well with activities requiring even minimal computer skills. Some faculty are frustrated by this small group of students and sometimes see this as a reason to stop using the Web or even email to communicate with students. The College of Medicine is trying to identify the computer skills that will help first-year students to be prepared to handle their assignments and is piloting a pre-orientation introduction to these computer skills.

ANALYSIS

Analysis of the UAMS information technology environment suggests six major areas for continuing consideration: a) the exploitation of computer and networking infrastructure; b) the increased importance of informatics resources available to clinical educators; c) the incorporation of new educational technologies in clinical education; d) centralized support for faculty and students; e) faculty and student computer literacy; and f) access to resources from any location.

Exploitation of Computer and Networking Infrastructure

UAMS should continue to exploit the substantial computer and networking infrastructure developed to support clinical care and research, in order to support education. Information technology is a core competency for academic health sciences centers and for physicians (Gewertz et al., 1997). Today's clinicians working in modern hospitals or clinics of academic health sciences centers can no longer avoid a reliance on computers and networks.

Increased Importance of Medical Informatics

Clinical educators should be encouraged to develop their skills with informatics and medical decision-making tools and then to model their use of these tools for students. The UAMS experience mirrors the findings of Salas (1998) in his study of medical schools and the incorporation of medical informatics. He found that institutions may have become proficient at providing access to educational materials and facilities, but there is a great gap between these services and the more complex incorporation of medical informatics into the professional lives of clinical educators and the educational experiences of their students. Those in the colleges and Academic Affairs Division who have worked to support computer literacy have for too long believed that introducing students to computer-based medical informatics tools would eventually create practitioners with these skills. However, after a decade of wishful thinking, it is apparent that students will not engage in the use of technology if such behavior is not valued by their clinical educators. The well-informed, technology-aware cadre of graduating students who will advance the use of technology in health care education and health care practice has not fully materialized.

New Educational Technologies for Clinical Education

As mentioned earlier, computer-based instruction has been much more successful in the preclinical years of the education of health care professionals than in clinical education. However, computer hardware and software have risen to a level of power and sophistication that can support the incorporation of videoclips of significant length and quality, high quality audio, and interactivity that can support a simulated clinic experience. Computer simulations, with virtual reality experiences following close behind, will become a training ground for health care professionals just as they had earlier become training grounds for pilots. The incorporation of true tactile simulation that enables not only visual virtual reality, but also, the feel of tugging, pushing, reaction, and resistance that is inherent in working with a human body, is now possible. Costs and equipment setups in the initial stages will keep high level virtual reality in the laboratory for a while, but it is not far off. Virtual reality will provide opportunities for practicing invasive and expensive skills such as surgical and diagnostic procedures without danger to the patient. These virtual reality programs will play a role in continuing medical education, as well as in undergraduate medical education and residency training, as ultimately a cost saver. The continual upgrading of skills necessary for practicing will help to drive virtual reality into the real world.

Centralized Support

Through the Academic Affairs Division, UAMS has followed a centralized approach for faculty development and support of computer-based instruction and testing. Five units— the Office of Academic Computing, the Office of Educational Development, Media Services, the Office of Academic Services, and the Library—support the bulk of the educational technology and information resources at UAMS. These units work closely together using a team approach to maximize resources and take advantage of the expertise of each unit. This approach is formalized in committees such as the Self-Directed Learning Program Committee and the Online Testing Team. The colleges seem generally content to work with this centralized group because the units have been responsive to the needs of the colleges. Individuals from the academic affairs units serve on various campus-wide computer technology committees as well as on committees within individual colleges. Daily experience confirms Chessare's (1998) finding that the lack of faculty development was one of the greatest obstacles to implementation of technology. There has also been work showing that computer technology and literacy workshops increased computer use and reduced faculty concerns about technology (Lewis et al., 1997). For these reasons, the academic affairs units stress faculty development. Centralized funding of the equipment, software, and human resources that support faculty development and student use of computers is, of course, very popular with the colleges.

Faculty and Student Computer Literacy

The computer literacy of faculty and students is critical, but the key lies with the computer literacy of the faculty. Although student computer literacy has long been an issue for the colleges at UAMS, faculty computer literacy has been viewed more as a preference than a requirement. Lewis et al. (1997) noted several contributing factors to a reluctance on the part of some faculty to embrace technological advances. These are: a) age of the faculty and administrators, b) inability to see potential, c) lack of funds for hardware and software acquisition, d) perceived threat to traditional faculty roles, e) fear of loss of employment, and f) perceived inability to control the teaching process. One or more of these factors have been observed as barriers to UAMS faculty development efforts on many occasions. At UAMS, a few faculty apparently hope to avoid computers as much as possible before they retire.

UAMS faculty, clinicians, and students could work together to create an environment that takes advantage of portable computers and palmtops in the clinical setting. Such measures as development of databases for logging patient contacts, providing access to printers with infrared attachments for printing from palmtops, and ultimately, installation of wireless network technology in clinical facilities would greatly enhance the usefulness of palmtops and portable computers for students and faculty.

Faculty must have an understanding of the implications of what they are asking students to do with computers. They must act as mentors to prepare students to use the computer-based instructional programs they assign and provide students with computer proficiencies needed in the clinical setting (Haque and Gibson, 1998).

Access to Electronic Resources Regardless of Location

Electronic resources should be accessible regardless of location whenever feasible, as Friedman's (1996) "virtual clinical campus" and digital libraries are rapidly becoming realities. He stressed that students in community clinics need the same access to resources as students located on campus. The educational and information resources, especially the electronic resources, available in the Library and the LRC should be even more widely available than at present. These resources must also extend into the AHECs, the associated hospitals, and UAMS off-campus programs. As mentioned above, this is costly, but within reach.

However, due to the disparities of speed between campus high-speed networks and modem access from homes and remote locations, there cannot be a single network-based mode for distribution of materials at this time. Thin-client technology, campus network connections, Web-based materials, checkout of CD-ROMs and other media, wireless technology, and palmtops will all be among the distributive access methods in the immediate future.

CONCLUSIONS

Successful integration of information and educational technology into health sciences education depends on the interest and commitment of the teaching faculty, the clinical educators, the support personnel, and the students themselves. The institutional and college administrations must be committed to funding sufficient personnel, hardware, and software to support faculty and students.

At UAMS, there are several trends and observations about the continuing role of technology in health care education:

1. Students are making good use of their home computers for Web access, for CD-ROMs checked out of the Library, and for programs on the remote access server.
2. The Library computer lab and small group rooms are increasingly used for small group study, testing, and faculty and student instruction and training.
3. UAMS has put much emphasis on computer-based examinations—it is easier than developing tutorials and it prepares students for board and certification examinations.
4. Distributed access to educational and informational resources can be provided to computer clusters on campus and to student computers in clinics and departments.
5. Early adopters have already "adopted"; it is now necessary to work with faculty who are not computer savvy and may not be particularly interested.

UAMS enjoys the benefits of a pervasive network and high-speed connections, but technology alone is not enough. The issue of computer literacy for both faculty and students is critical. UAMS and many academic health sciences centers have spent years concentrating on student computer literacy while providing little support for faculty literacy. Many faculty are not taking full advantage of the rich resources available to them. Increased faculty literacy would enhance their own informatics and educational skills, as well as provide students with needed mentors to model the use of computers in information seeking, education, and communication.

DISCUSSION QUESTIONS

1. How can a health care education institution promote computer literacy among its faculty? What incentives might prove effective or necessary?
2. What long-term effects could the improvement of information technology uses in health care education have on the health care industry in general?
3. How are the applications of technology and computers at health care education institutions similar to those at other types of higher education institutions? How do they differ?
4. How can the lessons learned from the University of Arkansas for Medical Sciences be applied to other types of higher education institutions?

REFERENCES

Chessare, J. B. (1998). Teaching clinical decision-making to pediatric residents in an era of managed care. *Pediatrics,* 101, 762-767.

Friedman, C. P. (1996). The virtual clinical campus. *Academic Medicine,* 71, 647-651.

Gewertz, B. L., Goode, L. D., Behrens, B. L., Fortuner, W. J., 3rd., Wallace, A. G., Williams, W. T., Jr., & Wilson, D. E. (1997). Tapping the power of information: An orientation for academic medical centers. *Academic Medicine,* 72, 677-681.

Haque, S. S., & Gibson, D. M. (1998). Information technology education for health professionals: Opportunities and challenges. *Journal of Allied Health,* 27(3), 167-172.

Henderson, J. V. (1998). Comprehensive, technology-based clinical education: The "virtual practicum." *International Journal of Psychiatry in Medicine,* 28, 41-79.

Lewis, D., Watson, J. E., & Newfield, S. (1997). Implementing instructional technology: Strategies for success. *Computers in Nursing,* 15, 178-190.

Salas, A. A. (1998). Computers and medical informatics in the curriculum. *Contemporary Issues in Medical Education,* 1(4), 1-2.

ADDITIONAL RESOURCES

Academic Medicine is a primary source of both practical and theoretical articles on medical education and medical informatics. *Computers in Nursing* addresses similar issues in the field of nursing. The American Association of Medical Colleges, Division of Medical Education Med-Ed listserv is an excellent source of information on medical education innovations. Subscriber information is listed on their Web site: http://www.aamc.org/meded/. *EduCause Review* and *Cause/Effect*, serial publications of EduCause, consider technology in higher education.

Section IV

Reflections on a Changing Environment

Chapter XVIII

Why Not Reengineer Traditional Higher Education?

Zane L. Berge
University of Maryland—Baltimore Country

INTRODUCTION

Just as the agricultural era gave way to an industrial society at the turn of the 20th century, an information society is now emerging as we move into the 21st century (Bell, 1993; Naisbitt, 1988; Toffler, 1980). With this shift in the means of production come drastic changes to every segment of society—including higher education (Rowley, Lujan, and Dolence, 1998). New delivery systems that increase the effectiveness of learning at a distance, new organizations such as virtual universities, and other models of teaching and learning are forcing higher education to change the way they do business (Mangan, 1998; Oblinger, 1997; Selingo, 1998).

Compared with that of the past 100 years, the rate of change occurring in society is unprecedented. There have been unparalleled increases in global competition, in customer expectations, and in new technology. These factors contribute to a lasting sense of crisis. Can traditional organizations in higher education respond to the changing environment by using the same approaches business has?

The traditional universities and colleges can be characterized as having: a residential student body; a recognized geographic service area from which the majority of student are drawn (a local community, a region, a state, or a nation); full-time faculty members who organize curricula and degrees, teach in face-to-face settings, engage in scholarship, often conduct public service, and share in institutional governance; a central library and physical plant; nonprofit financial status; and evaluation strategies of organizational effectiveness based upon measurement of inputs to instruction, such as funding, library holdings, facilities, faculty/student ratios, faculty qualifications, and student qualifications (Hanna, 1998, p. 69). However, technology is allowing non-traditional organizations to meet the curricular challenges many students are presenting (Whinston, 1994), including the need to develop learning materials that can be easily updated and configured for the particular needs of students, as well as the possibility of learning at any time and at any place. At the same time, the mode of industrial production within our society is being replaced with models that rely on the rapid growth in technology, an increase in the accessibility of information, a more critically aware population, and a shift from the production of goods to a service economy (Merron, 1995). These factors are causing significant change in education as well.

CASE QUESTIONS

- Consider fundamental changes in higher education from the past (e.g., coeducation) and the ways in which institutions of higher education responded. How are the changes brought on by the introduction of new technology similar or different?
- Does the introduction of new technology truly require a paradigm shift in higher education? Why or why not?
- In what ways are virtual universities forcing higher education to change the way it does business?
- What mechanisms are in place to facilitate reengineering in higher education? How is this similar or different from industry?

REENGINEERING IN BUSINESS AND EDUCATION

The development of national and international telecommunication systems has increased access to information and education. Customers now have many more choices than ever before. In business, the organizations that succeed are those that respond to heightened customer expectations within an increasingly technologically enhanced and fiercely competitive global market. In many instances, the first stage in their transformation was business process reengineering (Pappas, 1996). One definition of reengineering is:

> [...] the fundamental rethinking and radical redesign of business processes to achieve dramatic improvements in critical, contemporary measures of performance, such as cost, quality, service, and speed" (Hammer and Champy, 1993, p. 12).

Here fundamental assumptions are abandoned, old systems are thrown aside, and everything that is done starts over with a clean page. Radical redesign gets at the root of the issue, rather than making marginal changes to existing systems and procedures. It is not business improvement, but rather reinvention. It means a change in the very structure and culture of the organization. Dramatic change signifies quantum leaps in performance, not incremental changes. Reengineering is used to eliminate the old to make room for something completely different.[1]

For much the same reasons that businesses have had to change, so must education. In general, the delivery of education via technology and telecommunication systems has increased global competition—especially from start-up organizations and non-traditional suppliers of education. In addition, students are much more knowledgeable about their options for access to learning alternatives, and therefore they have higher expectations than they had before:

> Concepts of lifelong learning, individualized or personalized learning, and time-free, space-free "just-in-time" learning arrangements are emerging, all of which allow learning away from the traditional campus or worksite classroom. In this changing environment, particularly with the advent of learning at a distance, it is both difficult and exciting for students and institutions... (ACE, 1996, p. 5).

The combination of these factors has affected higher education to the point that some have considered that the very existence of the traditional university is in jeopardy.

Even in the face of this, traditional educational institutions have not reengineered themselves. Few organizations, including colleges and universities, change unless they feel directly threatened from outside the organization, often to the point that their very survival is in question (Meyer, 1997). There are several factors making such discontinuous change improbable within the traditional institutions of higher education. While not insurmountable, such issues as the promotion and tenure systems—designed to reinforce and perpetuate the status quo—are significant.

EDUCATION VERSUS BUSINESS: DIFFERENT STRUCTURES AND CULTURES

First, such radical change is improbable because there are no mechanisms in place to facilitate such change in higher education; in this way, higher education is quite different from industry (Stahlke and Nyce, 1996). One problem is that the hierarchical organizations designed to model the Industrial Age are built with more emphasis on assuring continuity than enabling change. Traditional universities have a robust capability to resist change. Another is the range of choices available to the traditional institution of higher education is limited by legislative mandate, regardless of economic consequences, or constrained by a tradition of service or a religious obligation that limits their ability to take advantage of strengths and excellence (Rowley, Lujan, and Dolence, 1997).

Second, the revolutionary change brought on by business process reengineering requires a different organizational and management structure and culture than is found in traditional institutions of higher education. The purposes for which people seek education are shifting and these needs are being supplied by emerging competitors that differ from the traditional university in a number of fundamental ways. The structure (who reports to whom within the organization, the boundaries in the organization, and people's roles and responsibilities) of higher education is not conducive to such change. The traditional, residential institution of higher education is generally characterized by fragmentation of processes, stifled innovation, inflexibility, unresponsiveness, and is focused on activity rather than results (Hammer and Champy, 1993). Essentially, the organizational structure, with its administrative and academic divisions in distinct and separate silos (Berge, 1993; Cohen, 1998; Harel and Partipilo, 1996), is the same as 100 years ago (Lewis and Smith, 1997).

In addition, the culture (which includes the norms, values, rules, and guidelines for behavior that support how people work together in the organization) also differs. Elements of the culture of traditional higher education go back at least 700 years to its European roots (Bucholz, n.d.), and thus its transformation would require changing the worldviews of its people. Of course, people don't give up ideas and culture easily (Nadler, 1995) because this requires that they change the accustomed habits of thought and patterns of behavior.

Success in business today is partially determined by the existence of an organizational culture that is highly adaptable and able to respond rapidly to the changing environment, has a strong, shared identity among people in the organization, and is a match between the culture and the environment:

> Working hard at the wrong thing is no virtue. When customers are kings, mere hard work, without understanding, flexibility, and enthusiasm, leads nowhere.

Work must be smart, appropriately targeted, and adapted to the particular circumstances of the process and the customer. Imagination, flexibility, and commitment to results are needed. If the results aren't achieved, you can no longer claim, "But I did what I was told and I worked very hard." It doesn't matter. You are accountable for results, not for effort (Hammer, 1997, p. 28).

The culture of higher education is not so adaptive and accommodating. Instructors who are experienced in teaching at a distance, for instance, state major barriers to their work in such terms as faculty or student resistance to innovation, resistance to online teaching methods, difficulty recruiting faculty or students, and lack of understanding of distance education and what works at a distance (Berge, 1998). These indicate a need for a different culture than exists currently in higher education.

DRIVERS FOR CHANGE

The purpose of a particular business varies with the industry in which that organization exists. However, an objective of every business is to make a return on investment for the owners. By contrast, the driving force in the traditional institution of higher education is its mission—not the "bottom line." Historically, colleges and universities were founded to generate new knowledge and to teach. The objective was not to make money, but rather to educate the citizenry through a comprehensive group of programs. This is particularly true for public institutions. Additionally, the more comprehensive colleges and universities have a commitment to the traditional liberal arts goals of helping students learn to think for themselves and to express their ideas intelligibly. Unfortunately, unfunded research and the cost of the faculty needed to teach comprehensive, liberal arts areas of study are a drain on the tuition money brought in by a smaller number of popular programs. Combined with this is the pressure students (and parents of traditional aged college students) place on institutions of higher education to offer programs of the highest standard that teach "job skills."

Traditional higher education faces new competition in the many organizations that place a much greater emphasis on the business, profit-motivated missions. These non-traditional providers "pick the low hanging fruit" of profitable programs and leave traditional universities to generate new knowledge and continue with the programs in the comprehensive educational system that cost rather than produce money. For the first time, technology allows these for-profit enterprises in higher education to ignore geopolitical boundaries (Heterick, 1995); there are no state or national lines on the Web. Furthermore, the lines that have historically divided the private, public, and nonprofit sectors have been blurring (Pappas, 1996). Partnerships between institutions of higher education and private sector enterprises are more common and will continue to grow in number and power.

NEW MISSIONS AND ORGANIZATIONAL MODELS IN HIGHER EDUCATION

By definition, higher education cannot reengineer because "if we get out of the education and research business, we are no longer in higher education" (Porter, 1993). On the other hand, some have argued that reengineering does not require changing the basic business objectives and mission of the educational organization. Nevertheless, the widespread use of technology has ushered in shifts in the vision for teaching and learning, and have an impact on the current model of higher education.

Along with social and demographic changes, these shifts are placing extreme external pressure on traditional educational institutions to change. For example, it is more common for students to expect: digital libraries rather than traditional libraries; professional certification rather than university credentials; shift from emphasis on teacher-as-expert education to their facilitating students in how to learn; just-in-time learning rather than classes offered only when the registrar schedules them; a rise in the use of distance education; desire of many professionals to earn degrees while remaining employed full-time; a shift toward viewing learning as a seamless, lifelong need; student and employer demands for more practical competencies.

Higher education today is changing in response to both global competition and more demanding customers. The changes are not found within the traditional institutions, however. Traditional administrators tinker:

> [...] with class size, increasing teaching loads, cutting sections with low enrollments, starting three-year degrees, redefining the core curriculum, modifying the reward system, and improving assessment" (Rowley, Lujan, and Dolence, 1997, p. 301).

These are stopgap measures that maintain the core university. The more significant change in higher education today is the emergence of new organizations that compete directly with traditional institutions and with each other for students. Much of this competition is spurred on by new technologies and telecommunication systems not in existence two decades ago.

Finally, Hanna (1998) identified seven alternative models to the traditional, residential post-secondary education: 1) extended traditional universities, 2) for-profit adult-centered universities, 3) distance education/technology-based universities, 4) corporate universities, 5) university/industry strategic alliances, 6) degree/certification competency-based universities, and 7) global multinational universities. A goal of each of these new models is to overcome one or more perceived weaknesses of the traditional university by changing a fundamental assumption about what a university should be and how higher education might operate in a global education and training marketplace. By adopting any of these models, would higher education cease to be higher education? If not, then why won't higher education reengineer itself accordingly?

CONCLUSIONS

As traditional colleges brace for competition from alternative suppliers—big-name competitors at a distance (Selingo, 1998)—will incremental changes be enough? Some argue it will not (Heterick,1993; Heterick, Mingle, and Twigg, 1997). Students seeking professional development and learning understand they have alternatives to the traditional. Is the future coming at traditional higher education too fast? Will traditional institutions of higher education become more customer centered, focusing on learning, or continue to regard their purpose to educate people—insisting on "my place at my pace" using an industrial model that is no longer appropriate? Will the traditional institutions of higher education embrace technology to help in ways business has done? Or will they use the new technologies to pave over their old cow paths?

The nation is in a time of transition from an industrial era to the post-industrial era. Still, in much the same way that the previous shift from an agricultural era to the industrial era did not mean all agriculture was abandoned, it is unlikely that all industrial activity will be immediately abandoned. To the extent that the public sector continues to desire an "educated citizenry," and is willing to pay for it, traditional institutions of higher education will be funded to supply comprehensive curricula. As such, although the traditional, residential higher education will remain, change will nevertheless occur. The use of information technology to improve education may involve incremental change:

> [...] contrary to the predictions of some 'reengineers,' [it] is likely to build on existing strengths and characteristics of the current . . . educational environment, rather than to radically change it" (Smallen, 1993, p. 26).

Still, when Thomas Edison was asked his vision for electric lights his response was:

> I shall make the electric light so cheap that only the rich will be able to burn candles (Halgrim, 1993).

Will traditional, residential education in the 21st century be found only at a few elite institutions and only for the wealthy?

What these shifts may signal for traditional institutions of higher education is that in the decades to come there will be significantly fewer of these organizations, with those surviving having changed significantly, using technology to enhance their purpose. Reengineering is often the origin of a transformed organization (Davidson, 1993; Pappas, 1996). Transformation can involve spin-offs, outsourcing, strategic alliances, and partnerships which are new to traditional institutions of higher education—the types of models being explored currently in competition with traditional higher education. Many institutions will enter into new contractual arrangements with for-profit corporations that serve the higher education sector (Beaudoin, 1998). The traditional institutions will be changed because of information technologies. They will facilitate access to information, organizing and displaying it in new ways that will facilitate communication among students, with their teachers, and others in the world. Traditional institutions of higher education, if they are to survive, must find ways, through reengineering or by some other means, to make the inevitable changes work to meet the needs of the learners in society who demand high quality, customized education, just-in-time learning, and convenient access.

DISCUSSION QUESTIONS

1. Are particular sectors of traditional higher education (e.g., community colleges, private institutions) more likely to reengineer themselves? Are newer institutions more or less likely to change?
2. Do different departments or schools within the university have more latitude in engaging in reengineering? Why is this the case?
3. How might the culture and practice of higher education differ if it undergoes radical reengineering?

REFERENCES

ACE (American Council on Education). (1996). *Guiding Principles for Distance Learning in a Learning Society.* Washington DC.

Beaudoin, M.F. (1998). A new professoriate for the new millennium. DEOSNEWS, 8(5). [Online.] Post to listserv@lists.psu.edu the command GET DEOSNEWS 98-00011.

Bell, D. (1993). *The Coming of the Post-Industrial Society.* New York: Basic Books.

Berge, Z.L. (in press). Educational technology in post-industrial society. In J.G. Webster (Ed.), *Wiley Encyclopedia of Electrical and Electronics Engineering.* NY: John Wiley & Sons, Inc., Publishers.

Berge, Z.L. (1998). Barriers to online teaching in post-secondary institutions. *Online Journal of Distance Learning Administration,* 1(2). Summer. [Online.] http://www.westga.edu/~distance/Berge12.html.

Berge, Z.L. (1993). Beyond computers as tools: Reengineering education. *Computers in the Schools,* 9(2/3) 167-178.

Bucholz, R.O. (n.d.) Be true to your medieval university tradition. [Online.] http://www.drake.edu/univannounce/medieval.html.

Cohen, E.B. (1998). Reengineering the university: A case study. *Journal of IS Education,* 1(5). [Online.] http://www.gise.org/JISE/Vol1-5/REENG.htm.

Davidson, W.H. (1993). Beyond re-engineering: The three phases of business transformation. *IBM Systems Journal,* 32(1), 65-79.

Halgrim, R. (1993). *Thomas Edison/Henry Ford Winter Estates.* Kansas City, MO: Terrell Publishing Co. ISBN 0-935031-67-7.

Hammer, M. (1997). The soul of the new organization. In F. Hesselbein, M. Goldsmith, and R. Beckhard (Eds.), *The Organization of the Future.* San Francisco, CA: Jossey-Bass Publishers. pp. 25-31.

Hammer, M., and Champy, J. (1993). *Reengineering the Corporation: A Manifesto for Business Revolution.* New York: Harper Collins Publishers.

Hanna, D.E. (1998). Higher education in an era of digital competition: Emerging organizational models. *Journal of Asynchronous Learning Networks,* 2(1): 66-95.

Harel, E., and Partipilo, G. (1996). Reengineering beyond the illusion of control. *CAUSE/EFFECT,* 19(2), 38-44.

Heterick, Jr., R.C., Mingle, J.R., and Twigg, C.A. (1997). The public policy implications of a global learning infrastructure. *Educom National Learning Infrastructure Initiative.* Denver, CO. November 13-14. [Online.] http://www.educom.edu/program/nlii/keydocs/policy.html.

Heterick, Jr., R.C. (Ed.). (1993). Reengineering teaching and learning in higher education: Sheltered groves, Camelot, windmills, and malls. Boulder, CO: *CAUSE,* Professional Paper Series #10.

Heterick, Jr., R.C. (1995). Overcoming Murphy. *Educom Review,* 30(2). [Online.] http://educom.edu/web/pubs/review/reviewArticles/30260.html.

Lewis, R.G., and Smith, D.H. (1997). Why quality improvement in higher education. *International Journal: Continuous Improvement Monitor,* 1(2). [Online.] http://llanes.panam.edu/journal/library/vol1no2/lewisarticle.html.

Mangan, K.S. (1998, June 18). 'Corporate universities' said to force business schools to change their ways. *The Chronicle of Higher Education.* [Online.]

Merron, K. (1995). *Riding the Wave: Designing Your Organization's Architecture for*

Enduring Success. New York: Van Nostrand Reinhold.

Meyer, J.H. (1997). *Re-Engineering the Land Grant College of Agriculture.* Davis: University of California.

Nadler, D. (1995). *Discontinuous Change: Leading Organizational Transformation.* San Francisco: Jossey-Bass, 1995.

Naisbitt, J. (1988). *Megatrends.* New York: Warner Books.

Oblinger, D.G. (1997). High tech takes the high road: New players in higher education. *Educational Record,* 78(1), 30-37.

Pappas, A.T. (1996). *Reengineering Your Nonprofit Organization: A Guide to Strategic Transformation.* New York: John Wiley & Sons, Inc.

Porter, J.H. (1993, Winter). Business reengineering in higher education: Promise and reality. *CAUSE/EFFECT,* 16(4). [Online.] http://www.cause.org/information-resources/ir-library/text/cem934a.txt.

Rowley, D.J, Lujan, H.D. and Dolence, M.G. (1998). *Strategic Choices for the Academy: How Demand for Lifelong Learning will Re-Create Higher Education.* San Francisco: Jossey-Bass Publishers.

Rowley, D.J, Lujan, H.D., and Dolence, M.G. (1997). *Strategic Change in Colleges and Universities: Planning to Survive and Prosper.* San Francisco: Jossey-Bass Publishers.

Selingo, J. (1998). Small, private colleges brace for competition from distance learning. *The Chronicle of Higher Education,* May 1, A33-35.

Smallen, D.L. (1993). Reengineering of student learning? A second opinion from Camelot. In R.C. Heterick, Jr. (Ed.), *Reengineering Teaching and Learning in Higher Education: Sheltered Groves, Camelot, Windmills, and Malls. CAUSE* Professional Paper Series, #10. Boulder, CO. pp. 21-26.

Stahlke, H.F.W., and Nyce, J.M. (1996, Winter). Reengineering higher education: reinventing teaching and learning. *CAUSE/EFFECT,* 19(4), 44-51.

Toffler, A. (1980). *The Third Wave.* New York: William Morrow.

Whinston, A.B. (1994, Fall). Reengineering education. *Journal of Information Systems Education,* 6(3), 126-133. [Online.] http://www5.pair.com/elicohen/JISE/Vol6/63/v63_1.htm.

ENDNOTES

1. While the basic concepts of transformation or reengineering are relatively simple, implementing them is a major undertaking within any organization: "It will generally involve: 1) overcoming organizational resistance; 2) adopting a different style of leadership; 3) introducing a new organizational culture; 4) empowering individuals; 5) developing flexible teams and self-oriented workgroups; 6) significantly and continually raising standards, many times through endeavors such as total quality management (TQM) programs; 7) redefining the organizational structure; 8) creating well-designed internal and external networks that rely on social interaction and electronic communications; 9) addressing a whole host of auxiliary issues such as new policy/procedure development, ongoing training and education, dealing with technophobia, and so forth; and, finally, 10) seeing that all of this fits together through good strategic planning and management" (Penrod and Dolence, 1992, pp. 9-10).

Chapter XIX

Forces of Change: The Emergence of a Knowledge Society and New Generations of Learners

Bizhan Nasseh
Ball State University

INTRODUCTION

Nothing in the history of humankind has permeated every aspect of life and culture as deeply and as rapidly as have the computer technology and the global network of the Internet. Over the last 10 years there has been a vast infusion of technology into communications, business, politics, social interactions, the workplace, and personal lives. Jobs in all sectors of society are being redefined to accommodate the new importance of information technology in society (Long and Long, 1998). Technology has made possible new forms of communication: thousands of virtual communities exist where members can share thoughts and knowledge independent of culture, country, religion, ethnicity, and economic status. In the workplace it is possible to conduct business with partners and clients without a physical presence. Technology's influence is both national and global.

As for the national influence, technology is changing the personal and professional lives of people, the operations of businesses, the communication techniques of society, the priorities of families, and the entertainment industry. Within the next few years, the population, institutions, and government will accept the extensive saturation of technology into every aspect of society as a national reality. With respect to the global influence, technology is also changing a geographically divided world into a global society and economy. A global society peopled with empowered citizens who can synchronously or asynchronously discuss issues and share knowledge can also collaborate on activities and interests and solve pressing problems.

Technology's influence is also felt in the education system. Nationally, K-12 education and higher education institutions are undergoing dramatic changes, and the development of global education has created an opportunity for learners around the world to access needed resources and learning programs. The educational system now presents the possibility of learning-on-demand without limitation of time, place, resources, and physical facilities.

The purpose of this chapter is to discuss how technology has been a key factor in the development of the knowledge society, the emergence of two new generations of learners (the Internet-generation and adult learners), and the subsequent shifts in the role and structures of institutions of higher education. The chapter illustrates how these factors are interrelated, and the ways in which the development of one is a force of change on the others, thereby facilitating the development of new educational identities at the national and international levels for institutions of higher education in the 21ˢᵗ century.

CASE QUESTIONS

- What are the expectations of the two new generations of learners (the Internet-Generation and adult learners) with regard to institutions of higher education?
- What new practices and educational structures are initiated by the emergence of the two new generations of learners?
- What are higher education institutions' roles and responsibilities in the generation, distribution, and utilization of knowledge in a knowledge society?

THE EMERGENCE OF A KNOWLEDGE SOCIETY

There has been exponential growth in investments in the generation of knowledge. For many nations, this is seen as a means to ensure a higher status in the global economy and improvement in the social interests such as education, health, and entertainment. The emergent status of knowledge in the national and global economy and society necessitates that nations create infrastructures, cultures, and educational systems that will enable the transformation from an information to a knowledge society. A knowledge society is a society with the power of scientific, technical, and professional knowledge and with knowledge workers to help people, organizations, and society to successfully meet the challenges of the 21st century. Just as education played a valuable role in the transition from an industrial to a service and information society, it is hoped that educational institutions can also make needed contributions to transform our information society to a knowledge society.

In this new century, a society's most important asset will be its ability to generate new knowledge from current knowledge, to share and distribute knowledge among organizations and communities, and to find innovative ways to utilize knowledge to improve the economy and society. Technology will continue to have even greater roles in the generation, distribution, and application of knowledge in the 21ˢᵗ century. Some countries have already taken major steps in the movement toward a knowledge society. In Finland, advancements in the communication technology infrastructure have made the cost of access and information transmission relatively low; now, attention is being paid to the content of that knowledge and its distribution. Canada is creating the Canadian Institute for a Knowledge Society, an organization committed to building a knowledge society. European countries as well are working as a unit, discussing and looking forward to the challenge of creating a knowledge community in Europe. In part, this is being done through conferences, such as "Quest for Competence—Toward a Knowledge Society," which bring together teachers, students, and business people.

In the United States, the National Information Infrastructure (NII), proposed by the Clinton-Gore administration, created a major opportunity for the development of infrastructure to access the Internet potentially from every home, school, library, community, and workplace in the United States. The NII has the potential to support the knowledge-age model of learning and business. In addition to the contribution of NII and educational institutions, other changes are necessary to facilitate a successful transformation to a knowledge society. These include some changes in the current political, social, and economic status of many people in the United States.

As society enters the 21st century, capital is no longer the most important resource and asset for organizations; rather, it is workers who have the power of knowledge that is most valued. Moreover, the most prosperous organizations will be those that provide a fertile environment and learning community for employees to obtain and share knowledge, to work collaboratively in teams, and to develop innovative ways of utilizing knowledge.

A knowledge society should therefore offer its citizens opportunities for lifelong learning, learning-on-demand, and adaptive and self-paced learning. In addition, society should have partnerships among education providers, business branches, industries, and government agencies in maintaining status as a knowledge society. Ultimately, it should recognize that knowledge workers are the most important asset of society.

A reasonable assumption is that, for the transformation to a knowledge society and preservation of a knowledge society's status, different branches of society—society as a whole, institutions of higher education, and individual members of society—should make major contributions. Some of the needed contributions from society in the development of knowledge society are to: develop a national policy that supports learning as a basic right of all citizens; promote equity in access to needed knowledge without limitation of social and economic status; support regulations for protection of intellectual property and innovation; enhance digital infrastructures and communities at local, national, and global levels. Additionally, society should create a National Knowledge Society (NKS) that facilitates generation, distribution, and innovative application of knowledge; develop links between NKS and education providers, businesses, industry, and government for needed knowledge generation, distribution, and application.

Some of the needed contributions from higher education institutions are to: generate new knowledge and share this knowledge with businesses, communities, and other institutions; react quickly to the educational needs of society at local, national and global levels; create lifelong learning centers in addition to traditional degree programs; develop partnership with other institutions and different branches of society; provide adaptive environments and programs to make all citizens eligible learners; and develop cultures, structures and programs that benefit and support a knowledge society.

Some of the needed contributions from individual citizens are to: create time for formal and informal learning; develop basic skills for accessing digital knowledge and participating in digital communities; develop desire for new knowledge and skills; share knowledge at the workplace and in the community; and support teamwork and contribute to a group's knowledge.

THE EMERGENCE OF TWO GENERATIONS OF LEARNERS

In the 21st century, the infusion of technology will affect two groups of students. The first group, the Internet-generation, includes the "traditional students" who come directly from high school to college for education. The second group, adult learners, are traditionally older and come back to or start college to learn new skills or update their current skills. These two groups—with different needs, styles, abilities, expectations, experiences, and social responsibilities—coexist in the current formal educational system. Knowledge of these two groups can help higher education institutions to develop effective pedagogical practices and educational programs.

Internet-Generation Learners

The Internet-generation students differ from other groups of learners in a number of ways. They are currently 10 to 20 years old, and have lived in the era of computers and the Internet (Tapscott, 1998). In 1998 an estimated 51 million students were in the K-12 educational system in the United States. This number will grow, and by the year 2004, more than 55 million will be studying in the K-12 school system. In the new century, this Internet-generation will enter into institutions of higher education with a different ideology and philosophy, and with different expectations about education, teachers, and institutions, as well as computer and communication technologies.

Members of the Internet-generation see computers and network technologies as tools for "edutainment"—part education, part entertainment—with the potential for many new discoveries. They see teachers as partners in a team that accomplishes the objective of learning. They expect the educational institution to be a place with needed resources, tools, and knowledge for discovery, research, and innovation. They see the learning process as innovative, creative, unique, and digitally focused, and they demand empowerment. They are ready to be lifelong learners and skilled knowledge workers in the knowledge society.

They are natural researchers, and they generously share their knowledge with the digital community, teachers, students, and institutions at the global level. They are adaptable to changes in computer and communication technologies and their applications in life, education, and work. They have positive attitudes toward the future and see it as an extension of today. They are ambassadors who have the potential to bring cultures, countries, and religions closer through digital communication, collaboration, and the sharing of knowledge. They are the most socialized generation in the digital world and the most isolated generation in the physical world through the Internet.

Understanding the Internet-generation is a very difficult task for the current educational system that is operated and directed by a generation with a different philosophy, culture, style, and ideology. Technology has played a major role in the life, education, entertainment, and communication of the Internet-generation, so educational programs designed for them might include: quality digital infrastructure and adequate access, bandwidth, computer power, and support for interactive multimedia Web-based resources and materials; the opportunity for asynchronous learning even for residential students; adaptable processes that can help students to personalize learning based on their talents, abilities, and styles.

Adult Learners

Today's society is unlike any other: now adults outnumber youths, the population is better educated than ever before, and there is more cultural and ethnic diversity (Merriam and Cafferella, 1991). With rapid changes in knowledge bases, needs for new skills, and the competitive global economy, educating the workforce has become increasingly important to preserve the status of American society. We are seeing more and more adults return to formal education, and lifelong learning is becoming an integrated part of their lives, especially considering the potential of technology to link educational institutions to home and work-sites (Zigerell, 1984).

This generation of learners is creating a huge market for the business of learning, and it demands a customer-oriented relationship with institutions of higher education. Many adult learners were originally schooled in the traditional mode, which is based on the campus, classroom, and teacher-centered and teacher-directed programs. Now adult learners face a system where the teacher is an expert who facilitates learning processes and activities, the institution is a place to acquire the skills and knowledge needed to prosper in their jobs and lives, technology is a tool to provide additional possibilities for learning and communication, and the learning process is innovative and student-centered, and learning activities are problem-centered and outcome-oriented.

Although it is difficult to attempt to characterize such a heterogeneous group, in large part adult learners have clear objectives for their participation in formal education; often have other commitments (such as family, work or community); have rich experiences that enable them to participate in the design of learning processes and activities; prefer self-paced and self-directed learning processes and activities; demand outcome-oriented education worthy of their time and investment; are unfamiliar with the digital world and might face challenges in adapting to technology and technology-based education; and are more problem-centered than subject-centered in learning (Knowles, 1980).

The success of institutions of higher education in attracting adult learners to their programs has a direct relationship with their understanding of the needs and expectations of adult learners. Programs targeted for adult learners might include orientation and training opportunities in technology-based and online education; adaptive educational programs that can be modified to an individual's styles, abilities, and environment; and programs designed to prepare people for the current job market and global economy. The structure of educational systems should take into account the demands of a technology-based, outcome-oriented, and student-centered education, and consider how programs can respond to the needs and expectations of both Internet-generation and adult learners.

FORCES OF CHANGE IN HIGHER EDUCATION

Considering the metamorphosis into a knowledge society and the changing nature and expectations of learners, it is important to consider the way institutions of higher education should be structured to accommodate these needs. Institutions of higher education have made major contributions to societal transformation by providing needed knowledge and by preparing economically, educationally, and socially capable intellectuals. In large part, society expects educational organizations to: generate new knowledge through research and share this knowledge with businesses, communities, other institutions, and society; develop programs that satisfy learning needs of a knowledge society; provide adaptive environments and programs to make all citizens eligible learners; create a lifelong learning center in addition to traditional degree programs; initiate social trends for solving some of today's problems such as drugs, familial dysfunction, violence, social and economic injustice, and environmental disasters; and endure new challenges posed by the development of a knowledge society.

In the 20th century, society made enormous investments in institutions of higher education's growth and development. In the 21st century, demands that institutions of higher education meet requirements of a knowledge society will create new, increasingly difficult challenges for these institutions, including accessing sources of knowledge, improving the content of knowledge and generating new knowledge, developing innovative ways for applying knowledge to social and economic improvement, developing learning environments and programs that make all citizens eligible for learning, and finally establishing relations between education, research, business, industry, government, and community.

In other words, regardless of the reasons individuals have for learning, institutions of higher education should provide needed environments, programs, and resources for learning throughout life for citizens without limitation of time, place, and social status. Computer and communication technologies have great potential for developing and delivering needed learning resources and programs.

In industrial and information societies, providing services and manufacturing has been based on the philosophy of group services and mass production. Even institutions of higher education offer systems and programs that focus on the student body as a whole, not on individual students. However, because of the significant role of each individual in a knowledge society, issues such as individual styles, abilities, experiences, limitations, needs, and social and economic status are very important. Institutions of higher education must develop adaptive learning programs and resources that make each individual eligible to participate in learning and able to grow both intellectually and personally.

In short, the growing presence of technology, with its national and global influences, profoundly affects the economy, society, and educational systems. The existing educational system—a hierarchical, teacher- rather than student-centered system—was developed over 100 years ago. Advancements in computer and communication technologies, changes in the student body, changes from a data society to an information society (and soon to a knowledge society), and tough competition in the global economy and education have brought about the need for changes in the traditional missions, cultures, structures, processes, and programs of higher education. Figure 1 presents a summary of the changes in higher education.

Thus, the new technology is not only altering the way education is implemented, but is fundamentally changing the very orientation and mission of the system.

Figure 1: Summary of Changes in Higher Education Institutions

Traditional Higher Education Institutions	Evolving Higher Education Institutions
Default mode (campus, classes, lectures)	Preferred mode (campus classes, virtual classes …)
Synchronous education	Asynchronous education
Process-oriented	Outcome-oriented
Teacher-centered	Student-centered
Geographic monopoly	Global education
Limited audience	Global audience
Focus on teaching	Focus on learning
Euro-American style	Multiculturalism
Standard programs	Adaptive programs
Local orientation	Global orientation
Traditional process	Business process
Degree programs	Degree and open-ended programs
Scheduled programs	Learning-on-demand
Center for traditional learning	Center of lifelong learning
Isolation	Partnership

COMPONENTS OF THE NEW PRACTICE IN HIGHER EDUCATION

The demand for educational expertise to support social and economic development is forcing higher education to look for new educational systems and delivery mechanisms (Oblinger and Maruyama, 1996). Institutions of higher education are creating new elements of practices, which are initiated by the possibilities of computer and communication technologies, needs of new generations of learners, and the development of a knowledge society. Nasseh (1999) writes:

> Institutions of higher education are recognizing that providing opportunity for lifelong learning is vital, asynchronous education is here to stay, cooperation and collaboration is the only way, and global education beyond the traditional geographic limits is the hallmark of learning in the 21st century (p. 2).

Institutions of higher education are increasingly utilizing the following elements of practice in order to satisfy learners' expectations, to access the market of education, and to survive tough global competition.

Asynchronous Education

In the 20th century, people physically came to institutions of higher education for information and knowledge. In the 21st century, information and knowledge can go to people without any geographic limitation. Students from South Africa, the United States, and Hong Kong can all register in the same course offered by Britain's Open University or American Duke University's MBA program. Many programs offer asynchronous education, a logical response to the need for learning-on-demand, without limitation of time and place. While geographic limitation was a strong reason for each institution to attract many local students in the past, continuous advancement in computer and communication technologies is supporting the growth of asynchronous educational programs.

Presently, more than 800 institutions in the United States, all competing for students not only from local and national levels, but also from around the world, offer Cyber-education. The Next Generation Internet, a federally led initiative, and Internet2, a university-led effort, will facilitate the expansion of Cyber-education even more in the 21st century. Nationally and globally, asynchronous education will create tough competition among traditional institutions and other education providers in accessing the market and attracting learners. Traditional campuses will continue to attract students, but even on-campus students will demand some asynchronous learning activities and courses in their schedules. Asynchronous education simply coincides well with demands of the market and load of life of most learners.

Marketing Educational Programs

Institutions of higher education are now advertising their programs through television, the Internet, and newspapers to identify themselves and their products to reach prospective learners on a local, national, and even international level. For example, The Community College Distance Network went national with $30,000 in contributions from each partici-pating college, and the first advertisements appeared in August 1998 in Chicago and Los Angeles, where there are large immigrant populations (Blumenstyk, 1998). The hope was to attract new students to more than 500 courses. This example of a customer-oriented advertisement to deliver messages to a specific target market and to introduce specific services and products is becoming more common in education. A higher educational institution's practice of marketing has the same purpose as business branches: they want to reach an audience and clients, and to build an identity in the field. These institutions are willing to spend big dollars for marketing from their annual budgets since education is becoming a much more competitive market that is going to demand more time and money and require an integrated approach (Lenington, 1996).

Competition

Global demands and needs for knowledge and skills have created a new mass market for education. In addition to competition among institutions of higher education, corporate universities are making life even harder for these institutions. Jean Meister, president of the Corporate University Exchange, said that there is an enormous network of corporate universities in the United States, some 1,500 of them with combined annual budgets of $30 billion (Denning, 1999). These corporate universities are offering competency-based and outcome-oriented educational training along with professional and certification programs. Some of them, such as the Arthur D. Little School in Boston, have formal degree granting powers. Others have developed partnerships with more traditional colleges and universities that provide standard course credits from institutions of higher education to students of corporate universities.

Corporate universities have programs and philosophies that meet the requirements and demands of most learners and employers. In addition to traditional degree programs, institutions of higher education should offer career professional and certification programs such as Duke's global MBA, Penn State's Executive Program, and Mercer University's Technical Certification programs. Asynchronous and synchronous offering of these types of programs can increase an institution's competitive edge in the market of education. The competition among and partnerships with corporate universities and other institutions of higher education will direct these institutions away from traditional educational systems and toward systems employing business processes and practices.

Partnerships

There are already many different types of partnership programs to attract learners, share technical and professional skills, utilize human resources, develop innovative programs and advanced computer applications, generate new knowledge by research, and strengthen the quality of learning resources. The Western Governors University (WGU) is a good example of partnership among institutions of higher education. Presently, 18 states are participating members. The main goal of WGU is to provide competency-based education toward degree, professional certificate, and technical educational programs. The University Corporation for Advanced Internet Development (UCAID), established in 1997, is another form of partnership for the development of better quality tools and resources. Also some universities, in collaboration with corporations such as Microsoft, Cisco, Oracle, and Novell, are offering certification programs and use experts from these corporations for teaching.

Partnerships for developing new programs, sharing expertise, and developing higher quality resources are incredibly important in competing for improving learning programs. Possible partnerships might include: partnership with local businesses, industries, government agencies, and K-12 school systems; partnership with global businesses, industries, and communities in need of expertise and competency, as well as for degree programs, certification programs, and internship programs; partnerships among institutions of higher education for sharing knowledge, experience, resources, and experts at local and global levels.

Benchmarking

Benchmarking is a way to develop quality indicators and to measure programs against similar programs offered by other institutions of higher education. While benchmarking has commonly been a tool for comparing and measuring methods in businesses and industry, many institutions of higher education now consistently practice benchmarking for improvement and competitiveness of their programs. For instance, in 1994 Penn State's information technology department compared its program against similar programs at five major research universities: UCLA, Texas, Illinois, Michigan, and Wisconsin (Augustson, 1994). The process of benchmarking applies to most deliveries, operations, and development programs. With tough global competition and restricted budgets, it is important to benchmark some of the critical and expensive programs against the best in the field for improvement.

Competency-Based Education

Considering the rate at which computer and communication technologies are penetrating all facets of life, everyone is required to possess two different types of competencies: basic competency in information technology and competency related to discipline and subject matter. For centuries, discipline-related competency has been the main criterion for the accomplishment of any discipline-related task. But presently, in most cases, the successful completion of a discipline-related task also requires an adequate level of competency in information technology. "Computer competency is becoming a prerequisite for people pursuing almost any career—from actuary to zoologist" (Long and Long, 1998, p. 13). For example, a faculty member in a natural resources department teaches an on-campus course on Chemical Spills. The faculty member should have knowledge of the soil, contaminants, cleanup techniques, related theories, and relevant methodologies. In addition, the faculty member should have adequate knowledge about using e-mail, bulletin boards, and Web applications and resources. This faculty member's students also need to have adequate basic competency to communicate and collaborate with the teacher and other students by computer, and to find needed resources on the Web. The demands and needs for basic competency will continue to include more branches of society in the 21st century. While the explosion of knowledge does create challenges, institutions of higher education can also benefit from the power and possibilities of computer and communication technologies to develop quality competency-based learning resources and programs. A computer application of a theory, a computer case study of an event, and a simulation program of a model can help students learn the subject matter in depth and use new knowledge and skills more effectively in real situations. Fortunately, every discipline has rich samples, events, and models that can be developed into computer case studies and simulations.

The movement toward competency-based education does not represent a call for converting liberal arts universities to vocational ones. It is, rather, a call for competency-based education in areas and subjects in which students need to develop practical as well as theoretical knowledge. The competency-based curricula that complement the liberal arts curricula can help students apply knowledge and perform more adequately in real situations. For example, Mercer University Information Technology Center, in collaboration with Innovative Community Technology Service, offers technical certification programs in Microsoft, Cisco, and Novell. The short-term certification programs fit perfectly with the needs for new skills of adult learners. The programs also provide practical knowledge for students in degree-oriented programs such as computer science and information technology. Competency-based education is another new reality for institutions of higher education in the business of education.

Institutions of higher education would benefit from incorporating these new practices as it will help them to support the changing educational needs of society as well as survive tough global competition for the educational market in the 21st century. The addition of new practices to the traditional system does not undermine what a higher educational institution has been; it is a logical response to the infusion of the technology in our life, work, and communication.

LOOKING TO THE FUTURE

The default mode of the traditional educational systems was developed over a century ago. These campus-based, hierarchical, teacher-centered systems recognize teaching as the main responsibility of institutions of higher education. But recently, an influx of technology, the need to retrain the workforce, demands for asynchronous education, and global needs for continuous learning have made education a mass and competitive market. Additionally, advancements in computer and communication technologies, changes in the student body, the transformation from a data society to an information society (and soon to a knowledge society), and tough competition in the global economy and education have brought about the need for changes in the current educational system. Institutions of higher education must redefine their missions, structures, cultures, and programs to meet the requirements of the 21st century society.

The coexistence of the Internet-generation and adult learners—with different expectations, abilities, styles, and needs—continues to change institutions of higher education's missions, cultures, practices, instructional deliveries, and business operations. Knowledge of these two groups' characteristics and expectations can help institutions of higher education to develop educational programs and learning resources that can satisfy both groups' objectives for participating in formal education.

The transformation to a knowledge society encourages institutions of higher education to be lifelong learning centers instead of traditional information providers with degree-oriented programs. Furthermore, it facilitates and supports equity in access to content of knowledge for all citizens without any social and economic restrictions. Scientific, technical, and professional knowledge will continue to be the competitive edge in the global economy and society in the 21st century. Institutions of higher education must sustain their vital roles in the generation of new knowledge, the distribution and sharing of knowledge, and the innovation in utilizing knowledge in the new century. The digital revolution and global network is going to create changes not only in terms of who learns, or how and when they learn, but also in terms of who the education providers will be.

The new century is conceivably full of the prosperity that can result from collaboration among institutions of higher education—collaboration that will prepare us intellectually to solve many problems inherited from the 20th century. The journey into and through the 21st century is full of unexpected failures and successes, unimaginable discoveries and developments, unthinkable innovations and creations. Our pioneers continue to invent a future that shapes and affects our lives, our communities, and our world.

DISCUSSION QUESTIONS

1. What are the potential challenges that educators will likely have to consider in facilitating the integration of education with technology?
2. What are some of the unanticipated consequences that might result from the implementation of new practices in higher education?
3. What are the similarities and differences between the Internet-Generation Learners and Adult Learners? Can technology accommodate both of their needs, or is one group more likely to benefit?

ENDNOTE

This chapter is dedicated to Dr. Clinton P. Fuelling (1937-1999), chair of the computer science department at Ball State University.

REFERENCES

Auguston, J. G. (1994, October & November). *Benchmarking: Real World Results from a Real World Attempt.* Paper presented at the meeting of EDUCOM'94, San Antonio, Texas.

Blumenstyk, G. (1998). Leading community colleges go national with new distance-learning network. *Chronicle of Higher Education,* 44, A16-A17.

Denning, J. P. (1999 May/June). Teaching as a social process. *Educom Review,* 34, 18-22.

Knowles, S. M. (1980). *From Pedagogy to Andragogy.* New York: Cambridge Books.

Lenington, L. R. (1996). *Managing Higher Education as a Business.* Phoenix: Oryx Press.

Long, L., & Long, N. (1998). *Computers.* New Jersey: Prentice Hall Inc.

Merriam, B.S., & Caffarella, S. R. (1991). *Learning in Adulthood.* San Francisco: Jossey-Bass Inc.

Nasseh, B. (1999). Are higher education institutions ready for the 21st century? *Journal of Distance Education Report,* 3(4), pp. 2-5.

Oblinger, D., & Maruyama, M. (1996). *Distributed Learning.* CAUSE Professional Paper #14.

Tapscott, D. (1998). *Growing Up Digital: The Rise of the Net Generation.* New York: McGraw-Hill.

Zigerell, J. (1984). *Distance Education: An Information Age Approach to Adult Education.* Columbus, OH: The National Center for Research in Vocational Education, The Ohio State University.

Chapter XX

Adopting Information Technologies for Instructional Environments

Siva Kumari
University of Houston

INTRODUCTION

The introduction of new information technologies has created a turbulent environment for change in higher education; this has caused institutions, faculty and administrators to rethink their roles, teaching venues, and delivery options in markedly new ways than those currently available. The promise that accompanies any such remarkable change also brings with it some realities as these ideas are tested, implemented and adopted. Neal (1998), an outspoken critic of the unbridled enthusiasm of technology, advocates investigating experiences of individual faculty members since they are the end-of-the-line implementers of technology in higher education. He says that their opinions about the benefits of technology should be of ultimate value in discovering useful and effective strategies that have the capacity for long-term survival.

This case study presents a synthesis of data derived from interviews with six faculty members in an urban public institution of higher learning. These innovators, who have been implementing information technologies in their teaching, provide valuable information about the possibilities and the restrictions, and discuss support structures that are needed to advance the adoption of this innovation on a larger scale. This chapter addresses four core areas of concern relating to the integration of IT in higher education. The first is to understand the factors that led faculty to adopt IT in their teaching. The second is to explore the interplay between particular technologies and teaching practice. The third to ascertain the relationship between teaching architectures and learning outcomes.

CASE QUESTIONS

- What factors influence the early adoption of technology by faculty?
- How can technology be used to create student-centered learning environments?
- What are the unintended consequences of using technology in teaching and learning?
- What are the rewards for using technology in the classroom environment? Does it reduce or increase the amount of time spent?

BACKGROUND

Urban Public University (UPU) is a state-supported public university located in a large urban city in the southern part of the United States that prides itself for its capacity to enroll and educate a diverse student body. It is a doctoral degree-granting institution, the largest in a system that includes three other universities. It offers 103 bachelor's degree programs, 119 master's degree programs, 53 doctoral degree programs and three professional degree programs through its 14 colleges. The teaching faculty in this university consists of 856 ranked faculty.

Six faculty members at this university were interviewed to address issues of integrating technology in higher education at a public university. They were identified through a search of the university's Web site for faculty who had won teaching awards, through Internet courses, from personal knowledge about those who have a reputation for innovation, and from recommendations of other faculty.

The faculty members interviewed for this chapter represent diversity in terms of academic disciplines and professional rank. To preserve confidentiality, only collective descriptions of the group are provided. These members include two associate deans of colleges who continue to teach. The other four include one tenured associate professor, one assistant professor seeking tenure in the year 2000, and two visiting assistant professors, one of whom has been recently promoted to an associate professor.

These faculty have been employed at this institution between four to 17 years and represent the winners of a number of teaching and distance learning awards. Many of these faculty members are also involved in an informal group, formed in 1994, that meets regularly to discuss and showcase integration of information technology (IT) into education. Those who do not teach entirely online are involved in integrating information technologies consistently into their courses. Some have participated in funded projects that resulted in technology-enriched learning resources. One faculty member is the editor of a journal that focuses on the integration of technology in his discipline. Four of the six have participated in Interactive Television (ITV) courses. Only one has never taught a completely online course.

Excerpts from the interviews are intertwined throughout this chapter. Each excerpt is preceded by FM1 (Faculty Member 1), FM2 (Faculty Member 2) to represent the person from whom that quote originated so that readers, if they wish to do so, can easily decipher whether or not the excerpts emanate from the same individual.

Factors that Led to the Adoption of Information Technology for Teaching

One of the much-touted benefits of IT is the potential for implementing new and highly flexible combinations of technologies to serve specific teaching needs of the instructor. The sophistication and level of IT implementation depends both on prior expertise with technologies, the operant teaching philosophy, unfulfilled teaching needs, and expressed student needs. This section explores these issues and "technology readiness" as a factor that prompted faculty to integrate IT into their teaching. Although "readiness" was inherent in these early adopters, this issue needs to be understood in context as institutions create support systems for other faculty. It is presented here to instigate a discussion about how to create effective systems of support for those who may not be "technologically ready" or "inclined."

A background in, facility with, and interest in computing were factors that led them to be poised and ready to adopt IT in their teaching. Five out of the six faculty members indicated a history of computing that formed the basis for and propelled them to use these newer information technologies. When technology teaching innovations arose in their own disciplines, they had an affinity to the technology and developed practical experience with implementation in teaching. The focus of the implementation was always how to use the technology as a teaching tool.

One faculty member described himself as a "tinkerer" and as someone who has a natural curiosity about the use of technology in the classroom. He recalled his history of implementing technologies incrementally that led him to use IT and continue the pattern of experimentation in three formats: face-to-face classroom, Interactive Television (ITV) and online teaching.

Another faculty member, whose expertise is educational technology, indicated that she was inspired by a colleague's presentation that demonstrated the use of Internet resources in teaching. This demonstration sparked an interest in and contemplation about how IT would serve her teaching needs. She recounted her path of experimentation that started by creating hyperlinks which eventually transformed into a full-fledged online course that has been offered several times.

Consistently, this group indicated that creating elaborate, technology-rich teaching resources for the benefit of their students was one of the main reasons that led them to implement IT. Since the majority of students are commuters and hold jobs outside the university, the fundamental benefit of IT to serve "anytime, anywhere" access to learning resources is valuable. In response to the learning needs of their students, they hosted lecture notes, in-class presentations, and links to additional content-related resources. Some aids were created to assist students in terms of the perceived deficiencies in learning skills essential to the effective consumption of curricular content:

> **FM5**: Many of my students lack certain skills. They don't know how to take notes in a lecture. They need that to help figure out what was important and what was not important. And online resources can help do that.

The creation of Web resources enabled one faculty member to change the dynamics of her face-to-face classes by enriching the teacher-student interaction:

> **FM6**: I always want to cover too much material. We have three hours of class once a week.... I found myself lecturing, imparting that knowledge... Now I can ask them to read that (material) on their own. I can ask then to explore topics that are interesting to them. And I can spend my time in class in a more dialogue kind of interaction rather than me talk, you listen, you write.

To summarize, the factors that led these faculty to adopt technology were a predisposition to using technology and a need to address teaching and student learning needs for which IT was a logical solution.

Use of Information Technology and Implications for Teaching

The experiences of these faculty members shed some light on the variables that need to be considered in iterative refinements when using particular technologies. A single technology implemented and employed with subtle variations could produce different outcomes. Pedagogy plays as important a role as the technology itself. One faculty member, for instance, might employ the pedagogical strategy of using students as moderators in Web-based conferencing and may observe dramatically increased volume of interaction in course communications among students. Another faculty member who self-moderates the Web-based conferencing may observe that course communications have remained similar to those in a traditional classroom. This section will present issues relating the manner and use of individual technologies that these faculty have adopted and their observations about the effects on teaching practices.

Email and Other Asynchronous Communications

Email continues to be a popular technology on college campuses and is relatively easy to implement in teaching environments as attested by the annual Campus Computing Project (Green, 1998). There is a continuous rise in the percentage of college courses using email. This percentage of use estimated at 54 percent in 1999, was 44 percent in 1998, 33 percent in 1997, 25 percent in 1996 and just eight percent in 1994. Email can be used to foster communication between the teacher and the student in relation to administrative and educational issues about the course.

One faculty member used asynchronous communications between face-to-face sessions as a means of providing the students with material to discuss between classes. The ensuing student-to-student dialogue formed the basis of further discussion during the next in-class session. Thus, out-of-class communication was used as an extension and a stimulant for in-class discussion. Others used email to engender communication where there was none before and/or to change the culture of student-teacher interaction:

> FM5: For commuter students, first of all, it means communication with faculty. I can hold office hours for most semesters and basically for the whole semester never see a student. ... And electronic technology can build a bridge that's important.

One faculty member used this "bridge" to gain more usable knowledge about her students:

> FM6: It's much easier to stay connected to your students. That's because we use the online hypergroups. And they know that I'm much easier to access. And I know that they are much easier to access.... And I guess knowing the students and knowing about whether they do understand the material has improved a lot.

Another employed asynchronous communications deliberately to increase the ability of students to use modern technologies in their learning activities and thus acquire the skills of communicating electronically:

> FM2: I've made it a point to encourage and in fact require students to use technology like email and to .....submit papers electronically.... I have encouraged, bribed, required them to become at least somewhat familiar with communication technologies and hopefully use them. So that every student that comes to my class has to have an active email account.

Other faculty used this technology to overcome the perceived lack of interaction when they taught Interactive Television (ITV) courses. Typically in these ITV settings, the students are in remote locations and view live broadcasts of the lecture. Students also have the option of watching taped broadcasts through the public television channel or through the library. After using email with ITV students, one faculty member suggested distance education students should be given email accounts and follow protocols that require them to check their email every so often. This would change the course and increase the communication with faculty:

> FM5: Without that, it's a correspondence course....We need to be very careful about maintaining academic quality. And I think the only way we can do that is with interactive communications.

Another faculty member, whose students typically view taped broadcasts of courses, made it a personal course policy that required students to use electronic communications:

> **FM2**: And so those folks (ITV students) then… the only communication I have with them is using the electronic medium. Those people do email and are expected to submit assignments and to raise questions using the technology.

Thus these faculty used email to encourage communications between them and their students where there were none before, to increase the quality of in-class discussion, and to encourage students to use email. The effect of increased communication while using IT has been elaborated upon by many.

Increased Communication and Use of Technology Requires Increased Time Commitment

Although communications have enormous value, there are indications that there is an analogous increase in the amount of time required to monitor, respond to, sustain, and manage incoming and outgoing course communications:

> **FM3:** They (colleagues) haven't a clue that I've spent far more time reading and responding to email messages than I would have spent on a lecturing course.

Rowntree (1995) refers to the potential negative effect that these time implications have to cause "tutor overload." Some aspects of this increased time commitment was validated by several faculty:

> **FM6:** There's an enormous amount of time commitment both on the part of the student as well as the faculty… You need to make it very clear that you will be online when you can be online. So I feel that pull on me to be there— to just live in cyberspace.

Another indicated that setting expectations in the course about reply-time, adhering to those policies, and resisting the temptation to reply to every message, is one way of countering the overload:

> **FM6:** I am online a lot. But I tell students I won't be online everyday and I won't reply 20 minutes later every time they send me an email or a post. They still expect it. But if you give it to them, they will expect it even more. They will be times when I get an email and I will let it sit just so that I am not reinforcing instant feedback.

However, conferencing technologies do have the potential of increasing the quality of teaching and learning. They allow students to share the deliberation process contemporaneously with fellow students and the faculty member in a manner that is impossible without these technologies. Traditional face-to-face interactions, in most instances, only allow the faculty member (and not fellow students) to see the product of the knowledge-negotiation process. However, when information is presented and circulated among fellow students, it promotes Socratic dialogues (Couples ,1996). Lippert (1997) termed such occurrences as the building of the learning agora. As this faculty member indicates, the results of such facilitation result in an increase in quality of student communication:

> **FM1:** They are more in-depth, they are richer. Students are able to participate more fully, more broadly, deeper ... they have more time to do research before they participate.

However, the technological skill level of the student should also be considered as a factor that could add to the faculty time load and as one that could potentially divert attention from the main content of the course. A faculty member in the humanities has reservations about re-teaching online following his first attempt:

> **FM5:** Students who took this course were not students who were fluent in technology. They were students who didn't know much about technology but wanted to learn.... I had to teach them much about their computer, much about downloading files, much about everything. ...each of these people would demand so many hours of my time, it was impossible...those 10 (students) took more time than 200 students.

Another faculty member reinforced this notion of increased time load on a per-student basis:

> **FM6:** I would not go back to not using technology but I wouldn't tell anybody— ... use this and it'll make your life easier. It doesn't. It's astonishingly compli- cated—keeping up with the needs of all these students.

One technique that could be used to disperse the traditional unidirectional flow of communication patterns (students to teacher) and thus share the workload is to establish a structure for student-to-student communications. This discourages the student-to-teacher paradigm and deflects a certain amount of responsibility to the students themselves:

> **FM6**: If they ask a question I will not be the first one to respond. And that if somebody posts a help question, needs some help, or asks for an idea, they (students) should respond. And when they realize that I am serious—don't jump in there and rush to be the guide—then it really changes the class.

To guide the occurrence of useful information exchange between students, it is important to set guidelines for participation at the outset, concerning the content of these messages. Posting guidelines for discussion in detail is only the beginning:

> **FM1**: I have found that if I do not give parameters of what kind of posting they should make, they would love to listen to themselves think. And nobody else does. And they don't have a lot to contribute, quite frankly. ...But when you give them parameters—which I do—I say that you should be referencing something with an authority, you should be referring people to a Web page, you should be telling us something about and giving us a citation. Then the quality explodes. It is so rich and so deep that people feel overloaded with so much— including me.

Setting clear expectations about email assignments prevents students from forming undue expectations. One faculty member requested that students send email after completing the assigned reading for the week. The students, however, not knowing that the faculty member was not going to respond to each of these assignments, were offended, a situation that could have been avoided by setting parameters.

Besides setting guidelines, managing the increased volume of communications, and reserving time to sustain these communications, there are time loads involved with creating other content-related online resources (Brahler et al., 1999). The following statements from two faculty members who have taught an online course between two and five times each sheds some light on the recurring time investment in modifying courses:

> **FM2:** I don't see the return on investment yet. Increasing rewards for time spent. Because I am very much in the development mode.
> **FM6:** It's a huge amount of time to begin with. But I think people are deceived by thinking that once you get it done then it's over. There are a lot of things I want to add… compared to face-to-face, week to week about twice as much. It's not fair to say it's a huge amount of time to begin with because that would depend on how much material you already had before you started.

Additionally, faculty teaching course loads are a factor. One tenured faculty member indicated that his course load—three in the spring and in the fall—was a big hindrance to finding the time to develop additional course materials. Without institutional commitment to provide course-release time, it requires greater personal time commitment to create and teach with integrated resources. Others cautioned against any misperceptions about low time commitments in the production of IT-based learning environments.

> **FM3:** I think some professors are beginning to jump on to this kind of technology thinking it's going to free them up and get them out of these large lecture classes. They might be looking at this thing as a way to give them more time. They are going to be in for a real shock when they discover the amount of time that's just involved putting all of this stuff together.

These faculty are investing their time to create new and different kinds of learning environments that capitalize on the abundant information resources for use in education. This requires them to gather, evaluate, and incorporate such resources into their teaching practices. However, the limiting factor here appears to be support that will allow these faculty to invest more time in creating refined iterations of their current courses, disseminate information of effective practices, and engage in creating other technology-enhanced learning architectures without having to expend personal time.

Students, in order to participate efficiently in these learning environments, need to possess a repertoire of basic skills. These include the ability to navigate the Internet, productively research information, judge the validity of sources, and effectively manage the retrieved information. Additional skills should include an awareness of ethical issues such as plagiarism and copyright violations. The common misconception in most institutions is the assumption that all students possess these skills. When students enter learning environments without these prerequisite skills, faculty will have to teach the technology as well as the content. This adds to the time required to maintain and teach these courses:

> **FM2:** I'm fielding a lot of basic questions on email, on Web access, on stuff like that—that I assume, or mistakenly assume, that they should have the basic competency in.

FM3: Searching the Internet is a topic that we really ought to address in some of the classes or at the library. They (students) waste a lot of time....If they spend 20 minutes learning how to do it effectively, they will save hours and hours of time.

Teaching Architectures and Learning Outcomes

Another main question that comes to the surface is to determine faculty perceptions of how technology has influenced their specific teaching and learning goals. It is important to look at both the positive outcomes of using IT as well as some of the drawbacks. Has IT enabled them to explore new teaching methodologies or learning outcomes? What, if any, are the incidental outcomes of teaching with technology.

One faculty member initially thought of IT as an extension, a technology for delivery and dissemination. Once the experimentation with this iteration was completed, however, the path of integration led to more complex questions. These questions led to the heart of the process of building nontraditional learning environments that are structured to engage students. How does one make the best use of the medium? These are questions that truly require rethinking the course and the events that occur within it in different ways. The interview excerpts below provide glimpses of some of the paradigm shifts that occur as a result of these questions:

> **FM2:** Initially it was a way of providing more information more easily or more information visually or more information without having to draw it on the blackboard each time...But as I get more into it, it's become less of an extension of a traditional classroom and more of a challenge to think of different ways of doing things and ...restructuring the learning process.
>
> **FM6:** I am pressured more to make that knowledge that they want. So I'm under more pressure to directly relate the knowledge to whom they are so that they'll want to use it and make it their own knowledge.
>
> **FM5:** That's where I think we have cutting edges, not delivery, not how can we deliver this course over the Internet, but rather a new kind of project that we literally could not do in the past.

Each course will require distinctive course architectures that include content, student activities, and communication processes to attain the intended course outcomes that are best suited for that course:

> **FM6:** The organizing... in the online class, I'm responsible for organizing that information for everybody (students) regardless of their learning style or who they are or background or what they want out of it. And, that's a lot of work— to anticipate what potential problems there might be and how they go through those. How... the technology fades away and the material comes to the front .... And revising it when it doesn't work.

Administrators focus on scalable models of technology implementation. While such models are necessary for large-scale cost-effective implementations, it is necessary to conceive newer teaching architectures for individual courses rather than merely converting existing materials to online formats. Teaching architectures, as used here, refer to the use of IT as an embedded resource in a course. It refers to the technical, instructional design and pedagogical elements incorporated in the learning environment (Chrisman & Harvey, 1998).

The number of students within a course also has an impact on the kind of teaching architectures one would use. One faculty member in the humanities who deals with classes of up to 592 students indicated that technology integration can be a rather complex undertaking with such large numbers. IT can be implemented through the creation of individual learning modules on core concepts that students can use to enhance their understanding. However, the same faculty member indicated that for courses where the student numbers were smaller, IT can play a role in equalizing access to original sources of information. Such access is a forgone conclusion in colleges with abundant resources, but a problem in an institution with limited resources for faculty to duplicate original documents for their students. Informational technologies can bridge that divide:

> **FM5:** Active learning. We want them (students) to take charge of their education, and this, if we do it creatively, can happen.

Access to computing or the lack of it may be an issue. Statistics are not available on how many students at this institution report Internet access at their homes or the least common denominator in computer hardware. Some of the colleges host their own computing laboratories for their students. In general there are 26 labs available for students in this institution. Some labs are limited to students within that particular college.

Student computing capabilities have an impact on the teaching architecture that is implemented. For instance, streaming media is not a viable option if the majority of students connect through low-bandwidth modems:

> **FM1:** I had a student literally in the middle of a jungle in Indonesia last summer. … he was connecting at about 8K half the time on Net-Meeting.

Online communication between students enables students to learn from each other as well and get to know their fellow students, thus forming the basis for an electronic learning community:

> **FM1:** And what students tend to appreciate is that they get to know people very well online. Which is an odd concept for a lot of people who have never been online or worked in this arena. But they establish rapport and get to know people in a way that they never would have time to in class.

The same faculty member continues about the learning benefits of these interactions that transform every student into a potential resource for information, a colleague and a critic—a closer emulation of the real world:

> **FM1:** And I think it is because they are learning so much from each other in Web-board postings because there is so much more there than you ever get in a classroom.

Sharing the content production aspect of the teaching architecture, some of the faculty mentioned incorporating the consistently proliferating information on Web sites into their courses:

> **FM2**: The textbook that I'm using has an online, publisher-supported, end-of-chapter quiz ….They (students) quickly discover that they can take the end-of-

chapter quiz in about two minutes. So it is painless for them. And their grades get emailed to me.

Others discussed new relationships with the publishers of textbooks to develop content. One faculty member used the content of the Web site that was associated with the textbook. Textbooks are increasingly including CDs and informational resources in their contents. Although this can be beneficial, one possible downside is "information overload." As a reviewer of textbooks for publishers, one faculty member indicated that the links were far too many and too overwhelming in some instances as opposed to a set of "magnet sites" or sites that host concentrated ranked information.

ANALYSIS

The use of information technology (IT) in higher education has transformative potential. Within an amazingly short period of time, IT has gone from the speculative revolutionary potential to transform universities to one that is increasingly devoted to discussing the realities and results of implementing these new technologies. Early in this "revolution," Noam (1995) and Tehranian (1996) argued that the inevitable and widespread adoption of IT will result in profound changes in the traditional structures and operational modes of the university. Currently predominant models of education require students to physically aggregate at the university to partake in an educational process in what some have referred as the "credit for contact model" (Dede, 1996).

Distributed IT systems, by contrast, will radically alter the direction of information flow and thus eliminate the need for the student to consider physical location or a particular university as a factor while selecting educational opportunities (Noam, 1995; Tehranian, 1996). This paradigm shift in access to education—to "anytime, anyplace learning"— requires a fundamental re-conceptualization of both the teaching and learning at the university (Brown & Duguid, 1995) and the business of operating a university (Denning, 1996; Eustis et al., 1998). Additionally, competitive new players, such as the frequently cited Microsoft University and McGraw Hill University, are challenging the sanctioned role of universities as providers of education (Anson, 1999). Such developments have incited calls for a re-engineering of the role of the faculty member by outsourcing some duties, such as production of learning environments (Chellappa et al., 1997; Couples, 1996; Young, 1997). Statements such as "former practices and roles have to give way to the digital juggernaut" exemplify sentiments that consistently reverberate through current educational literature in many disciplines (Taylor, 1998).

Much has been written about the process of integrating technology into higher education practices, the potential for change in pedagogy and learning environments (Berge, 1997; Boettcher, 1997; Boettcher & Cartwright, 1997; Bourne et al., 1997). By studying early adopters, we can begin to make preliminary observations about those issues. However, technology in and of itself does not produce invigorated learning environments, but it can be creatively employed to answer educational needs (Burbules, 1997; Chen, 1997; Clark, 1994).

CONCLUSION

From these interviews it is clear that Web-based technologies provide an infrastructure in which to implement new models of teaching and learning environments, and that innovators in a state-supported public institution are able to experiment with and without institutional support. It is also evident from the reports provided by faculty members who have experimented with these technologies that their use has made some of the more moderate prophecies for revolutionary change come true. The Web provides the faculty member with a means by which to create student-centered learning environments while eliminating the need for time and space barriers. It also appears from the perceptions of these faculty members that formal structures of support, both in technical terms and in the form of incentives, are needed if this innovation is to reach further into the fabric of this institution. Institutions need to consider renegotiating their financial paradigms, roles, and support structures to enable faculty to experiment with and successfully integrate these technologies that have the potential to result in evolved and sophisticated learning environments for students. While pockets of innovation are necessary and are welcome, some of the configurations of technology-enriched learning environments could be implemented elsewhere in the institution with minimal support. The following sentiment expressed by one of the faculty members in this sample succinctly expresses the frustration of innovators when their efforts are not formally rewarded and sustained:

> **FM1:** The innovators are being evaluated by the resistors in the tenure review process.

DISCUSSION QUESTIONS

1. In what ways does technology substitute for or supplant prior forms of communication (e.g., online office hours rather than face-to-face office hours), and in what ways does technology create new mechanisms?
2. This case describes the use of technology at an urban, public university. What different sorts of challenges and opportunities would be found at a private institution, or at a university in a non-urban setting?
3. This chapter described the experiences of faculty who had employed IT in their teaching. What might be the concerns of other faculty who do not use IT in their classrooms?
4. How could the impact of the introduction of technology be measured and assessed?

REFERENCES

Anson, C.M. (1999). Distant voices: Teaching and writing in a culture of technology. *College English*, 61(3), 261-280.

Berge, Z. (1997, May-June). Characteristics of online teaching in post-secondary, formal education. *Educational Technology*, 37 (3), 35-47.

Boettcher, J. V. (1997, November/December). Internet pitfalls: What not to do when communicating with students on the internet. *Syllabus*, 46-52.

Boettcher, J., & Cartwright, C. G. (1997, September). Designing and supporting courses on the Web. *Change*, 29(5), 62-66.

Bourne, J. R., McMaster, E., Rieger, J., & Campbell, J.O. (1997). Paradigms for online learning: A case study in the design and implementation of an asynchronous learning networks course. *Journal of Asynchronous Learning Networks*, 1(2), 38-56.

Brahler, C. J., Peterson, N. S., & Johnson, E. C. (1999). Developing on-line learning materials for higher education: An overview of current issues. *Educational Technology & Society*, 2(2). Available online: http://ifets.gmd.de/periodical/.

Burbules, N. C. (1997, Winter). Aporia: Webs, passages, getting lost and learning to go on. *Philosophy of Education*, 33-43.

Brown, J. S., & Duguid, P. (1995, August). Universities in the digital age. *Change*, 11-19.

Chellappa, R., Barua, A., & Whinston, A. B. (1997). An electronic infrastructure for a virtual university. *Communications of the ACM*, 40(9), 56-58.

Chen, L. (1997, July-August). Distance delivery systems in terms of pedagogical considerations: A reevaluation. *Educational Technology*, 34-38.

Chrisman, N. R., & Harvey, F. J. (1998). Extending the classroom: Hypermedia-supported learning. *Journal of Geography in Higher Education*, 22(1), 11-18.

Clark, R. E. (1994). Media will never influence learning. *Educational Technology Research and Development*, 42(2), 21-29.

Couples, C. (1996). Academic infotecture: Course design for cyberschool. Paper presented at the Annual Meeting of the Southern Political Science Association, Atlanta, Georgia. (ERIC Document Reproduction Service No. ED 403 854.)

Dede, C. (1996, April). Distance learning—Distributed learning: Making the transformation. *Learning and Leading with Technology*, 25-30.

Denning, P. J. (November/December, 1996). Business designs for the new university. *Educom Review*, 21-30.

Eustis, J., Gaylord, C., Hitchingham, E., Homer, K., & Taylor, D. (1998). Virginia Tech report: CNI's assessing the academic networked environment. *Information Technology & Libraries*, 17(2), 93-99.

Green, K. (1998). Campus Computing Project. Available online. Retrieved June 19, 1999, from the World Wide Web: http://www.campuscomputing.net/summaries/1998/index.html.

Lippert, P. J. (1997). Internet: The new agora? *Interpersonal Computing and Technology*, 5(3-4), 48-51.

Neal, E. (June 19, 1998). Using technology in teaching: We need to exercise healthy skepticism. *Chronicle of Higher Education*, 44(41), B4-B5.

Noam, E. M. (1995). Electronics and the dim future of the university. *Science*, 270(13), 247-249.

Rowntree, D. (1995). Teaching and learning online: A correspondence education for the 21st century? *British Journal of Educational Technology*, 26(3), 205-15.

Taylor, P. (October, 1998). Institutional change in uncertain times: Lone ranging is not enough. *Studies in Higher Education*, 23(3), 269-79.

Tehranian, M. (1996). The end of the university? *The Information Society*, 12, 441-447.

Young, J. R. (1997, October, 3). Rethinking the age of the professor in an age of high-tech tools. *Chronicle of Higher Education*, 44(6), A26-A28.

Chapter XXI

Fostering a Technology Cultural Change: The Changing Paradigms at the University of Minnesota Crookston

Dan Lim
University of Minnesota Crookston

INTRODUCTION

Many people in higher education wonder where the rapid changes in information technology are going to take them. Many more fear that the ongoing information technology explosion may eventually leave them behind. Due to entrenched mindsets and bureaucracy in higher education, fostering a technology cultural change requires paradigm shifts in all areas of administration, teaching, and research. A fundamental paradigm shift must happen in four areas before a technology cultural change can be set on a forward path.

This chapter focuses on four essential components of a paradigm shift in technology and higher education at the University of Minnesota Crookston (UMC). This case describes how a paradigm shift model can help to promote a long-term technology cultural change in a higher education institution. The model consists of technology commitment, technology philosophy, investment priority, and development focus. It has been used at UMC to bring about a reengineering of the entire institution to support a ubiquitous laptop environment throughout the curriculum and campus. The model has helped UMC achieve an overwhelming success in utilizing laptop computing and other technology to enhance learning.

CASE QUESTIONS

- Who is ultimately responsible for a technology cultural change in an institution of higher education?
- How does the institutional technology climate support or discourage the use of technology to enhance learning?
- What are the difficulties in integrating computer technology into curriculum?
- What types of strategies can be used to help faculty become more comfortable with computer technology?

CASE NARRATIVE

Background

Located in the fertile Red River Valley in Northwestern Minnesota, the University of Minnesota Crookston (UMC) is the fourth and youngest campus in the University of

Minnesota System. UMC became a four-year college in 1993. Surrounded by rich farmlands, UMC provides technology resources to enhance the regional economy and labor force. It produces technology-oriented graduates sought after by regional, state, and national businesses and corporations. UMC's location in the farming region of the Red River Valley has played a vital role in supporting the use of technology to create alternate delivery of courses and degree programs.

The University of Minnesota Crookston has numerous degree programs in Agriculture and Natural Resources, Arts and Sciences, and Business and Technology. Its technology implementation is supported by the Computing Services, Media Resources, Computer Help Desk, Instructional Technology Center, and Web Team units. In general, faculty at UMC have accepted that technology will become an inseparable part of teaching and learning in the classroom, and have responded well to computing and courseware training. Administrators and other staff at UMC have adopted the Web environment for daily communication and operation. In short, the organizational climate at UMC is structured to be supportive around issues of technology that can be used to enhance learning.

From the start, the UMC administration moved toward a technology-based position. In 1993, when it first became a four-year college, it immediately determined to have a ubiquitous laptop computing environment. The University requires and issues laptop computers to all its students. As the first laptop university in the nation, UMC has become a national showcase in ubiquitous laptop computing. Hundreds of delegations from across the nation and around the world came to learn about ubiquitous laptop implementation.

UMC also did away with middle layer bureaucracy and empowered working groups and committees to make decisions and execute various operations without further consultation. The total commitment to technology from the very top was the major step of embarking on a sweeping technology cultural change at UMC. Since the changes happened so quickly, faculty support and training was quite haphazard. The early adopters among the faculty did use the laptop environment for some limited learning applications. Most faculty, though, felt that the technology initiative was an added burden. The challenge of motivating and training the rest of the faculty to incorporate laptop technology into classroom teaching took center stage.

The challenge faced by the University of Minnesota Crookston was how to take full advantage of the ubiquitous computing infrastructure and have 100 percent of the faculty using the technology to enhance learning. A technology cultural change needed to take place among top management, technology personnel, faculty, and staff.

Technology Culture: A Model for Change

The technology cultural change model has embedded within in it four distinct paradigms that must shift simultaneously in order to enhance learning. The four changing paradigms are technology commitment, philosophy of technology, investment prioritization, and development focus. The four paradigms must shift together dynamically, meaning that stagnation in any one paradigm shift may affect the other three, potentially crippling the positive impact on learning.

Paradigm 1: Technology Commitment

If technology is going to change education the way it has changed workplace and lifestyle, it is imperative that a total commitment is made to involve and infuse technology into the curriculum. Educational technology as an add-on to the university budget is not enough. It has to be a significant part of the recurring budgetary process. The add-on paradigm in technology funding and implementation does not originate with the university mission. Technology is funded whenever there is extra money available. It does not matter how much money has been made available, nonrecurring funds cannot sustain a long-time wish list in technology implementation and integration. In fact, the larger a one-time funding is, the harder it is to continue and maintain any technology initiative, let alone keep up with the rapid changes that occur in the computer industry.

The funding of educational technology needs to be committed to a long-term recurring process so that technology implementation will not experience budget reduction or budget cuts. The "add-on" mentality must be replaced by an absolute commitment to technology before any serious plan that will impact learning can be implemented.

If technology is important to a university, it should be reflected in the university's mission. The budgetary process should allocate financial and personnel resources to reinforce technology as mission-critical to the university. Even if there is some nonrecurring funding, both the nonrecurring funds and their stipulating conditions should be worked into the university's mission and budgetary process.

A total commitment to technology and its integration into the curriculum was made at the University of Minnesota Crookston in 1993. The UMC administration's commitment to educational technology was reflected in the amount of resources allocated for it. The university Chancellor and his administration restructured the entire university organizational, financial, and human resources setup to make the bold technology venture work. Since funding was the most crucial factor, a significant reallocation of financial resources to fund campus-wide laptop use and technology integration sent a strong message to the entire university faculty and staff that the technology initiative was not a temporary fix but a long-range mission-critical component for the university.

Staff restructuring and hiring of new technology staff to implement and support the laptop initiative was the next crucial step. The entire campus quickly understood the administration's unwavering commitment to technology. In view of more instructional technology support, faculty were more willing to commit themselves in terms of time and resources to integrate technology into classroom learning. The presence of more technology staff in important committees continued to reinforce the administration's commitment to total technology integration at all levels within the university.

Ongoing organizational restructuring to support technology was vital to counter any doubt about the university's commitment. The sweeping changes in technology and the explosion of the Internet required the university organizational structure to "reinvent" itself as often as possible. Organization structure is as good as the administrators who form it. At the University of Minnesota Crookston, the administrators were a community of learners of sound administrative support and technology skills. The top management, consisting of the Chancellor, Vice-Chancellors, and Center Directors, were constantly attending technology workshops and utilizing cutting-edge technology at work. They not only set a contagious example, but also formed a tremendous driving force through their technology-enriched office.

Paradigm 2: Technology Philosophy

Another paradigm shift required for technology cultural change in schools is that education should "drive" technology rather than vice versa. Technology is a tool that should be built around how teachers teach. Teachers should not have to adjust their lesson plans to suit some computer software. Wherever possible, technology should be implemented to help make the work of teaching easier, or at least, more enjoyable. Administration and computing staff must not implement technology without consulting teachers. The learning outcomes and teachers' instructional agenda should play the central role in determining what software to procure and how it will be implemented. The question is not if a university has the necessary technology but if the technology is meeting the needs of teachers and students. Technology should not dictate how teachers teach, but teachers should determine what technology is best suited for achieving specific learning outcomes.

Although technology is the main driving force at the University of Minnesota Crookston, the administration recognizes that technology must be driven by learning outcomes and by the faculty. The emphasis is to improve or strengthen the learning design. Unless faculty know what they want students to learn, they will not know what is the most appropriate technology tools to use or how to assess whether technology indeed makes a difference in learning. After all, faculty are hired to teach and help students learn. If teaching is what they have committed to, it is only logical to help them focus on their content area before any matching technology tools can further enhance their work.

Since UMC required and issued laptop computers to all students with the objective to enhance learning, the administration has realized that integration of technology into curriculum is crucial to keep the entire laptop initiative on track. The technology "operational" feasibility among faculty can only be improved if the concerns of faculty are addressed and needs met. The decisions on hardware, infrastructure, software, and training must have strong faculty input. The most "intelligent" software does not do any good if no one uses it. The ultimate goal is not to "sell" a particular brand of technology to the faculty, but to use the most appropriate technology to "sell" learning to the students.

The administration at UMC found that an individual technology plan for each faculty member works best. Technology staff conducts ongoing needs assessment of faculty technology needs. Instead of viewing faculty as groups, the staff take time to work with individual faculty to work out an individual technology plan over a certain period of time in terms of meeting their needs, customizing training, and providing timely instructional and technical support. In essence, the technology personnel bring technology to faculty and build it around the way they teach and the way they expect their students to learn.

Paradigm 3: Investment Priority

The next paradigm shift is toward investing heavily in teacher training and development instead of leaving little funds available for training after buying hardware and software. It is better to spend more on training teachers to fully utilize available software than purchasing additional software whose packages teachers may not even have time to open. It is common that teachers hardly use a technology application for the simple reason they do not know how to use it. Training and development should not be an afterthought. It should be a vital part of any successful implementation plan for technology in education.

The major obstacle most higher education institutions face in technology integration is general faculty resistance toward using computers to teach. Comprehensive planning and implementation of aggressive training programs are crucial to overcome faculty resistance toward computers. Training must become the central component in strategic technology planning and its budgetary process. Resistance toward the use of computers can be attributed to the lack of time, anxiety toward computers, or lack of training.

Training needs should also play a part in software selection. At the University of Minnesota Crookston, the choice of authoring platform was based on educational principles used in software interface, customization flexibility, and built-in functionality that makes training and development easier for general faculty. Appropriate technology incentives help faculty get started and maintain momentum in courseware development. Timely recognition rewards also reinforce continual commitment toward technology integration among faculty. Technology staff must recognize that the faculty plays the key role in technology integration. They must do whatever it takes to make software transition and integration as transparent as possible for the faculty.

Paradigm 4: Development Focus

Since technology is more conspicuous than teaching and learning, it is easy to focus solely on technology as if it alone can lead to success. It is education that provides the concept, content, and design for developing a sound educational technology. Administration and instructional technology staff should concentrate their efforts in promoting the need to improve teaching and learning. The need for technology will take central stage as soon as teachers become excited about improving instructional design. As long as extensive access to technology is provided, teachers who are motivated to improve teaching and learning will take full advantage of using appropriate technologies to enhance learning. Promoting technology without relating it to teaching and learning may increase resistance or anxieties among teachers because they feel learning and using technology is an added burden.

At the University of Minnesota Crookston, technology has taken center stage since the 1993 campus-wide implementation of laptop computer use. Students got into the habit of using the laptops almost immediately while faculty needed some gentle "pressure." After three years, when most of the faculty finally embraced the use of laptop computers in the classroom, many faculty were torn between technology and teaching. They found themselves spending too much time on technology issues at the expense of teaching. It became a vicious cycle that the more technology was promoted, the less likely faculty were going to increase using it to enhance learning.

In 1997, the UMC administration realized that the focus of technology-enhanced instructional development should not be centered on technology. Instead, the focus should be on learning innovation. Faculty should spend most of their time designing learning and developing content. Training workshops in instructional systems design were conducted to help faculty plan learning and identify the right technologies. One-on-one consultations were held with faculty to identify their teaching needs and development areas. Faculty could visualize the need for technology when they became excited about using matching technologies to implement their new learning design and content.

One approach that helped change this paradigm was using interactive authoring templates. In order to help faculty to concentrate most of their time on designing and developing content rather than worrying about learning or troubleshooting technology, a set of specific interactive authoring templates was created for the faculty to develop interactive online learning applications. These templates were designed to save faculty time and frustration from authoring interactive learning activities from scratch. Some templates were derived from interactive modules already developed by some faculty. They were made into templates for other faculty to reuse over and over again. The templates were placed in catalogs built into an authoring software package. Faculty only had to select the desired authoring template, enter the content, and post it on the Local Area Network or the Web for students to self-learn, practice, or review for exams. Generally, faculty spent between 15-30 minutes to generate an interactive exercise posted on the Web.

ANALYSIS

The changing technology culture, represented by a paradigm shift from a technology focus to a learning focus, at the University of Minnesota Crookston has changed the attitudes of faculty members toward technology training workshops. Three four-day interactive courseware camps held in the past summer were quickly filled up by faculty, many of whom would not attend even a short workshop. Using the technology cultural change model, the interactive courseware camps were focused on determining what and how faculty wanted to teach and building a set of interactive technologies that would deliver their design. Faculty were allowed to select designs and technologies that fit their content and the way they wanted to deliver, as well as using resources with which they would feel comfortable.

The downside to the above approach is twofold: it takes longer for some faculty to adapt to using more advanced technologies, and it is more difficult to support their development because of diverse technology packages. Although it may take longer and more effort to support faculty technology development, it is important to encourage faculty to trust the process of letting learning "drive" the implementation and integration of technology into curriculum. This new technology culture among the faculty is fragile, though. It will quickly revert back to the old paradigms if administration and technology staff are only concerned with quick results or more streamlined courseware development.

Universities and colleges that do not have a high level of technology and staff support may need to find a scalable model of fostering technology cultural change. The scenario described in this chapter is applicable to traditional campuses if the central administration, departmental administration, faculty, and technology staff share the same vision of promoting a technology cultural change in the four areas described in the model. A shared vision will help in the design and implementation of a scalable model that will foster the necessary paradigm shifts.

CONCLUSION

The technology culture at any institution of higher learning is shaped and formed whether or not a conscious effort has been made to steer it toward enhancing learning. If a conscious effort is made, it should be conducted strategically, effectively, and holistically. The four-component model of fostering a technology cultural change has been used with success at the University of Minnesota Crookston. It was an innovative approach that helped to bring about a ubiquitous mobile computing environment at UMC in 1993. It became even more innovative and revolutionary by setting teaching initiatives as the driving force behind technology integration in higher education at UMC. Other institutions of higher learning may want to consider using or adapting the UMC model to reengineer technology implementation and integration at their campuses. However, it is important to keep in mind that this model is not static. It must continue to evolve, renew, or eventually reinvent itself in other forms.

DISCUSSION QUESTIONS

1. How can administration move from an add-on paradigm to a total commitment paradigm in technology resource planning?

2. What are the pros and cons of requiring and empowering teachers to develop their own learning applications?
3. Why is technology training usually not given adequate funding?
4. What kinds of incentives might be used to help motivate faculty to use technology to enhance teaching and learning?

ADDITIONAL RESOURCES

Oblinger, D.G. (Ed.). and Rush, S.C. (1997). *The Learning Revolution: The Challenge of Information Technology in the Academy.* Bolton, Mass: Anker Pub.

Benchley, R.S. (1999). The results are in: ThinkPad universities assess their first 'connected' years. *Multiversity*, Spring.

About the Authors

EDITOR

Lisa A. Petrides

Lisa A. Petrides is an assistant professor of education in the Department of Organization and Leadership at Teachers College, Columbia University. She is the coordinator of the Education Leadership and Management EdD-MBA program, a joint degree program offered by the Educational Administration Program and the Columbia Business School. Dr. Petrides is also a senior research associate at the Community College Research Center at Teachers College. Her teaching and research interests are in the areas of management systems and information technology, information and decision-making, higher education and workforce preparation, and issues of access and equity in education. She has worked as an information management consultant, developing management information systems for government contracts and business management. She currently works with a wide array of Internet-based technologies for classroom teaching. She received a PhD in education from Stanford University and an MBA in information systems and policy from Sonoma State University, and worked as a postdoctoral fellow at Educational Testing Service in the Educational Policy Research Division.

CONTRIBUTING AUTHORS

Zane L. Berge

Zane Berge is currently director of training systems, Instructional Systems Development Graduate Program at the University of Maryland System, UMBC Campus. His scholarship is in the field of computer-mediated communication and distance education and includes numerous articles, chapters, workshops, and presentations. Most notable are Berge and Collins' recently published books. First, in 1995, was a three-volume set, *Computer-Mediated Communication and the Online Classroom*, that encompasses higher and distance education. Following that was a four-volume set of books, *Wired Together: Computer-Mediated Communication in the K-12 Classroom*, and most recently, he and Schreiber edited *Distance Training* (Jossey-Bass, 1998).

Christopher Blandy

Chris Blandy provides expertise in digital video production for CD-ROM, Web and videotape; HTML; and multimedia software. He serves as a WebCT trainer and consultant.

Blandy has been employed at the University of Texas in various technical support roles since 1995. He is a recent graduate of the University of Texas and holds a BA in Economics.

Sheryl Burgstahler

Sheryl Burgstahler is an affiliate associate professor at the University of Washington where she is also assistant director of Information Systems, Computing & Communications. Burgstahler directs project DO-IT (Disabilities, Opportunities, Internetworking, and Technology), funded primarily by the National Science Foundation, U.S. Department of Education, and the State of Washington. DO-IT employs adaptive technology, computers, and the Internet to help people with disabilities succeed in academics and careers. She has written numerous articles that spread the word about making computers and Web resources accessible to people with disabilities. She is the primary author of the *New Kids on the Net* Internet training series for students and teachers.

Andy Busuttil

Andy Busuttil works as the senior staff development officer in the Centre for Higher Education and Development at the University of Western Sydney. His passion is ethnomusicology and he has a consuming interest in organizational development, social systems and the impact of global contexts on subsystems and vice versa. He is interested in the impact of technology on the educator-student relationship and the development of educator skills. In his staff development work his focal interests are the development of leadership skills among managers and the development of team and organizational planning processes. He has a master's of higher education.

Dubravka Cecez-Kecmanovic

Dubravka Cecez-Kecmanovic is professor and founding chair in information systems at the Faculty of Management, University of Western Sydney Hawkesbury. She has been teaching graduate and undergraduate courses in information systems since 1970. She is also a founder of the Research Group Information Systems—Knowledge Management in Organisations. Her research interests are in computer-mediated communications and Web-based learning and teaching, knowledge management, information systems development methodologies, and groupware technologies.
She holds an MS in system sciences and information systems from the University of Belgrade and a PhD in computer science and information systems from the University of Ljubljana.

Mark Lowry Decker

Mark Lowry Decker is the lead instructor and advocate for WebCT. He is also the quality assurance manager for UTCD 2000, a role he filled in 1998 and 1999. He came to ACITS from the Center for Social Work Research. At UT, he has provided research and administrative support to the Faculty Computer Committee, the Multimedia Instruction Committee, the Telecommunications and Networking Committee, and the Long-Range Planning for Information Technology Steering Committee. He received his BA from Texas Tech while majoring in English and psychology and has a master's degree in social work from UT with an emphasis in administration and planning.

Gunapala Edirisooriya

Gunapala Edirisooriya is associate dean at the College of Education, East Tennessee State University. He has been associated with the higher education sector his entire adult life, as a student, instructor, or administrator, except for a stint of four years during which he worked as a research and evaluation specialist in a large urban school system. Altogether he has attended or worked for nine universities in Sri Lanka, Great Britain, Nigeria, and the U.S. In addition, he has served the World Bank and the Government of Sri Lanka as a consultant on educational planning. His current research focuses on educational data management. He received his PhD from the University of Delaware.

Dorothy E. Finnegan

Dorothy E. Finnegan is an associate professor of education in the area of educational policy, planning and leadership in the School of Education at the College of William and Mary. She is an anthropologist and has taught undergraduate anthropology in the past and now teaches in the graduate higher education program. Her research interests include American and Belgian faculty careers, legal issues in higher education, and the history of higher education.

Ann F. Harbor

Ann F. Harbor is IT strategic planning and administration director for information systems at University of Memphis. She leads the campus-wide technology planning process which mandates daily involvement at various levels across the campus and within the Information Systems division to help gauge trends, progress, issues, or assess other institutional and divisional needs. She holds a master's in educational leadership and a bachelor's in psychology and has extensive background in human resource management. She is a member of SCUP and EDUCAUSE.

Jan K. Hart

Jan K. Hart has been chair of the Library Learning Resource Center at University of Arkansas for Medical Sciences since 1988. She is currently nearing completion of an EdD in Higher Education at the University of Arkansas at Little Rock. Her interests are medical informatics, student/faculty computer literacy, faculty development, and implementation of information and educational technology. She holds a Masters in Library Science from the University of Denver, and an MEd in instructional resources from the University of Arkansas at Little Rock.

Robert Heckman

Robert Heckman is an associate professor at the School of Information Studies, Syracuse University. He teaches courses in strategic management of information resources, management principles, and professional issues in information management. He developed one of the first university courses on information technology acquisition, and he has directed three studies for the Society of Information Management (SIM) on current practices in software contracting and the management of information technology procurement. He previously worked for over 20 years in the information industry. He served as vice president and division head for the Mellon Bank Datacenter Group, one of the largest providers of information services to the financial industry.

Ali Jafari

Ali Jafari is director of CyberLab and associate professor of Computer Technology at Indiana University Purdue University Indianapolis (IUPUI). Professor Jafari has worked in the field of Information Technology and distance learning since 1985 as a software designer, system architect, and researcher. He has designed and directed several major research and development projects including the Interactive Multimedia Distribution System (http://www.imds.iupui.edu/, 1996), the Oncourse Environment (http://oncourse.iu.edu, 1999) and the Angel Enterprise System (http://angel.iupui.edu/, 2000).

Joyce P. Kaufman

Joyce Kaufman is professor of political science at Whittier College and director of the Whittier Scholars Program. Kaufman worked with the ICONS project since its inception and initiated bringing the ICONS project to California high schools, as well as the INMP project to Community Colleges throughout the country. Her publications include being the Guest Editor, *International Negotiation: A Journal of Theory and Practice*, special issue on "The Teaching of International Negotiation," Vol. 3, No. 1, 1998, and "The International Negotiation Modules Project: Integrating International Simulation into the Geography Classroom in the Community College," in the *California Geographer*, Vol. XXXVII, 1997.

Sharon Khanuja-Dhall

Sharon Khanuja-Dhall is a global information technology quality leader at GE Capital. Her work involves project planning, team facilitation, functional and technical requirement analysis, and process mapping to the application of quality models and frameworks. She has worked for Arthur Andersen in the Operational Consulting Group where she managed and participated in reengineering engagements. She is currently completing her MA in organization psychology at Teachers College, Columbia University. She holds a BS from Syracuse University's Information Studies and Technology School.

Siva Kumari

Siva Kumari is a research assistant professor at the University of Houston where she is developing courses for an online certification program in information processing technologies. Kumari currently teaches a course entitled "Integrating Technology into the Curriculum." She has been working with educators to integrate information technologies into education since 1994. Her doctoral research involved the study of higher education faculty using Web-based teaching.

Brian Lewis

Brian Lewis is professor and director of the School of Communication at Simon Fraser University. He teaches courses in information technology, media industry structures, technology and policy, as well as digital video production courses. His early research work applied a cultural perspective to how various countries are policing and implementing their new information infrastructures. Recent work, with Richard Smith and Christine Massey, has analyzed the micro and macro policy environments surrounding the development and implementation of telelearning technology at post-secondary sites throughout Canada.

Dan Lim
Dan Lim earned a PhD degree in educational administration from Andrews University, Michigan, in 1998. He had received training in software engineering and instructional design. He specializes in interactive authoring tools, graphics and interface design, JavaScript/DHTML Web development, and interactive courseware development. His special research areas are interactive paperless learning, interactive online testing, learning games, and interactive courseware models. Besides assisting and training faculty in instructional technologies and courseware development, Dr. Lim teaches computer and instructional design courses to traditional and online students.

Gregory A. Malone
Gregory A. Malone is the technology computer systems coordinator at Cabrillo College in Aptos, California. His previous positions included teaching, research and evaluation, and management at schools and colleges in northern California and the Caribbean. His teaching and research interests are in educational psychology, instructional technology, program evaluation and measurement, and psychological statistics. Malone is conversant in grant writing, educational program evaluation, higher education and K-12 staff development and teaching, research methodology, statistics, and a broad range of applications of instructional technologies.

Christine Massey
Christine Massey is a PhD candidate in the School of Communication at Simon Fraser University in Burnaby, British Columbia. Her research interests are in the study of organizational and technological change in the university, and the evolving role of universities in a knowledge-based society.

Dave Maswick
Dave Maswick is a graduate of the School of Information Science and Technology at Syracuse University where he received an MS in information management. He currently serves as associate dean of information services and director of information technology at Bard College in Annandale-On-Hudson, New York. Maswick has participated in numerous technologically based educational initiatives as a consultant, designer, instructor and student.

Gary E. Miller
Gary E. Miller is associate vice president for distance education and executive director of the World Campus at Pennsylvania State University. He also serves as affiliate associate professor of adult education. He currently serves on the Executive Committee of the International Council for Distance Education and the Board of Directors of the Midwest Universities Consortium for International Activities, Inc. Dr. Miller holds a doctor of education degree in higher education from Penn State. He is the author of *The Meaning of General Education: The Emergence of a Curriculum Paradigm* (Teachers College Press, 1988). He has also chaired the Commission on Principles of Good Practice in Continuing Education for the National University Continuing Education Association.

Bizhan Nasseh

Bizhan Nasseh is a special assistant for educational technology and adjunct faculty of computer science. He has bachelor's degrees in criminology and in economics, a master's degree in computer science, and a doctoral degree in education from Ball State University. He has research interests in computer-based distance education. He has extensive experience in faculty development, academic application development, distance education, training programs, and computer and communication technologies. For the past 20 years, he has worked in information technology in different capacities at Ball State University.

James I. Penrod

James I. Penrod is the first vice president for information systems and CIO at University of Memphis. He was one of the first dozen chief information officers to be appointed in an institution of higher education and has served in that capacity at three other institutions. He holds a PhD in institutional management, a master's in biostatistics and a bachelor's in mathematics. He has been active in professional organizations for many years, serving on a variety of boards and committees such as CAUSE, EDUCOM, (now EDUCAUSE) and SIM.

Rosalind Latiner Raby

Rosalind Latiner Raby is the director of the consortium, California Colleges for International Education, and has worked in the field of internationalizing community college curriculum for over the past decade. She has been the community college coordinator of the INMP project since its inception. Her most recent publications include: "Community College Models: Ideals for Educational Reform" in *Introducing Community Colleges to South Africa*, Ed. A.H. Strydom & L.O.K. Lategan, University of the Free State: Bloemfontein South Africa (1998), and *Looking to the Future: A Report on International and Global Education Activities in California Community Colleges*, Chancellor's Office of the California Community Colleges (1998).

Pablo Reguerin

Pablo Reguerin is the coordinator for information management and finance at the National Center for the Accelerated Schools Project. He has worked as a senior admissions counselor for the University of California, Santa Cruz on projects dealing with access to higher education, and worked with the University of California's PUENTE Transfer Program on student advising, counselor training, and strategy development that aimed to increase transfer success at several community colleges throughout California. He has also worked as an information management consultant in higher education settings and taught various workshops on database design and information management. He received a master's in education from the Department of Organization and Leadership at Columbia University, Teachers College.

Jamie Rodgers

Jamie Rodgers is a principal consultant with PricewaterhouseCoopers (PwC) in Toronto. His specialties are project management, business process improvement, and information systems design and implementation within the financial services industry and government. Prior to PwC, he was with Andersen Consulting. Jamie pursued his MS in information resources management at Syracuse University in parallel with his management consulting duties.

Kevin Ruthen

Kevin Ruthen is a consultant at IBM Global Services Banking Finance and Securities Division. He recently obtained his master's of information resource management from the School of Information Studies at Syracuse University, where he also received his bachelor's of science in information management. Ruthen is president and co-founder of Sportcon Consulting. Prior to IBM, he was a project manager for Prudential Securities in the New Technology Equity Trading Systems area.

James H. Ryan

James H. Ryan serves as Penn State's vice president for outreach and cooperative extension. He oversees the coordination of the University's external outreach initiatives and has responsibility for Continuing Education, Distance Education, Public Broadcasting, and Cooperative Extension. He has served as a faculty member in public administration and held various administrative positions in academic affairs, institutional advancement, and student personnel with Indiana University and at the State University of New York at Buffalo. He received his baccalaureate, masters, and doctoral degrees from SUNY, Buffalo. His doctorate is in the sociology of education and higher education administration, with an emphasis on organizational development.

Morrie Schulman

Morrie Schulman is a systems analyst for the CIT. He was the principal investigator for the Web Tool Selection Committee, participated in the licensing of WebCT and is its systems administrator. He has been with the CIT since 1997, when he returned to the University after running a small business for 20 years. He holds a master's degree in educational psychology with emphasis on program evaluation and is near completion on a second master's degree in library and information science. He has worked as an educational program evaluator and has taught at Austin Community Schools and Austin Community College.

Scott R. Sechrist

Scott Sechrist is an associate professor and program director of the Nuclear Medicine Technology Program at Old Dominion University in Norfolk, Virginia. He has taught several courses in radiation physics and medical terminology via the TELETECHNET program at Old Dominion University. This program is an integrated television, computer, and audio system providing undergraduate and graduate instruction throughout Virginia and to additional sites throughout the United States. He received a grant from the American Cancer Society to create computer-based smoking prevention programs for preschool-aged children. He is a doctoral candidate in the higher education program at the College of William and Mary in Williamsburg, Virginia.

Andreea M. Serban

Andreea M. Serban is the director of institutional assessment, research and planning at Santa Barbara City College. Prior to joining Santa Barbara City College, Dr. Serban had research and faculty positions at University of Redlands, Rockefeller Institute of Government, State University of New York System Administration, Institute for Educational Sciences and University of Bucharest. Her research interests are in the areas of performance funding, reporting and measurement, and state budgeting for higher education. Her experience

254 About the Authors

includes policy analysis, higher education planning and finance, qualitative and quantitative research, mathematics and statistics, data analysis and management, and applications of computer technologies.

Kandis M. Smith

Kandis M. Smith is the special assistant to the vice president for academic affairs at the University of Missouri System. She received a PhD in higher education from the University of Missouri-Columbia. Her current research interests are in the areas of teaching and information technology, issues of equity and diversity, and development of collaborative programming. She is currently working with a number of diverse groups to develop innovative uses of technology to enhance teaching and learning.

Richard Smith

Richard Smith is assistant professor of communication in the Faculty of Applied Science in Simon Fraser University, Burnaby, British Columbia. He is also director of the Centre for Policy Research on Science and Technology (CPROST) at Simon Fraser University at Harbour Centre, in Vancouver, British Columbia. His research looks at the innovation process for new products and services in telecommunications and financial services industries, policy studies of new applications for information technology for universities as well as the primary and secondary school environment, and the role of social capital in the management of innovation and collaborative research and development. He holds MA and PhD degrees from Simon Fraser University in Burnaby, Canada.

Robert S. Stephenson

Robert S. Stephenson, an expert on the biophysics of insect photoreceptors, is associate professor in the Department of Biological Sciences at Wayne State University in Detroit, Michigan. For the last three years he has taught a successful online physiology course at Wayne State. The course has both lecture and Internet-only sections, and is based on 550 Web pages, as well as RealVideo asynchronous broadcast of the videotaped lectures and an electronic discussion board. Dr. Stephenson is the founder and chief architect of the Harvey Project, an open course project to develop free, online rich content for teaching physiology. He holds a PhD from MIT and is a Sun Microsystems certified Java programmer.

Gary Wee

Gary Wee is vice president and director for a leading European bank in derivatives and global relative value. His background includes 12 years of trading various fixed-income and equity portfolios, and he has several years of experience with financial system design and architecture. He co-founded Tux Communications Inc., a company which develops and markets products focused on real-time data publishing and Internet-based collaborative technology. He completed an MS in information management at Syracuse in 1999.

Index

A

Useful resource for all IS faculty!

Annals of Cases on Information Technology

Volume 2/2000

Annals of Cases on Information Technology

IDEA GROUP PUBLISHING
Publisher in information science, education, technology and management
http://www.idea-group.com

Editor-in-charge:
Mehdi Khosrowpour
Pennsylvania State University

ISSN 1098-8580 * Published annually
Annual subscription rate:
$35 Individuals; $165 Libraries

MISSION

Annals of Cases on Information Technology is a refereed, international journal whose mission is to provide understanding and lessons learned in regard to all aspects of information technology utilization and management in organizations.

COVERAGE

Annals of Cases on Information Technology (ACIT) documents 15-20 comprehensive ACTUAL REAL LIFE CASES based on individual, organizational and societal experiences related to the utilization and management of information technology. Cases published in the Annals will deal with a wide variety of organizations, such as business settings, government organizations, educational institutions, library settings, medical facilities, etc. Topics covered include (but are not limited to):

- Distance Learning
- End User Computing
- Web-Enabled Technologies
- Human Side of IT
- Internet Technologies
- Data Management
- Information Security & Ethics
- Legal Issues of IT
- IT in Developing Countries
- IT in Government
- Issues of Emerging Technology
- Multimedia in Education
- IT in Libraries
- *and many more!*

> "I am convinced that the Annals of Cases on Information Technology will be very well received and helpful to IS faculty."—**Maeve Cummings, Pittsburg State University**

For more information on this international journal, please visit the
Idea Group Publishing Web site at http://www.idea-group.com

Journal of
End User Computing

Editor-in-Charge:
Dr. Mo Adam Mahmood
University of Texas, El Paso

*ISSN 1063-2239 * Published quarterly*
Annual subscription rate: $85 Individuals;
$219 Institutions

MISSION:

The **Journal of End User Computing** (JEUC) is a refereed, international publication featuring the latest research findings dealing with end user computing concepts, issues, and trends. It provides a forum to both academics and information technology practitioners to advance the practice and understanding of end user computing in organizations. The journal publishes empirical and theoretical research concerned with all aspects of end user computing including development, utilization, and management. The journal is especially interested in those studies that show a significant contribution by relating end user computing to end user satisfaction, end user productivity, and strategic and competitive advantage.

COVERAGE:

JEUC covers topics with a major emphasis on the productivity, strategic and competitive advantage derived from end user information processing. Some of the topics covered include:

- ◆ EUC success factors
- ◆ EUC management
- ◆ EUC hardware and software
- ◆ end users and downsizing
- ◆ EUC productivity

- ◆ EUC risk factors
- ◆ EUC satisfaction and usage
- ◆ end user supports and training
- ◆ information centers
- ◆ EUC, piracy and copyright

- ◆ EUC quality assurance and management
- ◆ EUC and strategic/competitive advantage
- ◆ information resource management and end users
- ◆ managing emerging EUC technologies
- ◆ EUC in various management functions
- ◆ EUC controls for security and privacy
- ◆ and other related topics

An excellent addition to your library —please recommend it to your librarian!

For more information on this international journal, please visit the
Idea Group Publishing Web site at http://www.idea-group.com

New Author Invitation

The ultimate scholarly recognition in one's discipline can be realized by editing or authoring a book. Editing/authoring a book in one's research area also provides for knowledge dissemination in the discipline. During the past 12 years, Idea Group Publishing (IGP) has worked with many scholars and researchers in publishing high-quality publications in all aspects of the information technology discipline, and IGP is always in search of new editors/authors for new publications. I would like to take this opportunity to personally invite you to consider editing a new book in your area of interest for IGP.

Editing a book requires a systematic approach to bringing together a group of scholars with the same research interest to collaborate on a single project. Unlike authoring a textbook, editing a book requires certain leadership and coordination, as well as tremendous guidance from the publisher of the work. IGP can provide you with the needed support to get your ideas organized, to identify contributing authors, to review contributions, and to put together a high quality publication!

IGP editors and staff will work with you through the many phases of publication—from the inception of your idea for an edited book to its completion and publication. IGP provides the following support services to its editors:

❖ Expert support in formalizing your idea for an edited book in your area
 of expertise.
❖ Full assistance from our experienced staff during development of your book
❖ Fastest and most efficient production turnaround for your publication
❖ Most effective worldwide promotion and sales for your book through our more than
 200 wholesalers and jobbers in the United States, Canada and over 50 other countries

Should you be interested in editing/authoring a book in your area of expertise and research, please submit a prospectus (2-4 pages) that should include the following items:

- Suggested titles (3-5)
- An introduction to the subject area
- Overall objectives and mission of your proposed book
- The audience for such a book
- Existing publications (competitors)
- Tentative table of contents
- Timetable for the entire project

Please send your proposal to:
Mehdi Khosrow-Pour, Senior Academic Editor
Idea Group Publishing
1331 E. Chocolate Avenue, Hershey, PA 17033-1117, USA
Tel: 717/533-8845 • Fax: 717/533-8551
or preferably through e-mail to <mehdi@idea-group.com>